CRITICAL INSIGHTS

The Scarlet Letter

CRITICAL

INSIGHTS

The Scarlet Letter

Editor
Brian Yothers
University of Texas at El Paso

SALEM PRESS
A Division of EBSCO Information Services, Inc.
Ipswich, Massachusetts

GREY HOUSE PUBLISHING

Publisher's Cataloging-In-Publication Data
(Prepared by The Donohue Group, Inc.)

Names: Yothers, Brian, 1975- editor.
Title: The scarlet letter / editor, Brian Yothers, University of Texas at El Paso.
Other Titles: Critical insights.
Description: [First edition]. | Ipswich, Massachusetts : Salem Press, a division
         of EBSCO Information Services, Inc. ; Amenia, NY : Grey
         House Publishing, [2018] | Series: Critical insights | Includes
         bibliographical references and index.
Identifiers: ISBN 9781682176887 (hardcover)
Subjects: LCSH: Hawthorne, Nathaniel, 1804-1864.Scarlet letter. | Hawthorne,
         Nathaniel, 1804-1864--Criticism and interpretation. | Puritans
         in literature. | Transcendentalism in literature.
Classification: LCC PS1868 .S39 2018 | DDC 813/.3--dc23

First Printing

Contents

Resources

About This Volume

Brian Yothers

Few American novels generate as wide a range of approaches as Hawthorne's *The Scarlet Letter*, and this volume reflects that diversity of opinion and subject matter. In *The Scarlet Letter*, Hawthorne addresses issues as wide-ranging as the changing status of women in nineteenth-century America, the relation of nineteenth-century New Englanders to their Puritan past, the ethical and aesthetic theories of romanticism and transcendentalism, the nature of sexual relationships and morality, the meaning of childhood, the relative value of religious faith and skeptical doubt, and indeed the entire structure of human relationships. The thirteen chapters in this volume explore the full range of issues that have been so crucial to criticism and scholarship on *The Scarlet Letter* over the last century and a half.

Critical Contexts

In the opening Critical Contexts section, Samuel Coale provides a narrative of the history of the critical response to *The Scarlet Letter*, built around the insight that unlike most of the other books now acknowledged as major midcentury American works, *The Scarlet Letter* has never been out of critical favor. Coale explores the significance of this observation to understanding Hawthorne's ability to speak powerfully to multiple audiences, both in his own lifetime and throughout the decades following his death.

Robert C. Evans's Critical Lens essay shows just how many vantage points there are for considering the meanings of *The Scarlet Letter*, illustrating the varying approaches that formalist, Marxist, feminist, and poststructuralist critics, among others, might take to the text. The variety of approaches that find correspondences in *The Scarlet Letter* can perhaps help to explain the longstanding critical prominence of Hawthorne's most famous book.

Anupama Arora's comparison of Hawthorne's *The Scarlet Letter* and Jhumpa Lahiri's *Unaccustomed Earth* likewise shows how enduring Hawthorne's work has been. Lahiri, one of the United States' most prominent immigrant writers in the twenty-first century, found that Hawthorne's nineteenth-century novels and stories could provide a critical backdrop for her own work. Arora traces the lines of influence from Hawthorne to Lahiri and shows that the work of one of twenty-first-century America's most eminent immigrant writers is closely, if obliquely, connected to that of Salem's nineteenth-century custom house surveyor. Nor, as Arora points out, is Lahiri alone, as the major Indian-American writer Bharati Mukherjee has also engaged directly with *The Scarlet Letter* in her 1993 novel *The Holder of the World.*

The final chapter in this section, Brian Yothers's "Puritans and Transcendentalists: *The Scarlet Letter* in New England Culture," shows how Hawthorne's representations of both his Puritan forebears and transcendentalist contemporaries are shaped by the history of New England and by Hawthorne's desire to provide a new history of the region. Yothers draws upon earlier readings of Hawthorne as a New England historian by Michael Colacurcio, and he suggests how Colacurcio's important insights might be applied specifically to *The Scarlet Letter.* Yothers suggests that the governing consciousness of *The Scarlet Letter* owes significant debts to both the Puritans and the transcendentalists, even as it includes significant elements of critique of both traditions.

Critical Readings

At the start of this section, Jane Zwart considers an aspect of *The Scarlet Letter* that may not be immediately evident to casual readers, but which appears everywhere around the margins of the story. Hawthorne's story is not, like Lydia Maria Child's *Hobomok*, a novel primarily engaged with the contact between indigenous and European Americans, but as Zwart shows, the question of New World colonization is never far from the foreground, even as Hawthorne's engagement with transatlantic writing is always present. For Zwart, an engagement with postcolonial criticism and theory becomes essential for a full understanding of Hawthorne's story.

John Wenke's chapter also considers the ways in which *The Scarlet Letter* looks beyond the conventional boundaries of Puritan society, in this case by exploring how "The Custom-House" introduction opens up Hawthorne's novel to a wider, more cosmopolitan set of concerns than those immediately visible through the bulk of the novel, and he also shows how the cosmopolitan strands that the "Custom-House" introduction introduce appear throughout the entire book, enabling Hawthorne to develop a transhistorical voice that moves beyond the limitations of time and place. Wenke shows that Hawthorne's quintessentially American novel is deeply engaged with the wider world.

Jonathan A. Cook also reminds us of the importance of the "Custom-House" introduction, delving into the role that this part of *The Scarlet Letter* plays in helping us to understand Hawthorne's own role in the heated political controversies of his time, and showing how Hawthorne's story as a political appointee shapes the story that he tells in *The Scarlet Letter.* Notably, Cook points out that the novel's significance is heavily shaped by political events in Hawthorne's lifetime, an insight that complements powerfully Zwart's and Wenke's postcolonial and cosmopolitan readings of the book.

Brad Bannon's chapter is concerned with the ways in which Hawthorne intersects with the intellectual and artistic world of international Romanticism. For Bannon, Hawthorne's multiple points of connection with British and German Romanticism figure largely in his work, and help to justify the traditional, if at times neglected in the twenty-first century, classification of Hawthorne as an American Romantic. Bannon shows that Hawthorne's vision is informed by British Romantics like Samuel Taylor Coleridge

The matter of Hawthorne's classification, and that of *The Scarlet Letter* in particular, is also crucial to Casey R. Pratt's chapter. Pratt considers how Hawthorne's book fits within the model of the American Romance, a consideration that had, as Pratt shows, considerable explanatory power for critics in the 1950s and 1960s, but which had fallen out of favor for some critics in the 1980s and 1990s. Pratt explores how thinking of *The Scarlet Letter* as a romance rather than a novel can help us to understand Hawthorne's formal experimentation more fully.

A third chapter to explore the evolving critical constructs applied by American literary scholars to Hawthorne's 1850 book is Christopher N. Phillips's consideration of *The Scarlet Letter* as a representative American Renaissance text, a role that was claimed for it initially in F. O. Matthiessen's *American Renaissance*, the text that first elucidated the concept. For Phillips, this reflection on Matthiessen's concept becomes an opportunity to consider how feminist criticism in particular has reinvestigated and reinterpreted the idea of an American Renaissance.

We may sometimes put so much pressure on the larger cultural issues shaping Hawthorne's work that we lose track of the reasons why it has spoken to such a wide readership over the years. Nancy F. Sweet's essay addresses precisely this issue, as she considers how Hawthorne's work shaped and was shaped by popular American fiction. Sweet's treatment of popular fiction builds on a history of reading Hawthorne in tandem with his wider literary context, notably in such studies as David S. Reynolds's *Beneath the American Renaissance* and Michael T. Gilmore's *American Romanticism and the Marketplace*.

Steven Petersheim takes a related tack in writing about *The Scarlet Letter* as an example of the complementary genres of utopian and dystopian fiction. For Petersheim, Hawthorne's story bears witness to the ways in which one author can oscillate meaningfully between the paired concepts of utopia and dystopia, at times implying that utopia is unrealizable, and at times finding openings for the utopian impulses that so often appear across time and physical space in literature. Petersheim shows that while dystopian elements may predominate in *The Scarlet Letter*, Hawthorne also leaves room for the attractions of utopianism.

Even as *The Scarlet Letter* has functioned as a quintessentially canonical American text in its own right for over a century and a half, it has also served to spur the development of numerous adaptations in the world of film. As a scholar of both nineteenth-century American literature and film, David Greven considers the filmic afterlife of *The Scarlet Letter*. He surveys a range of filmic adaptations of Hawthorne's book, from the 1930s United States to a 1970s German production filmed in Spain, and back to the United States for Roland Joffé's widely panned 1995 adaptation, placing particular emphasis on the changing gender politics of *The Scarlet Letter*'s afterlife. As Greven notes, the wide range of responses to *The Scarlet Letter* in film includes widely varying levels of quality among the responses.

As a group, these chapters illustrate the profundity of the impact that *The Scarlet Letter* has made on the literature and culture of both the United States itself and the English-speaking world. Hawthorne's book, which is so deeply engaged with questions of interpretation, is itself an example of how productive the process of literary interpretation can be. If Hawthorne's characters can never quite find a conclusive meaning for the *A* on Hester's dress, even as they know the initial reason for its placement, it is small wonder that Hawthorne's enigmatic tale of adultery, deception, and moral judgment continues to elicit a multitude of sometimes contradictory, sometimes complementary responses.

On *The Scarlet Letter*

Brian Yothers

Nathaniel Hawthorne's *Scarlet Letter* sits near the center of a very short list of novels to which Jonathan Arac's term hypercanonization can be applied without the slightest exaggeration. In his study *Huckleberry Finn as Idol and Target: The Functions of Criticism in Our Time*, Arac adduced Mark Twain's *The Adventures of Huckleberry Finn*, Herman Melville's *Moby-Dick*, and *The Scarlet Letter* itself as the ultimate examples of this phenomenon, which he defined as the state in which "a very few individual works monopolize curricular and critical attention," and which he considered to be a distinguishing feature of American literary study (133). Although Arac found the fact that *The Scarlet Letter* and *Moby-Dick* dominate our sense of what constitutes prose literature from the nineteenth century troubling, he also found the dominance of *The Scarlet Letter* to be among the most important features of our understanding of the literary past in the United States.

This dominance of *The Scarlet Letter* becomes curious when we consider a point that both Arac and critics from John H. McElroy in the 1960s, with his description of *The Scarlet Letter* as "literally conventional from first to last" (89) to David S. Reynolds in the late 1980s, with his careful accounting for the roots of Hawthorne's art in popular literature, have made: in many respects, Hawthorne's narrative resembles a great deal of other nineteenth-century American literary production. Stories of Puritan New England, stories of adultery, stories of religious hypocrisy, and stories rich with overt symbolism were common in nineteenth-century America, a fact that makes the dominance of *The Scarlet Letter* in twentieth- and twenty-first-century school curricula in the United States seemingly improbable. Most recently, Richard Kopley has shown that Hawthorne drew substantially for plot elements and scene setting on the long-forgotten historical romance *The Salem Belle*, by Ebenezer Wheelwright.

So how might we account for the central place that this novel occupies in our understanding of American literature? *The Scarlet Letter* contains a great deal of the furniture that we associate with mid-nineteenth-century American literature: it is rich in symbolism, it attempts to create a chronological depth for North American history that can challenge the longer recorded history of Europe, Asia, and Africa, and it reflects on profound economic, political, moral, and religious changes in the brief span of colonial and early United States history. It is no surprise that writers like F. O. Matthiessen, Richard Chase, and Charles Feidelson, who defined the distinctive qualities of American literature as consisted in the centrality of the romance genre and the importance of complex symbolism, would find *The Scarlet Letter* to be a crucial touchstone for understanding American literature. The range of reasons to find *The Scarlet Letter* compelling has been far broader than just symbolism and ambiguity, however. In the 1950s, Darrel Abel could read Pearl as the figure of the "Universal Child"; Frederick Crews could find Hawthorne's work to be suggestive of Freudian psychoanalysis in the 1960s; Nina Baym could find incipient feminism in Hawthorne's work in the 1970s; and Sacvan Bercovitch could find it broadly explanatory of the mix of dissent and consensus in American culture in a series of books published from the 1970s to the 1990s. *The Scarlet Letter* continues to speak to readers of many different critical orientations, as both this brief overview of the criticism and the chapters that follow illustrate.

One of the mistakes that readers make in approaching *The Scarlet Letter* is to treat it as if it begins with Hester Prynne's departure from the prison-house and her initial ascension to the scaffold. What this approach to reading Hawthorne's novel ignores is that he has devoted nearly 20 percent of his book to a narrative that at first glance seems only loosely related to Hester's story of ambiguous sin and possible redemption.

Appropriately, this volume includes several pieces that draw attention to the "Custom-House" as more than a quaint framing device. Hawthorne was a highly accomplished writer of short fiction by the time he composed *The Scarlet Letter*, and had he wished to dispense with such a lengthy introduction and proceed directly into the story of Hester Prynne, he surely would have. Yet the "Custom-House" is both a rich work in its own right and an essential complement to the body of Hawthorne's account. When Hawthorne's younger, and deeply admiring, contemporary Herman Melville considered what made Hawthorne's short fiction engaging in his 1850 review "Hawthorne and His Mosses," Melville chose to focus as much on Hawthorne's humor and "geniality" as on his devotion to the "power of blackness" (Melville 242-43).

After the "Custom-House," the contours of the plot come into view: a young woman, Hester Prynne, has given birth to a child who cannot possibly have been fathered by her absent husband, and she is being publicly punished for this transgression at the start of the narrative. She refuses to reveal the identity of the father of her child, a fact that seems to have an especially strong effect on Arthur Dimmesdale, her young minister. Her punishment is to wear a scarlet letter *A* on her breast, which she has sewn in a manner that seems defiantly ornate.Meanwhile, a mysterious stranger, Roger Chillingworth, arrives in town, and it soon becomes apparent that he is Hester's husband. Chillingworth has spent time as a captive and a physician among the Native American peoples of the region, and he gains status in the community as a physician. As it becomes clear that Dimmesdale is the father of Hester's child, it also becomes clear that Chillingworth is engaging in a perverse psychological experiment at Dimmesdale's expense. A parallel development is the growth of Hester's daughter, Pearl, who instinctively seems to reject the moral judgments of her parents in favor of her own intuitions, and we soon see that Hester shares these rebellious intuitions. Dimmesdale, despite standing with Hester and Pearl on the town's scaffold at night, refuses to confess his role in Pearl's conception in the daylight. After Hester Prynne and Arthur Dimmesdale have decided to escape immediately following Dimmesdale's delivery of the Election Sermon, Dimmesdale suffers his final collapse, confesses his paternity of Pearl, and dies. Pearl goes on to live as an heiress in Europe, but Hester ultimately returns to New England to expiate her past. Throughout, the question of what to do with the letter that Hester has been commanded to wear—to embrace it, reject it, or reinterpret it—is paramount in the narrative.

How one views the *A* on Hester's bosom in the novel reveals a great deal about one's own preconceptions, and, similarly, how one views Hawthorne's novel reveals a great deal about one's understanding of the literary history of the United States. Americanists from the 1950s generation like Richard Chase and Charles Feidelson tended to find a profound message in the visual symbolism of the novel, and they tended indeed to argue for the book's distinctness from the genre of the novel altogether, preferring to describe it as a romance.

Perhaps no reading of Hawthorne's book in the last half-century has been more influential than Sacvan Bercovitch's suggestion that *The Scarlet Letter* is American literature's central example of the politics of "structures of consensus founded on the possibility of dissent" that Bercovitch used to suggest the ways in which nineteenth-century American books could both voice and coopt dissent, ultimately reinforcing the existing social order (159). For Bercovitch, the "office of the Scarlet Letter" (the title of his book on *The Scarlet Letter*) is at once to point to contradictions in the existing social order and to contain those contradictions in order to forestall any sort of revolutionary eruption. Hester is permitted to question everything about the Puritan society in which she lives, so long as she does so privately, but she is not permitted to change it.

So what do we know about these people about whom Hawthorne was so ambivalent, and for whom later literary and cultural critics and historians have made such imposing claims? The Puritans, although they can easily be seen as a monolithic group, were actually characterized by a substantial range of opinion, and this wide range of opinion lurks in the background of Hawthorne's story. In the opening chapter of Hester Prynne's story, we are introduced not only to Hester herself but to Anne Hutchinson, perhaps the most famous woman in seventeenth-century New England. Hutchinson's commitment to the idea of a direct personal relationship between the Christian deity and the individual believer can in some ways resemble Hester's daring reimagination of her relationship to her community, and even Pearl's refusal to accept the community's strictures altogether.

How we view the Puritans matters a great deal to how we view *The Scarlet Letter*: if we take the early twentieth-century view of Puritans as joyless bigots, desperately concerned that "someone, somewhere, may be happy," as H. L. Mencken quotably put it (qtd. in Kemeny 234), then Hawthorne's book reads as a kind of investigative report on the corrupt foundations of the American project. In that case, *The Scarlet Letter* reads as a call to renounce a moralistic version of social and sexual relations, preferring instead a model of individual empowerment. If we note the visionary and rebellious qualities that characterized Puritanism itself, as discussed by Andrew Delbanco in *The Puritan Ordeal*, we may arrive at a more complex sense of the novel's relationship to the Puritan tradition.

The *A* on Hester Prynne's bosom is far from the only crux for interpretation in the novel, and central to how we understand the nature of Hawthorne's work is how we understand Hester herself, and what Hawthorne's depiction of Hester tells us about his, and his novel's, attitude toward the roles of women in seventeenth- and nineteenth-century Massachusetts alike. Nina Baym has registered the most compelling argument in favor of what she considers Hawthorne's feminism, even as many readers have detected something more akin to misogyny in Hester's portrayal. For Baym, Hawthorne can reasonably be described as a feminist. She argues "unless a feminist perspective requires asserting that women are perfect, his observations might be seen as attempts to intervene on the feminist side" ("Revisiting" 117) and Baym's eminence in the field of feminist literary scholarship has helped to ensure that the debate over Hawthorne's feminism or lack thereof will likely continue.

Hester becomes a vastly more interesting figure when we consider that she can be both the prophet of a new sexual and social dispensation and a believer, at least to a degree, in the dogmas of the society and faith into which she was born. Hester gestures repeatedly in the direction of free thought, both in the ideas that the narrator describes as passing through her mind, and in the words that

---

she says to Dimmesdale and Chillingsworth in their conversations in the woods. At the same time, Hester feels herself connected to her community in ways that do not allow her to break free of it completely. For some critics, such as Sacvan Bercovitch, this points to a strong conservative thread in the novel; it might also suggest Hawthorne's desire to probe the basic human need for community as opposed to extreme individualism.

Three passages in particular illuminate Hawthorne's treatment of Hester and what she might mean for his understanding of women in the social sphere and how he might oscillate between traditional understandings of social roles and the possibility of reinterpreting those roles.

> Her breast, with its badge of shame, was but the softer pillow for the head that needed one. She was self-ordained a Sister of Mercy; or, we may rather say, the world's heavy hand had so ordained her, when neither the world nor she looked forward to this result. The letter was the symbol of her calling. Such helpfulness was found in her,—so much power to do, and power to sympathize,—that many people refused to interpret the scarlet A by its original signification. They said that it meant Able, so strong was Hester Prynne, with a woman's strength. (161)

Hawthorne's narrator here considers the complexity of Hester's position in the years following her judgment for adultery at the hands of a Puritan court. On the one hand, she is permanently marked by her "badge of shame," but on the other, she has become a figure of considerable power. Because she has suffered deprivation and social ostracism, she has become a more powerful and compassionate figure. This does not excuse the cruelty of her punishment, but it does suggest that Hester possesses a moral power that can transcend the intentions of her judges. We might also note who is performing the act of interpretation that Hawthorne describes here: Hester has been condemned by the elites in Salem's Puritan-dominated community, but members of the very community that witnessed and enforced her shame now find her to be an exemplar of female capacity.

"I freely forgive you now. May God forgive us both! We are not, Hester, the worst sinners in the world. There is one worse than even the polluted priest! That old man's revenge has been blacker than my sin. He has violated, in cold blood, the sanctity of the human heart. Thou and I, Hester, never did so!"

"Never, never!" whispered she. "What we did had a consecration of its own. We felt it so! We said so to one another! Hast thou forgotten it?" (195).

Here *The Scarlet Letter* lines up closely with one of Hawthorne's central themes: the inviolability of human selfhood. Hester's justification for her adulterous affair with Dimmesdale emphasizes that although they might have transgressed a moral command, Hester and Dimmesdale have not engaged in cruelty, and they have not violated the privacy of another's conscience, as Chillingworth has done.

Among the most moving passages in *The Scarlet Letter* is the narrator's account of how she turns her suffering and exclusion into an ability to console others and to offer a vision of a brighter future. Hester has been set apart from Puritan society but nonetheless fills a vital role for others who have experienced exclusion or loss. The narrator describes Hester's efforts on behalf of others:

> Hester comforted and counselled them, as best she might. She assured them, too, of her firm belief, that, at some brighter period, when the world had grown ripe for it, in Heaven's own time, a new truth would be revealed, to establish the whole relation between man and woman on the surer ground of mutual happiness. Earlier in life, Hester had vainly imagined that she herself might be the destined prophetess, but had long since recognized the impossibility that any mission of divine and mysterious truth should be confided to a woman stained with sin, bowed down with shame, or even burdened with a life-long sorrow. The angel and apostle of the coming revelation must be a woman, indeed, but lofty, pure, and beautiful; and wise, moreover, not through dusky grief, but the ethereal medium of joy; and showing how sacred love should make us happy, by the truest test of a life successful to such an end! (263)

Hester's status as a prophet is tempered by Hawthorne's tendency to give with one hand and take away with the other when considering her ideas. Hawthorne's narrator recounts Hester's visions of the future sympathetically, even as he ultimately suggests that Hester is not herself able to realize her most daring visions, in part because she has accepted the judgment that she is "stained with sin." It is noteworthy, then, that Hester is never fully able to rest in her most daring speculations on matters of faith and polity. She is in a perpetual dialogue with the Calvinism that provides the context for her thought and existence, and even her most radical departures from that Calvinism reflects something of the impress of that Calvinism, a point that both Lawrence Buell and Michael J. Colacurcio have made regarding Hawthorne himself (Buell 271; Colacurcio 305).

Hester's doubleness in *The Scarlet Letter* can perhaps reflect a related duality on the part of her creator. One of the most compelling recent readings of Hawthorne's career, Robert Milder's excellent critical biography *Hawthorne's Habitations*, reflects on the difference between Hawthorne's notebooks, which as Milder points out are surprisingly focused on the material world and social relationships rather than on the sort of dark philosophical musings that we associate with Hawthorne's fictions and his highly allegorical short stories and novels. Following one of Hawthorne's earliest biographers, his own son Julian, Milder shows that Hawthorne can appear to be two separate people in his literary corpus and in his personal notebooks (Milder 4-8).

Milder's observation in this regard echoes the response to Hawthorne's work of one of his earliest critics, Edgar Allan Poe. As one of early America's most fecund and imposing literary critics, Poe praised Hawthorne in no fewer than three reviews, but by the third review, his panegyrics were tempered by a bracing critique of what he saw as Hawthorne's excessive fondness for allegory and a corresponding weakness in his treatment of plot and character, concluding that Hawthorne should "Get a bottle of visible ink, come out from the Old Manse, cut Mr. Alcott, hang (if possible) the editor of *The Dial*, and throw out of the windows to the pigs all of his odd numbers of *The North American Review*" (qtd. in

Wineapple 195). Poe's advice was directed toward Hawthorne's short stories in *Mosses from an Old Manse*, and it seems reasonable to suggest that *The Scarlet Letter* addresses some elements of Poe's critique. Although Hawthorne certainly makes considerable use of symbolism in *The Scarlet Letter*, there is also a level of attention to everyday life that seems to temper the romance of some of his more mysterious tales from the 1840s and that perhaps bridges something of the gap that Milder has noted between Hawthorne's fictional and nonfictional writing and that Melville noted in 1850 between humor and darkness in Hawthorne's prose.

The Scarlet Letter is a text that builds pigeonholes for itself and perpetually breaks out of them. It walks a fine line between reformism and conservatism, religion and secularism, feminism and traditionalism, without allowing itself to be exclusively identified with any of these impulses. Among the greatest mistakes we can make in reading Hawthorne's novel is to restrict ourselves in just the ways that Hawthorne's narrative is constantly urging us not to: reading *The Scarlet Letter* as too final a triumph for one set of ideas or practices over another is to ignore Hawthorne's own careful refusal to provide easy answers. If Dimmesdale as a tormented Romantic artist placed in a Puritan world draws us, Dimmesdale as a self-dramatizing male who refuses to share Hester's fate should equally repel us. If Hester presents us with a vision of the possibility of future self-fulfillment in a post-Puritan culture, she should also suggest to us the value of a society in which individuals feel strongly their bonds of responsibility to others in the community. Criticism on *The Scarlet Letter* has emphasized the multiple conflicting interpretations of the titular letter "A" as a symbol; we read Hawthorne and his story well when we realize that the novel itself draws together and keeps separate similarly conflicting impulses.

Works Cited

Abel, Darrel. "Hawthorne's Pearl: Symbol and Character." *ELH* vol. 18, no. 1 (1951): 50-66.

Arac, Jonathan. *Huckleberry Finn as Idol and Target: The Functions of Criticism in Our Time.* U of Wisconsin P, 1997.

Baym, Nina. "Revisiting Hawthorne's Feminism." In *Hawthorne and The Real: Bicentennial Essays*. Edited by Millicent Bell. Ohio State UP, 2005: pp. 107-24.

_____. *The Scarlet Letter: A Reading*. Hall, 1986.

_____. *The Shape of Hawthorne's Career*. Cornell UP, 1976.

Bercovitch, Sacvan. *American Jeremiad*. U of Wisconsin P, 1978.

_____. *The Office of the Scarlet Letter*. Johns Hopkins UP, 1991.

_____. *The Puritan Origins of the American Self*. Yale UP, 1975.

Buell, Lawrence. *New England Literary Culture: From Revolution to Renaissance*. Cambridge UP, 1986.

Colarcurcio, Michael J. *The Province of Piety: Moral History in Hawthorne's Earlier Tales*. Harvard UP, 1984.

Chase, Richard. *The American Novel and Its Tradition*. Doubleday Anchor, 1957.

Crews, Frederick. *The Sins of the Fathers: Hawthorne's Psychological Themes*. Oxford UP, 1966.

Delbanco, Andrew. *The Puritan Ordeal*. Columbia UP, 1989.

Feidelson, Charles. *Symbolism in American Literature*. U of Chicago P, 1953.

Kemeny, P. C. "Power, Ridicule, and the Destruction of Religious Moral Reform Politics in the 1920s." In *The Secular Revolution: Power, Interests, and Conflict in the Secularization of American Public Life*. Edited by Christian Smith. U of California P, 2003.

Matthiessen, F. O. *American Renaissance: Art and Expression in the Age of Emerson and Whitman*. Oxford UP, 1941.

Melville, Herman. *The Piazza Tales and Other Prose Pieces, 1839–1860*. Edited by Harrison Hayford, Alma A. MacDougall, and G. Thomas Tanselle. Northwestern UP and The Newberry Library, 1987.

McElroy, John H. "The Conventionality of *The Scarlet Letter*." In *Melville and Hawthorne in the Berkshires*. Edited by Howard P. Vincent. Kent State UP, 1966.

Milder, Robert. *Hawthorne's Habitations: A Literary Life*. Oxford UP, 2013.

Reynolds, David S. *Beneath the American Renaissance: The Subversive Imagination in the Age of Emerson and Melville*. Oxford UP, 1989.

Wheelwright, Ebenezer. *The Salem Belle, A Tale of 1692.* Edited by Richard Kopley. Pennsylvania State UP, 2016.

Wineapple, Brenda. *Hawthorne: A Life.* Knopf, 2003.

Biography of Nathaniel Hawthorne_____

Brian Yothers

Unlike many of his literary peers in the nineteenth century, Nathaniel Hawthorne both enjoyed acclaim and popularity during his lifetime and continued to be regarded as a major literary figure after his death. In many ways, a more appropriate face for American literature in the nineteenth century could hardly be imagined. He had a New England heritage that was both venerable and haunted, and he was born on the Fourth of July, the day which had also come to serve as the birthday of the United States for people in the early republic. In addition to admiring his prose, many of his contemporaries greatly admired his appearance: men and women alike commented on his striking good looks throughout most of his life. He also was intimately connected to a network of the most substantial figures in nineteenth-century American literary culture: Ralph Waldo Emerson (his sometime landlord), Margaret Fuller, Herman Melville, Henry Wadsworth Longfellow (his college classmate), George Ripley, Bronson Alcott, Harriet Beecher Stowe, Henry David Thoreau—the list could go on and on. Moreover, he was deeply admired by other contemporaries, notably Edgar Allan Poe.

Nathaniel Hathorne (he would add the "w" to his name only at the age of 23) was born on July 4, 1804, the descendant of prominent figures in early New England, notable among them his great-great-grandfather William Hathorne and his great-grandfather John Hathorne. John Hathorne was grim figure who made his major contribution to New England history by presiding as a hanging judge during the Salem witchcraft trials, and William Hathorne played a leading role in the persecution of religious dissidents in early Massachusetts, especially the Quakers. If William and John Hathorne's intolerance offered reasons for Nathaniel to feel shame about some of his ancestors' behavior, the prominence of the Hathorne family in Salem society meant that Nathaniel was also well poised to become a person of substance in nineteenth-century

New England. Hawthorne's life was not without challenges. If he was extraordinarily talented, descended from an illustrious family, and strikingly handsome, he also suffered from frequent experiences of financial distress, approaching poverty at times. In part, these financial straits had to do with the business failures of the author's father, also named Nathaniel, a ship's captain who died abroad when the young future author was only four years old (Wineapple 21).

The younger Nathaniel Hathorne grew up in Salem, and he pursued his education among a distinguished group of classmates at Bowdoin College in Maine, including Longfellow and the future president of the United States, Franklin Pierce. Despite his lineage and connections, success proved elusive, and Hawthorne's first novel, *Fanshawe: A Tale*, was published anonymously in 1828 and was greeted with little interest by his contemporaries. Starting in the previous year, meanwhile, the author had begun to spell his name with a "w": Nathaniel Hathorne had become Nathaniel Hawthorne.

Hawthorne made his fame as a writer of short stories, earning both critical and popular acclaim for short fiction early in his career. Indeed, until he published *The Scarlet Letter* in 1850, he was almost exclusively known as an author of tales and sketches, and once readers get beyond *The Scarlet Letter,* they are still most likely to encounter him as an author of short fiction. Hawthorne published in the major literary journals of his day, including John O'Sullivan's *Democratic Review*, James Russell Lowell's *Pioneer*, and Rufus Wilmot Griswold's *Graham's Magazine* (previously edited by Edgar Allan Poe), and Sarah Josepha Hale's *Godey's Ladies Book* (Wineapple 173-74).

Hawthorne's two major books before *The Scarlet Letter* were collections of short stories that drew upon his magazine fiction, *Twice-Told Tales* (1837), which included such frequently anthologized stories as "The Minister's Black Veil," "Wakefield," and "The Maypole of Merrymount," and *Mosses from an Old Manse* (1846), which included perennial classroom favorites "Young Goodman Brown," "Rappaccini's Daughter," and "The Celestial Railroad." During the period when Hawthorne was publishing his early short stories, he met two extraordinary sisters, Elizabeth and

Sophia Peabody, and became friends with both of them, ultimately beginning a romantic relationship with Sophia that culminated in their marriage. In the early years of their marriage, Nathaniel and Sophia Hawthorne lived at the Old Manse in Concord, Massachusetts, with Ralph Waldo Emerson as their landlord.

Hawthorne's relationship with Sophia points, as Robert Milder notes, toward aspects of Hawthorne's attitudes toward gender that can be troubling for readers in our own time. Milder points out that Hawthorne tends to spiritualize women both in his fiction and in his letters to Sophia even as he evinces considerable ambivalence toward the bodily aspects of female sexuality, and indeed seems to feel uncomfortable with sexuality in general (Milder 143).

A crucial interlude in Hawthorne's literary development was the time he spent at George Ripley's utopian community at Brook Farm where just before his marriage, he attempted to work with his hands as part of an ambitious utopian experiment. The ideas embraced by the inhabitants at Brook Farm were a combination of intellectual self-culture and the physical pursuit of a simple life on the land. The leaders at Brook Farm, Ripley, Bronson Alcott, and Margaret Fuller, envisioned a society in which manual labor and a simple lifestyle could contribute to a richer life of the mind for all men and women.

While drawn to the reforming vision of the Brook Farm experiment, Hawthorne ultimately rejected it as a model for a reformed society, and one of the more unkind remarks in the "Custom-House" introduction to *The Scarlet Letter* is that to "a man who had known Alcott," the customs house officials could come as a relief (25). The part of Hawthorne's biography that is most visible in *The Scarlet Letter* is his career as a political appointee, a customs house surveyor whose job depended on patronage from the political party in power at the moment. Hawthorne came into the position through Democratic Party patronage in 1846, and his lost his job when Zachary Taylor and the Whigs expelled the Democrats from power in 1848.

Losing his job turned out to be an excellent career move for Hawthorne as a writer, as he was able to complete his first novel, *The Scarlet Letter*, and to publish it in 1850. With the publication of *The*

Scarlet Letter, Hawthorne achieved not only "wide and continuous acclaim" from critics, but also a significant level of financial security (Wineapple 216). Hawthorne capitalized quickly on his success as a novelist, publishing *The House of the Seven Gables* (1851) and *The Blithedale Romance* (1852) in quick succession, along with a third short story collection, *The Snow-Image and Other Twice-Told Tales* (1852). Coming so quickly after the publication of *The Scarlet Letter*, these publications helped to ensure that Hawthorne would be seen as a central figure in what F. O. Matthiessen was to call the American Renaissance, the period from 1850 to 1855 that Matthiessen saw as redefining the shape of American literature.

Perhaps the most eminent of Hawthorne's nineteenth-century admirers from our twenty-first-century vantage point is Herman Melville, whose interest in Hawthorne was so intense that it has frequently been said to have an erotic quality. Melville corresponded with Hawthorne regularly during 1850 and 1851 as he was composing *Moby-Dick*, and he wrote his most substantial work of literary criticism in the form of a review of Hawthorne's *Mosses from an Old Manse* entitled "Hawthorne and His Mosses." Melville praised Hawthorne particularly for his ability to blend humor and tragedy in his body of work, and he saw Hawthorne as the most significant of his contemporaries among American authors.

One of Hawthorne's most frequently condemned remarks appears in a letter from 1855 to his publisher, George Ticknor. Hawthorne bemoaned the existence of a "d—d mob of scribbling women," whom he regarded as crowding writers like himself out of the literary marketplace "with their trash" (Ticknor 141). It is certainly true that Hawthorne reacted negatively to the popularity of much women's writing, but it is also noteworthy that he admired Fanny Fern, who was among the most popular of his female contemporaries. Regarding Fern, he wrote to Ticknor that she "writes as if the Devil was in her" and affirmed that when women writers "throw off the restraints of decency, and come before the public stark naked, as it were,—then their books are sure to possess character and value," concluding with his desire to convey to Fern "how much I admire her" (Ticknor 142-43). Hawthorne's reflections on Fanny

Fern's work seems to suggest that his critique of some nineteenth-century women's writing was based less on misogyny than on his sense that some of the popular writing of the midnineteenth-century was inauthentic in its representation of human experience.

Hawthorne's early years at Bowdoin College played an important role in shaping his later literary career, as he published a campaign biography in 1852 of his college friend Franklin Pierce, now often described as one the weakest presidents the United States has had, and not infrequently blamed for contributing to the spread of slavery and the coming of the United States Civil War. Indeed, in recent years, Hawthorne's biographers and critics have become particularly uneasy about his reaction to the American Civil War. His most substantial piece on the subject, "Thoughts in War-Time, by a Peaceable Man" (1862) is as pacific as its title suggests, but it also fails to recognize the weighty moral issues at stake in the Civil War. Hawthorne thus came to be regarded late in life as a rather conservative writer, and among the traits that is most frustrating to his twenty-first-century admirers is his inability to contend with the issues of racial equality and justice that had become increasingly important in the United States in the 1850s and 1860s. The Hawthorne who could exercise extraordinary moral intelligence in relation to the Puritan past in New England seemed to lose something of that capacity when faced with the moral crisis of the Civil War.

Hawthorne's last novel, *The Marble Faun; or The Romance of Monte Beni*, moved in directions that had been suggested by *The Scarlet Letter* and some of his short stories, but this novel has never been as widely discussed or taught as Hawthorne's earlier New England novels. It deals quite profoundly with matters of art and moral responsibility, however, and in recent years it has been recovered as an instance of nineteenth-century American transatlanticism that looked forward to the Italian settings of Henry James.

Hawthorne's ill health during the early 1860s culminated in his death in 1864, in the company of his lifelong friend from Bowdoin College, former US president Frankin Pierce. Hawthorne left some important work uncompleted at his death, notable *Septimius Felton;*

or, The Elixir of Life, which was published posthumously in 1872, and he also left a rich array of letters and notebooks reflecting upon his experiences and travels. Hawthorne's literary legacy would be preserved in part by his family: his son, Julian Hawthorne contributed substantially to the knowledge that we have about his personal life and views. Hawthorne was also unique among nineteenth-century American writers, as Samuel Coale points out in his chapter in this volume and in his longer study *The Entanglements of Nathaniel Hawthorne*, in that he never really fell out of critical favor. In the late nineteenth century, Henry James could devote a volume to Hawthorne's work, and serious authors have looked back to this ambivalent descendent of the New England Puritans ever since.

Works Cited

Coale, Samuel. *The Entanglements of Nathaniel Hawthorne.* Camden House, 2011.

Matthiessen, F. O. *American Renaissance: Art and Expression in the Age of Emerson and Whitman.* Oxford UP, 1941.

Milder, Robert. *Hawthorne's Habitations: A Literary Life.* Oxford UP, 2013.

Ticknor, Caroline. *Hawthorne and His Publisher.* Houghton Mifflin, 1913.

Wineapple, Brenda. *Hawthorne: A Life.* Knopf, 2003.

CRITICAL
CONTEXTS

The Scarlet Letter Casts Its Shadow_____

Samuel Coale

The headline in the arts section of the *New York Times* on September 12, 2017, proclaimed, "A Revenge Tragedy Colored by Brecht; Susan-Lori Parks's Riff on 'The Scarlet Letter' Returns to the Stage with a New Vitality" (C5). According to the critic, Ben Brantley, Parks's play, which features a scatological pun in its title that might have surprised Hawthorne, riffs on 'that great 1850 novel about Puritan guilt and repression.' Wherever you look, the letter shimmers yet again.

Since its publication in 1850, *The Scarlet Letter* has never been out of print. Unlike that of his contemporaries, such as Melville, Dickinson, Whitman, Stowe, and to a lesser degree, Emerson and Poe, Hawthorne's work, once embraced by the academy, has always been discussed, critiqued, studied, and analyzed, and has found its place in virtually every high school curriculum. As Hyatt Waggoner asserted in 1979, "Never forgotten, Hawthorne has never needed to be rediscovered" (*Presence* 143). The letter itself still shimmers as a public icon from politics to popular culture. Bruce Daniels revealed that, as of 1997, American literary critics have ranked Hawthorne as the first among American writers and that *The Scarlet Letter* exists in twenty-nine editions.

What I would like to do in a broadly chronological manner is to explore the various critical approaches *The Scarlet Letter* has been subject to over the years from the first polarized assessments in the nineteenth century, where critics and admirers wrestled with the seeming incompatibility of Hawthorne's "elegant" style and the morbidity of his tales, to the more contemporary positions of feminist criticism, political commentary, and the various contexts of cultural studies. I'd also like to suggest that the book has been easily hijacked by all manner of critical reception because of its peculiar power, its text webbed with secrets, silences, subterfuges, evasions, psychological probings, social hierarchies, and speculations.

These have been tackled by nineteenth-century commentators, modernist critics, postmodernist and deconstructive critics, and more contemporary ones. The text seems to be doing its own critical work for us as Hawthorne assembles and disassembles the dualisms of allegory and laces his work with contradictions and multiple perspectives. As Margaret B. Moore suggested in 1998, "His conclusions were tentative. That is the reason he spoke more in the subjunctive mood rather than in the indicative" (256).

We live in a critical time, Rita Felski wittily reminds us, where the spirit of Paul Ricœur's "hermeneutics of suspicion" still lingers as critics interrogate, pummel, assault, and batter various texts in terms of their complicity with the status quo, their hidden treacheries and accommodations, their spurious ideological underpinnings, and their reinforcement of political power. *The Scarlet Letter* responds to all of these things, each embedded in Hawthorne's text and his ideas about creating an American romance as opposed to the socialrealist British writers of his time, such as Charles Dickens and Anthony Trollope.

American critics at the time of *The Scarlet Letter* were eager to crown a "great" American writer to compete with the all-pervasive British imports, and Hawthorne quickly filled that void. He became the Great American Romantic Icon, isolated, solitary, a brooding Byronesque creature doomed to his own shadow of seclusion and reticence. His polite style hid psychological and cultural terrors, his mantle of respectability, and the morbidity and menace of his manuscripts. His allegorical framework with its Christian attributes appealed to his readers while at the same time he was eroding its very essence.

Fashions and attitudes changed, but *The Scarlet Letter* maintained its central place in American literature. Hawthorne's reputation as a gothic writer only grew over the years, even as both Melville and James couldn't decide whether or not he harbored a deep dark metaphysical blackness or whether he was just conjuring up aesthetic effects for their atmosphere and coloring. In the modernist era, when Freud and his vision of universal repression took American culture by storm, Hawthorne's best romance provided the perfect candidate for analysis and dark unconscious possibilities, complete with "unreliable narrators, conflicting viewpoints, fragmented narratives and metafictional devices. . . ." (Felski 42).

Phenomenological perspectives could focus on Hawthorne's fetishizing of objects—scarlet letters, houses with seven gables, veiled ladies, and Roman ruins. New Critics, desperate to find an ultimate unity in all things, grappled with ironies and paradoxes and what seemed to be Hawthorne's neo-Orthodox sensibilities. When the linguistic turn heralded by deconstruction arrived in the 1970s, his style, already deconstructed and deceptive, played yet again right into critics' hands. Feminist critics praised Hester Prynne's independence as opposing the hierarchical patriarchy of her day, minimizing how much the Calvinist society permeates her own outlook on the world. She did keep Roger Chillingworth's true status a secret and wore her letter proudly as its interpretation shifted from "Adulterer" to "Angel," proclaiming her own artistry in its gold and crimson incarnation. Hawthorne's politics, particularly regarding his stance on the Civil War in "About War Matters," were raked over the coals in his evenhanded assessment of the North and South that, like his friend President Franklin Pierce, could be taken for upholding the status quo when tempers and patriotism erupted on both sides, a dualism, however disrupted, that couldn't be shaken in the heat of war. While much of the critical reception shifted and changed, *The Scarlet Letter* withstood and thrived on all of it.

Upon its publication *The Scarlet Letter* was praised and celebrated more than it was castigated and condemned. Readers were fascinated by its focus on adultery and its very nineteenth-century anti-Calvinist point of view. Dr. George Bailey Loring and the Reverend Arthur Cleveland Coxe (though to see them as opposites, one positive, the other determinedly negative, elevates Coxe's opinion more than necessary) provide a too-easily polarized response to the romance.

Loring's impressionistic and convoluted essay is saturated with the concepts of Christian sin and redemption, though he praises Hester's courage and excoriates Dimmesdale's secret repentance, his lack of any ultimate wisdom, and his self-proclaimed criminality:

"It would be hard to conceive of a greater outrage upon the freezing and self-denying doctrines of that day, than the sin for which Hester Prynne was damned by society, and for which Arthur Dimmesdale damned himself" (169). For Loring, the Puritan sin lay in condemning human passions, "the foundation of all that beauty which seeks its expression in poetry, and music, and art . . . " (169). Such passions were crimes. Dimmesdale learns nothing from his excruciating self-punishment. Siding with Hester as opposed to society's hard and cold laws on virtue and chastity, Loring insists that "Between the individual and his God, there remains a spot, larger or smaller, as the soul has been kept unclouded, where no sin can enter . . ." (171). Here lies the nineteenth century's belief in the democratic center in each individual that transcends society's rules and remains virtually immaculate. For him, Hester's line, "What we did had a consecration of its own," however much a product of conflict and social stigma, encapsulates her ultimate beauty and holiness, however marked by guilt, surrounded by a self-righteous society with "the stiff, formal dignities of our early New England Colony" (169).

Not so the Reverend Coxe who proclaims his sense of outrage. He denounces "the nauseous amour of a Puritan pastor," which degrades American literature and encourages "social licentiousness . . . Is the French era actually begun in our literature?" (182). Mon Dieu! True, Dimmesdale as a character may be interesting, but filth besmirches his soul. As for Hester, "a frail creature of his charge, [her] mind is represented as far more debauched than her body" (182).

Coxe's rant does nail the nineteenth-century dilemma when it came to Hawthorne's fiction that his style is chaste, delicate, and decorous, but his tale is morbid, immoral, and unclean. How can one support the other? Can they ever be reconciled? In a sense this conflict has permeated much of Hawthornian criticism and the challenges of his several biographers: the solitary morbid soul who yet held several public political appointments; the dark-dyed vision embodied in a dedicated family man; the dark night of the soul—Dimmesdale's, Hester's—embodied in a perfectly decent and wholesome style.

Orestes Brownson, the transcendentalist who became a Catholic, upbraided *The Scarlet Letter* because it reduced serious theological concerns to mere psychology, another dilemma that plagued the nineteenth century. For him Hester never repents and, therefore, doesn't take her very real sin seriously enough: "We are never to forget that sin is sin . . . But in the present case neither of the guilty party repent . . . they hug their illicit love; they cherish their sin . . ." (177). While Coxe and Brownson remain critical outliers in regard to the romance, much of their attitude continues to the present day which, in popular culture, sees the scarlet letter as a proclamation of guilt, a symbol of punishment and shame, representing "the persecuting spirit" (2) that Philip Roth in his novel, *The Human Stain*, identified as embedded in American culture.

Critics from the beginning commented on Hawthorne's fascination with damaged souls, the existential estrangement between human beings, the severe consequences of concealment, his analytical probing of each of them as if studying them under a microscope and searching for their deepest inadequacies and self-delusions, their unrelievable sense of solitude and separation and their ultimately unfathomable experience of sorrow and suffering, of secret misdeeds and fantasies. Many also pointed out the ruthless playing out of impersonal laws—social, personal, cultural, historical—akin perhaps to the Greeks' sense of fate and self-destruction. They admire Hester's perseverance and courage, while pointing out her submission to Chillingworth's demands that she keep his secret.

Many have also commented upon the structure of Hawthorne's fiction as allegorical, setting up abstract ideas in opposition to one another as opposed to full-blooded characters. The nineteenth century relished allegory, particularly before the Civil War, since most of its writers were familiar with it from their own Christian education and background. Human passion battled patriarchal hierarchies; the heart clashed with the head; sin contended with sorrow as theological perspectives confronted psychological explanations. The coldly analytical Chillingworth dogged the haunted steps of the self-wounding minister and his secret bouts of flagellation, a penance that always struck me in its masturbatory repetition as sexually charged.

Hawthorne set up various tableaux—the three scaffold scenes, for instance—to focus on these encounters, seemingly siding with Chillingworth's idea that all has resulted from a "dark necessity," whereas the modern reader more skeptically assigns this vision to Chillingworth and not entirely to Hawthorne. Modern criticism has explored the conscious breakdown of such frameworks in Hawthorne's self-proclaimed "blasted allegories"—again the ambiguities: blasted because of a failure of form? Blasted as in condemning allegory as such?—revealing how master and slave depend on one another to establish each other's role.

The Scarlet Letter dovetailed nicely with modernism's Freudian notions of repression and unconscious compulsions. Newton Arvin struck the note of the soul-haunted, troubled author of such a book, wrapped in solitude and forever isolated from his fellow creatures, a romantic stereotype that has survived the various critical approaches, however attacked, undermined, and rendered too simplistic if not wrongheaded. Hawthorne's excavation of his characters' souls exemplified Freud's examination of his patients. Psychological depth provided the ultimate key to understanding Dimmesdale's withering, self-imposed self-abasement (albeit in private), Chillingworth's ruthless pursuit of his quarry's secrets, and Hester's obstinate faith in her own self-worth, however compromised, and artistry. Each played off the other's guilt and dependence, rigorously entangled, however earlier allegorical criticism viewed them as stalwart representatives of certain human traits.

The Scarlet Letter also became the perfect candidate for the New Critical approach to paradox, irony, and ambiguity in producing a perfectly unified work of art, created in the shadow of a neo-Orthodox Christian faith and outlook, but as Lionel Trilling in "Our Hawthorne" decided, his work had become an anachronism and was limited and marginal in relation to someone like Kafka's, since Hawthorne "always consented to the power of his imagination being controlled by the power of the world . . . the modern consciousness requires that an artist have an imagination which is more intransigent than this" (454). The shadow of allegory as an old-fashioned, rigid, and discredited structure still fell upon *The Scarlet Letter* and led Alfred Kazin to declare, "This is why there are so many theological and psychoanalytical interpretations of Hawthorne; they fill the vacuum created by our modern uncertainty about the use and relevance of Hawthorne's art" (458). Both believed in Hawthorne's exploration of dark psychological depths but would have agreed with Mark Van Doren who suggested in 1949 that only in *The Scarlet Letter* did Hawthorne really probe deeply, achieve the perfect balance in his fiction, and then forever after avoided those depths, a backhanded compliment if there ever was one.

F. O. Matthiessen celebrated the optimistic romantic essayists and poets, placing the likes of Hawthorne and Melville off to the side as a kind of tragic chorus that "mainstream" American literature transcended. His Hawthorne comes across as politically conservative and very much a supporter of the status quo, a kind of ancestor to V. S. Naipaul's idea that one should hate the oppressor and fear the oppressed. However true, if we were to take this perspective literally, it suggests political paralysis and inaction, assisted in Hawthorne's case by his delight in ambiguity and irony. Matthiessen's was the search for the voice of the age, the true American sensibility and soul in its remarkable aesthetic expressions such as Whitman's "Song of Myself" and Emerson's poetry and essays. In such company Hawthorne was bound to look timid and tame.

Matthiessen's New Critical approach to *The Scarlet Letter* embraced the various dualisms and polarities: progress versus the status quo, egalitarian democracy versus traditional hierarchies. Dualism threaded his lukewarm appreciation of Hawthorne, both prying his work loose from the rigid nineteenth-century category of allegory and at the same time appealing to it as well. His vision encompassed "devices of multiple choice," not the mere dualistic nature of allegory: Hawthorne "does not literally accept his own allegory, and yet he finds it symbolically valid because of its psychological exactitude" (277). This underscored Hawthorne's fascination with mesmerism (and the charismatic power of Hester, Dimmesdale, Chillingworth, and Pearl), which he morally despised for allowing one human being to gain power over another and yet psychologically recognized the visceral reality of it.

The modernist symbol, often opaque, multifaceted, mysterious, and infinitely suggestive, transcended allegorical bindings, but such Manichean strictures were never totally abandoned by Hawthorne critics and led to future simplistic categories: Hester, the liberally minded protofeminist free spirit; Pearl, the quirky "devil's child"; Chillingworth, the single-minded, obsessive, and evil scientist-doctor; and Dimmesdale, the self-hating, self-eviscerating Puritan. Hawthorne's tableaux and especially the three scaffold scenes contributed to this allegorical framework.

The New Critics thrived on polarities with their roots in the allegorical tradition. Their vision of the aesthetic unity of texts arose from the often precarious balancing act between these various dualisms. And even in relatively recent years Magnus Ullen conceived of the importance of allegorical markers in *The Scarlet Letter* along with the more modernist notion of dialectical interchanges and entanglements. In Hawthorne criticism allegory never dies, however reshaped, rekindled, undermined, underscored, and overstated.

Post-New-Critical analysts discovered different approaches. Kenneth Dauber relied on the new waves of critical theory, especially deconstruction, to explore Hawthorne's fiction. Edgar A. Dryden added to the expanding interest in Hawthorne's vision of the American romance as a particular genre in opposition to the socially realistic novel. Nina Baym contributed to the new interest in feminist criticism. All three of these critical categories erupted into an avalanche of book-length studies and critical articles, laying waste to the New Critical belief in unity, balance, and the more or less immaculate self-enclosed quality of literary texts.

Deconstruction, the "linguistic turn," took all of American literary criticism by storm with its emphasis on undecidability, indefiniteness, deferral, disruption, and the way the prison-house of language led only to other cells and texts. Texts became transparently porous and pointed not to well-balanced polarities but to Hawthorne's linguistic indeterminacy, his rhetorical strategies, and the slipperiness and elusiveness of language itself. Critics interrogated texts searching out their weak spots, their evasions, their unresolved and unresolvable contradictions, and their glaring inconsistencies and uncertainties. Readers and texts became entangled, almost willfully engaged, scrutinized, seduced, and abandoned. *The Scarlet Letter* proved to be a perfect case study for this mode of critical reception, already fashioned as a very "porous" text.

Kenneth Dauber assaulted unity and wholeness in literary texts. For him texts wrote the author: "the forms of fiction impose themselves . . . To write is to repeat what has already been written. [Hawthorne's] work exists as a cultural imposition before he begins. It is a tyranny he cannot resist" (41). His attack on Calvinism with self-righteously autonomous individuals and society's rules and regulations locking horns can also be seen from the perspective of Foucault's idea of power's inhabiting all human creatures, not merely as some exterior oppression. Themes are not so much integrated as dispersed. *The Scarlet Letter* wars with itself, wandering in dark corridors of the mind. Hawthorne oscillates: "He presents himself divided against himself, mocking one half with the other" (34) as does language itself. Division rules. Synthesis crumbles. Old categories such as allegory are "so undirected the reader may overcome it with any number of explications of his own. [The reader] works his will on the text" (16-17). Suddenly Hawthorne criticism, which had seemed old-fashioned, outmoded, and stale, burst into new life as Dauber was one of the first to delve into the deconstructed depths of romance.

Other critics struggled to define the American romance as its own special genre, one Hawthorne had helped create and cultivate. Hawthorne's "neutral territory," which he describes in "The Custom-House" at the beginning of *The Scarlet Letter,* allows for strange and supernatural events to mingle with the everyday world, pits characters against one another who do represent certain types but are never reduced to them, lures readers into the shadows of the upper story of the Custom-House and the beckoning dark woods where witches and devils may linger, stages stark scaffold tableaux at midnight, points to strange astronomical signs in the night sky, suggests the diabolical potions and powders that Chillingworth has learned from the Indians, hints at the demonic nature of Pearl's spontaneity and sudden outbursts, explores the dark roots of New England Calvinism that have contributed to mysterious superstitions and terrors, discovers the revelation of something deeper in the reflections that appear in mirrors, and spreads rumors of the Black Man's book and Mistress Hibbins's witchcraft. The craft and ambiguities of such a structure as the American Romance also helped spawn the fictions of others, such as James, Faulkner, Morrison, McCullers, O'Connor, Oates, Didion, and Jackson.

Perhaps Dryden best summarizes the lure of the American romance. Building on works that focused on dualisms, polarities, psychological conditions, and the symbolic in Hawthorne's fiction, he employs the Keatsian dialectic between enchantment and disenchantment, being seduced by the sound of the nightingale and the bucolic scene on the Grecian urn, only to finally pull away and suffer the loss of that romantic ideal of sublime harmony. As a result he suggests, "dreams and reality are unable to coexist as one always seeks to invade and transform the other" (138). Hester and Arthur dream of escape and have escaped into the forest to make love beyond and outside the Calvinist boundaries of social realities and constrictions. Hawthorne's persistent use of mystery, secrets, silences, backgrounds, motives, and unconscious compulsions seduces the reader, sets her up to try and fathom the unfathomable depths of haunted minds, enchanted both by fascination and multiple interpretations. Disenchantment will soon follow—Keats cannot forget the very real possibility of his own death while imagining the continued singing of the nightingale forever—and Dimmesdale will die, but for one sweet shining moment Hester and Arthur seem eternally bonded and self-forgiving.

Nina Baym viewed Hawthorne as a feminist writer, describing Hester and others as courageous, brave, and at times outspoken souls who take on the stringencies of patriarchy and outwit (if only momentarily) the hierarchical reigns of male politicians, mesmerists, reformers, and monks. She traces how Hawthorne grew as a writer and celebrated human passion as opposed to a repressive society in *The Scarlet Letter*, a theme that over the years has been narrowed to celebrating the marginalized as always preferable to mainstream society, muddying how much of the Calvinist ethic has seeped into Hester's soul as much as she does valiant battle to overcome it.

The self in conflict with society has always been the staple of fiction, but Hester is not as one-dimensional as some critics have made her out to be, excluding Baym and others. In "Revisiting Hawthorne's Feminism," she insists, "In this essay I swim against the tide to argue—again—for Hawthorne as a feminist writer from *The Scarlet Letter* onward" (541). That critical tide had deconstructed a feminist "essentialism" in relying on the hermeneutics of suspicion across the board, but Baym continues her very strong case. Hester's flaws and failures do not automatically invalidate her ideas and perceptions. She is a much more complicated character than that: "To say that Hawthorne's women have more heart than his men does not imply that they have less brain" (553).

Emily Miller Budick discussed the romance form as employed by women writers, such as Carson McCullers, Flannery O'Connor, and Toni Morrison, and how the "Hawthorne Tradition" has influenced them. The women celebrate family and community more than male writers who focus on individual autonomy and patriarchy. From such a position Hester maintains her position as the true hero of *The Scarlet Letter,* particularly because of what she was up against. This conception, however simplified, has not really changed over the years, however modified and nuanced.

Monika Elbert asserted that the feminist perspective is less rigid than the male one and that it views all perspectives as subjective and shifting. It firmly rejects polarized platitudes, such as male versus female, black versus white, past versus present, and insists that such bifurcation is a "male-induced construct" (12) that oversimplifies and constricts actual experience. We can see how this outlook derives from the Calvinist tradition in its rigid view of the saved and the damned, the elect and the doomed, and the male and the female. Such dualisms are arbitrary and underscore the patriarchal hierarchy of society.

Two other critical approaches flourished in the 1980s and are still going strong. The New Historicist method placed novels and their characters within a historical context, thereby linking them to and as products of specific eras. This also involved critical looks at Hawthorne's politics. *The Scarlet Letter* explores the effect and consequences of a Calvinist theocracy on Boston in the seventeenth century. At the same time, written as it was in 1850, it fully reveals the nineteenth century's denigration of and judgment of the strict and harsh Calvinist era, which looked more rigid than it might actually have been because of Hawthorne's attack on his ancestors' involvement in the Salem witch trials. The second emerging critical advance examined the role of racism in all texts, the kind that infiltrates them even if particular African Americans are not mentioned. As Toni Morrison made clear, freedom in America has always been white; slavery has always been black. And that inflexible polarity, however socially constructed, remained virtually unassailable. The devil in *The Scarlet Letter* is embodied by the Black Man in the forest, a demonic creature waiting to seduce the very Calvinists who had conjured him up in the first place.

While he does not deal specifically with *The Scarlet Letter*, Michael J. Colacurcio examines and analyses the moral history and culture of the Calvinist era as seen through Hawthorne's eyes. Instead of allegorical symbols or symbolically allegorical dualisms, Colacurcio was convinced and convincing that Hawthorne was determined "to expose the moral premises which shaped the experience of the past" (150). Colacurcio had no faith in broad, general, and often vague psychological conditions, extracted from a historical context and presented as if they were universal and common to all, but instead concentrated on the historical era, thus creating a wider, more specific cultural milieu for Hawthorne's fiction: "Hawthorne repeatedly allowed the Puritan language of diabolical simulation and, more generally of the 'invisible world' to control the limits of his own psychological investigations" (285). This helps account for Hawthorne's use of archaic language to try to mimic Calvinist conversations and beliefs. Circumstances reveal their distinct historical roots; they are not meant to be simply allegorical. This method provided a context that the New Critics and deconstructionists had either played down or avoided. American beliefs in self-reliance, the autonomy of individuals, and the religious traditions of salvation and domination become historical markers, not just symbolic states.

Sacvan Bercovitch maintained that Hawthorne's ambiguities cancelled one another out and established a status quo-oriented equilibrium that sought synthesis in the future, not in the historical present. Hester's return to Boston reveals her hope for reconciliation and compromise, assimilated into the community as a sign of future progress toward cultural unity and harmony. Such an approach, I think, minimizes the tragic consequences of the romance and the shadows of Chillingworth's "dark necessity" that forever haunt the text. Bercovitch celebrates "a rhetoric of reconciliation that was rooted both in the ambiguities of legal language and in a providential sense of mission" (66). Arthur may be dead, but he still resides in Boston where Hester will take up her final resting place.

As Arthur Riss argues, "Where once Hawthorne had no politics, now it seems that all he has are bad politics," linking it to Jonathan Arac's notion of "'a politics of issueless patience'"(17). Larry Reynolds tackles the "issueless" issue head on, placing him directly within the blatant racism of his times, examining his loyal support for President Franklin Pierce, who in trying to straddle both North and South enflamed both, describing Hawthorne's version of John Brown as a violent outlaw who should have been hanged, and disagreeing with the flagrant and outright abolitionism of several of his Concord neighbors such as Emerson and Thoreau.

The Scarlet Letter, which exposes the flaws in Calvinist society and in individuals, obviously discredits the Puritans' rigid and theocratic rules and regulations, but nowhere is there any real challenge to the system except in the colorful prominence of Hester's *A*, her willfulness in clinging to Pearl as her child, and her certainty that what she and Dimmesdale did "had a consecration of its own." It may result in a distinctly autonomous personal politics, but it does nothing to change the system. The case can be made that in returning to Boston after Arthur's death and in living in isolation on the outskirts of Boston before that event, she is as much upholding the Calvinist order as attempting to defy it. Strong political positions for Hawthorne smacked of the obsessive quests and positions of many of his male characters, which often led to "the notion of righteous violence" (203) in the shadow of a cause and ultimately eroded their common humanity.

Racism infiltrates all walks of American life, once raising questions whether or not a slave was even a person. Riss castigates the position that political liberalism tries to blur all racial distinctions in an effort to both overcome and uphold them. "Liberalism . . . brands any specific meaning or identity as arbitrary and contingent," he insists, "and thus attempts to transcend such particularism" (123), as Hawthorne supposedly does in his many contradictory and ambiguous definitions of Hester's *A*. From this point of view, ambiguity can be understood as upholding the patriarchal system, supporting slavery, keeping women in their place, projecting a political state of noninterference and indifference, creating "neutral territories" in a way to avoid harsh political and personal decisions, and keeping secrets intact instead of taking direct stands on specific issues. I agree with all of this but at the same time believe that Hawthorne's tragic awareness of the human condition in all its contradictions and misplaced polarities provided the perfect antidote to a blind faith in progress, Manifest Destiny, Jacksonian Democracy, and that much-blessed myth of individual autonomy.

All these critical approaches to *The Scarlet Letter* remain in circulation today, despite the ups and downs of critical fashions and fads. I agree with Richard Millington who describes *The Scarlet Letter* as the "romance as revision" (59), where characters and readers, however psychologically and culturally limited, continually reinterpret the letter and revise its significance from *Adultery* to *Able* to *Angel* to *Art* to *Arthur* and beyond. The women, Hester and Pearl, grow and mature. The men, Dimmesdale and Chillingworth, wither and die. Revision suggests an ultimate humanity in the wake of certain male obsessions and compulsions. Richard Brodhead suggests that "what we see . . . is a mind playing across objects, allowing them to enkindle reflections and projections onto them its own thoughts and feelings . . . The scarlet letter itself becomes, in effect, a character, insisting upon itself . . ." (16, 56). Perhaps this helps to account for the book's lasting popularity and its ability to withstand all levels of critical reception and cross-examination. The letter already shifts and shimmers before critics can even get their hands on it. It embodies the changing patterns of human consciousness and historical and cultural circumstances. And in the future, I suspect, it will continue to do so.

Works Cited

Arvin, Newton. *Hawthorne*. Little, Brown, 1929.

Baym, Nina. *The Shape of Hawthorne's Career*. Cornell UP, 1976.

_____. "Revisiting Hawthorne's Feminism." In *Hawthorne and The Real: Bicentennial Essays*. Edited by Millicent Bell. Ohio State UP, 2005, pp. 107-24.

Bercovitch, Sacvan. *The Office of the Scarlet Letter*. Johns Hopkins UP, 1991.

Brodhead, Richard. *The School of Hawthorne*. New York UP, 1986.

Brownson, Orestes. Review of *The Scarlet Letter*, Brownson's *Quarterly Review*, (1850) in *Hawthorne: The Critical Heritage*. Edited by J. Donald Crowley. Routledge, 1970, pp. 175-79.

Budick, Emily Miller. *Engendering Romance: Women Writers and the Hawthorne Tradition, 1850-1990*. Yale UP, 1994.

Colacurcio, Michael J. *The Province of Piety: Moral History in Hawthorne's Early Tales*. Harvard UP, 1984.

Coxe, Arthur Cleveland. "The Writings of Hawthorne," *Church Review* (1851). Crowley, pp. 179-84.

Dauber, Kenneth. *Rediscovering Hawthorne*. Princeton UP, 1977.

Daniels, Bruce. "Bad Movie/Worse History: The 1995 Unmaking of *The Scarlet Letter*." *Journal of Popular Culture* (1999), pp. 1-11.

Dryden, Edgar A. *Nathaniel Hawthorne: The Poetics of Enchantment*. Cornell UP, 1977.

Elbert, Monika. *Encoding the Letter "A": Gender and Authority in Hawthorne's Early Fiction*. Haag &Herchen, 1990.

Felski, Rita. *The Limits of Critique*. U of Chicago P, 2015.

Hawthorne, Nathaniel. *The Centenary Edition of the Works of Nathaniel Hawthorne*. Edited by William Charvat et al. Ohio State UP, 1962-1997. 23 vols.

Kazin, Alfred. "Hawthorne: The Artist of New England." *Atlantic Monthly* (1966).

Loring, George Bailey. Review of *The Scarlet Letter*. *Massachusetts Quarterly Review*, (1850). Crowley, pp. 168-75.

Matthiessen, F. O. *American Renaissance: Art and Expression in the Age of Emerson and Whitman*. Oxford UP, 1941.

Millington, Richard. *Practicing Romance: Narrative Form and Cultural Engagement*. Princeton UP, 1992.

Moore, Margaret B. *The Salem World of Nathaniel Hawthorne*. U of Missouri P, 1998.

Morrison, Toni. *Playing in the Dark: Whiteness and the Literary Imagination*. Harvard UP, 1992.

Reynolds, Larry. *Devils and Rebels: The Making of Hawthorne's Damned Politics*. U of Michigan P, 2008.

Riss, Arthur. *Slavery and Liberalism in Nineteenth Century American Literature*. Cambridge UP, 2006.

Roth, Philip. *The Human Stain*. Houghton Mifflin, 2000.

Trilling, Lionel. "Our Hawthorne." *Hawthorne Centenary Essays*. Edited by Roy Harvey Pearce. Ohio State UP, 1964:429-58.

Ullen, Magnus. *The Half-Vanished Structure: Hawthorne's Allegorical Dialectics*. Uppsala University, 2001.

Van Doren, Mark. *Nathaniel Hawthorne*. William Sloane, 1949.

Waggoner, Hyatt H. *The Presence of Hawthorne*. Louisiana State UP, 1979.

Hawthorne's *The Scarlet Letter*: One Passage from Multiple Perspectives

Robert C. Evans

During the thousands of years that humans have been producing, enjoying, and studying literature, numerous approaches to analyzing and understanding it have arisen. Often these approaches have had much in common, but sometimes they have radically differed. The ancient Greek philosopher Plato (ca. 428-348 BCE), for instance, deeply distrusted literature because he thought it often sprang from, and encouraged, irrational emotions. On the other hand, his great pupil Aristotle (384-322 BCE) wrote an especially powerful and influential defense of literature, *The Poetics*, in which he argued, in impressive detail, for the beauty, morality, and intellectual value of important works of literary art. By time of the Roman poet Horace (65-8 BCE), Aristotle's arguments had pretty much won the day, so that Horace's own treatise, *The Art of Poetry*, is often a how-to manual that takes many of Aristotle's arguments for granted. Horace mainly offers practical advice about effective writing. Finally, another ancient critic—usually called "Longinus" (first century CE)—turned Plato's ideas inside out, insisting that truly great, ennobling, and lofty literature deserved to be called "sublime" (that is, "elevating").

So: four important ancient theorists and four fundamentally different approaches to literary works. Plato found literature potentially dangerous; Aristotle valued it as art and knowledge; Horace merely assumed its worth and offered advice about how to write effectively; and Longinus considered the best literature powerful, uplifting, and spiritually grand. Later, even more ways of thinking about and analyzing literature have been developed. These have included, for instance (in roughly chronological order), approaches that might be called (1) thematic, (2) historical, (3) formalist, (4) psychoanalytical, (5) archetypal, (6) Marxist, (7) structuralist, (8) feminist, (9) deconstructive, (10) reader-response,

(11) dialogical, (12) New Historicist, (13) multicultural, (14) postmodern, (15) Darwinian, and (16) ecocritical. Of course, many other approaches might easily be mentioned; for instance, the sheer variety of different kinds of psychoanalytical criticism can be intimidating. But by now the basic point is clear: literature can be, and has been, approached from numerous, often competing and contradictory points of view.

Many advocates of these differing approaches have argued for the superiority of their own approaches. Traditional historical critics, for instance, often resisted the rise of formalism; formalism in turn was attacked by Marxists and other kinds of theorists; psychoanalytical (i.e., Freudian) and archetypal (i.e., Jungian) critics still fundamentally disagree; deconstruction conflicts with structuralism; New Historicism takes aim at traditional historical criticism; and so on. Which approach, then, should a reader choose? Which is the "correct" approach? Attempts to answer these questions have produced enormous, sometimes exhausting, debate that has often been productive but can occasionally seem fruitless. Positions have often been clarified through debate, but few partisans have ever been truly persuaded by other points of view. Sometimes true believers have simply been unwilling to find any value in theories other than their own.

One solution to the question of which approach is the "right" approach is called *critical pluralism*. Pluralists assume that each different way of reading literature is like each particular tool in a toolbox. Is a hammer superior to a screwdriver? It is if one wants to hammer a nail, but a screwdriver is superior if one wants to twist in a screw. Is a saw superior to a wrench? It is if one wants to cut through something rather than twist a bolt, but a saw doesn't help much if twisting a bolt is the goal. In short, pluralists argue that each approach has potential merit *depending on the job one wants to accomplish*. A hammer need not conflict with a screwdriver, just as formalism need not conflict with historicism. A microscope is no "better" than a telescope or a pair of glasses: each has its own purpose and value depending on the task one wants to achieve. One advantage of pluralism is that it encourages readers to see from *multiple* perspectives and thus recognize both the strengths and limitations of numerous theories. By reading texts with *various* theories in mind, and by being willing to let each theory help illuminate the advantages or disadvantages of the others, readers (pluralists would argue) can achieve much richer, more nuanced understandings than if they insist on reading in only one particular way.[1]

Pluralism in Practice: A Passage from *The Scarlet Letter*

Consider, for instance, a passage from the first chapter of Nathaniel Hawthorne's *Scarlet Letter*. In this section, Arthur Dimmesdale, a young, respected local minister in Puritan New England in the mid-1600s, is urged by his superiors to address one of his parishioners, Hester Prynne, who has just been released from prison. They want Dimmesdale to persuade Hester, a young woman who has just given birth out of wedlock, to identify the child's father. So far she has refused to name him. Only she and Arthur know that Dimmesdale himself is the father:

> Such was the young man whom the Reverend Mr. Wilson and the Governor had introduced so openly to the public notice, bidding him speak, in the hearing of all men, to that mystery of a woman's soul, so sacred even in its pollution. The trying nature of his position drove the blood from his cheek, and made his lips tremulous.
>
> "Speak to the woman, my brother," said Mr. Wilson. "It is of moment to her soul, and, therefore, as the worshipful Governor says, momentous to thine own, in whose charge hers is. Exhort her to confess the truth!"
>
> The Reverend Mr. Dimmesdale bent his head, in silent prayer, as it seemed, and then came forward.
>
> "Hester Prynne," said he, leaning over the balcony and looking down steadfastly into her eyes, "thou hearest what this good man says, and seest the accountability under which I labor. If thou feelest it to be for thy soul's peace, and that thy earthly punishment will thereby be made more effectual to salvation, I charge thee to speak out the name of thy fellow-sinner and fellow-sufferer! Be not silent from any mistaken pity and tenderness for him; for, believe me, Hester, though he were to step down from a high place, and stand there beside thee, on thy pedestal of shame, yet better were it so than to hide a guilty

heart through life. What can thy silence do for him, except it tempt him—yea, compel him, as it were—to add hypocrisy to sin? Heaven hath granted thee an open ignominy, that thereby thou mayest work out an open triumph over the evil within thee and the sorrow without. Take heed how thou deniest to him—who, perchance, hath not the courage to grasp it for himself—the bitter, but wholesome, cup that is now presented to thy lips!"

The young pastor's voice was tremulously sweet, rich, deep, and broken. The feeling that it so evidently manifested, rather than the direct purport of the words, caused it to vibrate within all hearts, and brought the listeners into one accord of sympathy. Even the poor baby, at Hester's bosom, was affected by the same influence; for it directed its hitherto vacant gaze towards Mr. Dimmesdale, and held up its little arms with a half pleased, half plaintive murmur. So powerful seemed the minister's appeal, that the people could not believe but that Hester Prynne would speak out the guilty name; or else that the guilty one himself, in whatever high or lowly place he stood, would be drawn forth by an inward and inevitable necessity, and compelled to ascend the scaffold.

Hester shook her head. (67-68)

How might different kinds of literary theorists deal with this passage? What specific assumptions about literature would lead them to respond in particular and distinctive ways? Perhaps the best way to proceed is to begin at the beginning, with Plato.

Ancient Theories and Theorists

Plato, who supremely valued objective, rational truth and disdained irrational, selfish emotions, might sympathize with the Puritan authorities' interest in upholding the law and discovering the identity of the unnamed other law-breaker. He would almost certainly hope that Dimmesdale, having already failed to rely on reason to control sexual passion, would now himself confess the truth and thus set a good example of rational conduct. Plato's first concern would be with proper moral behavior, with each individual putting the interests of the community ahead of his own.

Aristotle, who valued the art and skill needed to produce well-crafted literary works, would surely appreciate the well-designed irony of the quoted passage. Hawthorne skillfully makes this moment as excruciatingly ironic as possible for Dimmesdale. It is hardly accidental, for instance, that Dimmesdale speaks from a physically lofty position and literally looks down on Hester, even though he knows that he is her moral and spiritual inferior. Aristotle would admire this touch of Hawthorne's artistry as well as much other similar evidence of Hawthorne's creative skill.

Horace, himself a poet, was especially interested in making sure that creative writers wrote well and did not make fools of themselves. Among much other advice, he counseled writers (1) to adopt a "middle" style (neither too complicated nor too vulgar), (2) to try to appeal to as broad an audience as possible, (3) to follow custom but to be willing to innovate cautiously, and (4), as Aristotle had already suggested, to write in ways that revealed talent, skill, and thoughtfulness. Surely Horace would have admired the general stylistic clarity of the quoted passage as well as its general "realism": the characters behave in ways Hawthorne's first readers would have found easy to comprehend. All the characters fit certain customary stereotypes: the older male authority figures, the supposedly virtuous young man, the young woman whose "mysterious soul" is "sacred even in its pollution," and the innocent baby. *The Scarlet Letter* was written in ways that have been proven to have broad, enduring appeal, and everything Horace would have admired here would probably also have been admired by Aristotle.

Longinus believed that only writers with lofty, noble souls can write in elevating, ennobling ways, sweeping readers off their feet by using powerful language imbued with high ethical ideals. Although Longinus might not find the language of this particular passage especially "sublime," he would certainly be interested in its striking concern with ideal spiritual behavior, high ethical obligations, and deep commitment to truth. The moral and spiritual seriousness of the issues this passage raises would have impressed both Longinus and Plato, although a key difference between them was that Plato considered most literature trivial and irrational while Longinus considered the best literature serious and inspiring.

Modern Theories and Theorists

Many positions outlined by the four key ancient theorists were repeated, developed, and even blended by subsequent theorists and critics. Most of the more striking recent developments in literary study and analysis have occurred since 1800. Of these, **thematic criticism**—the notion that literature is especially interesting in terms of its key concepts or central ideas—has been especially common. This approach, which resembles Plato's emphasis on the content (rather than the form) of literary works, has always been appealing to many readers. Literature, after all (unlike, say, music, painting, sculpture, or architecture) obviously involves concepts and ideas because its raw materials are words rather than sounds, colors, or physical surfaces. Thematic critics might be interested in such key themes of the quoted Hawthorne passage as the following: What is morality? What is immorality? What moral obligations does Dimmesdale have to Hester? What obligations does Hester have to her society? What is the role of religion in this passage and in *The Scarlet Letter* in general? Does the quoted passage suggest anything about "human nature"? Practically any idea or issue relevant to the passage would interest thematic critics, who typically examine texts for what they "say" rather for the literary methods they use.

Traditional **historical** critics might point out how almost everything mentioned in the quoted passage is rooted in, and conditioned by, particular historical conditions, including Hawthorne's personal history, the history of the Puritans in New England, and American history in general. To understand the passage properly, readers would (according to historical critics) need to know historical facts regarding such matters as the power of seventeenth-century New England clergy, the importance of religion in this setting, the power of men over women during this period, the prohibition against extramarital sex in this particular time and place, the greater likelihood of pregnancy during a period before effective birth control, the shame of being a single mother in the Puritan era, the shame during that era of impregnating a woman out of wedlock, the idea that a man should take responsibility for the children he fathers, and so forth. To comprehend the passage correctly, one would need to know about the history of Hawthorne, his own era, and the era he depicts.

Formalist critics, interested (like Aristotle, Horace, and Longinus) in literary craftsmanship, would find practically every single element of the quoted passage intriguing. Formalists typically favor "close reading," in which even a text's minutest details— including punctuation, sentence structure, and particular word choices—are seen as contributing to an overall "complex unity" and literary effectiveness. Formalists are especially interested in literary irony, since irony inevitably involves the complex union of two different meanings: a surface meaning and a different, often contrary, meaning. For example, Dimmesdale is "introduced ... openly" but is actually hiding his true identity. He is asked to speak about "the mystery of a woman's soul" when it is his own soul that is especially mysterious. Hester's soul is supposedly "polluted" when in fact this is far truer of Dimmesdale's. His speech is supposedly of great spiritual importance to Hester, but of course this is even truer of himself. And so on. The quoted passage is fraught with numerous such ironies, especially in the words Dimmesdale speaks to Hester. All these ironies reveal Hawthorne's artistry, partly because they are implied rather than overtly stated. The ability to *suggest* meaning, rather than spell it out, is a talent formalists prize.

Psychoanalytic critics, influenced by the ideas of Sigmund Freud (1856-1939), would be especially interested in relations between the unconscious and conscious minds of the characters. Thus, the reference to the "mystery of a woman's soul" implies the mystery not only of Hester's psyche but especially the mystery of Dimmesdale's. He acts and speaks in ways intended to hide what he is actually feeling, a fact that helps explain why his blood leaves his cheeks and why his lips tremble. His unconscious fears and guilt affect his bodily responses, and nearly everything he says to Hester implies his consciousness of his own secret guilt. Having succumbed to sexual desire for Hester, he now tries to present a reasonable, responsible front to the public, but his sense of guilt hampers his performance. In Freudian terms, he first gave in to his id (irrational desires) when he had sex with Hester, tries now to pretend to be a man of reason (directed by his rational ego), but is tormented by his conscience (his superego). The three most important aspects of his entire psyche are unbalanced and in conflict.

Archetypal critics, influenced by the ideas of Carl Jung (1875-1961), might argue (like Horace) that this passage presents a number of stereotypical (or archetypal) characters who behave as we might expect such characters to behave: the adult authority figures, the somewhat immature young man, the beautiful young woman, and the innocent baby. These kinds of characters have appeared in countless literary works throughout history, because these kinds of characters (according to archetypal theorists) reflect real, enduring, and inevitable types of human beings—types that can be found in all cultures everywhere and in all eras. When the blood rushes from Dimmesdale's cheeks and his lips tremble, these changes happen because Dimmesdale is a typical human being, not because of any unique or unusual aspect of his own particular psyche. Human nature, for archetypal critics, is pretty much the same everywhere and always, and effective literature often deals with the most common, most inevitable of human thoughts and emotions, to which nearly all humans can relate. The fear Dimmesdale suffers in this passage is one of the most primal of all human emotions, just as the sexual desire he felt for Hester is another.

Marxist critics, influenced by the materialist, anticapitalist, antireligious ideas of Karl Marx (1818-1883), would probably emphasize the way the quoted passage reflects the dominance of a totalitarian religion in New England Puritan society—a religion closely tied to (and enforced by) the official government. Hawthorne depicts a clear theocratic hierarchy, with the governor at the top, Reverend Wilson beneath the governor, and Reverend Dimmesdale further down the line of official power. Although Wilson addresses Dimmesdale as his "brother," a word which may imply their alleged spiritual equality, a Marxist would say that Puritan New England was anything but a society of genuine social and economic equals. The church and churchmen were powerful because the church was rich. Hester has become a victim of this wealthy theocratic society partly because she is relatively poor; a richer person (especially someone *very* rich) might have avoided prosecution for adultery. A very rich person would have had to worry less about the power of the "worshipful Governor" (a phrase that nicely implies the link in Hester's society between religious and political authority). Marxists might argue that Dimmesdale and the other powerful men stand above Hester both literally and figuratively because their dominance is rooted not only in real wealth but also in powerful and unquestioned religious superstitions. Marxists have often seen religion as an "opiate of the masses" that keeps weak people weak by offering them false hopes and deceptive consolations. Marxists might say that Hester, by rebelling against the theocracy of her era, points the way toward the possibility of a deeper, more pervasive social revolution in her time (and ours).

Theories and Theorists since the 1960s

Feminist critics, like Marxists, often take an explicitly political approach to literary texts. They are often interested not only in objectively examining the ways women are depicted in literature but also in using literary criticism to improve the lives of present and future women. Feminists would almost certainly note that this passage depicts a lone woman being oppressed by an explicitly patriarchal power structure. No women could serve as ministers or governors in Puritan New England, so it is hardly surprising that women in particular were politically and socially weak. Hester, according to this view, is not merely a wayward individual but represents the vulnerability of all women in her culture (including, ironically, any woman who might join in persecuting her). Patriarchal societies (according to feminists) tend to stereotype women *as* women rather than treating them as particular individuals. Thus it isn't surprising that the passage refers to the need to speak "in the hearing of all *men*" about the "mystery of a *woman's* soul" (italics added), as if women are somehow especially mysterious and therefore threatening creatures who need to be understood and controlled. The idea that a woman's soul is somehow especially "sacred" is (a feminist might argue) typical of the patriarchal habit of treating women either as whores or as holy rather than accepting their real complexities as actual human beings.

Structuralist critics argue that human beings make sense of reality by seeing it in terms of binary opposites, such as hot/cold, high/low, white/black, male/female, and so on. These opposites often have much in common; they reinforce one another and thus create overarching "structures" of meaning. Structuralist critics therefore look for the underlying binaries that help structure any given text. Among the mutually reinforcing binaries in the quoted passage from Hawthorne are these: man/woman; speech/silence; social power/social weakness; virtue/sin; pure/polluted; public/private; heavenly/earthly; innocence/guilt; honesty/dishonesty; good/evil; respected/disrespected; self-respect/shame; high/low; adult/child; psychological strength/psychological weakness; soul/body; and any number of other, similar contrasts. Key to structuralism is the idea that particular binaries tend to fall into patterns or structures based on similarities. Thus, the quoted passage from Hawthorne focuses on a man who speaks because he enjoys social power and is presumed to be virtuous, pure, innocent, honest, good, and so on, while the woman he addresses is silent and powerless and is presumed to be sinful, polluted, guilty, dishonest, or evil. Perceiving one set of binaries helps readers perceive many other related binaries that reinforce the entire structure.

Deconstructive critics, on the other hand, argue that distinctions between binaries are never quite as simple as they seem. The contrast between black and white, for instance, ignores all the many shades of gray that intervene, and the same thing is true of other simple binary distinctions, such as distinctions between hot and cold or tall and short; subtle gradations tend to be overlooked. Moreover (according to deconstructors), most binaries imply value judgments, in which one half of a pairing tends to be privileged over the other half. But deconstructors call attention to the inherent instabilities and complexities present in almost any simple pairing. In the quoted passage from Hawthorne, for instance, who is *really* weak and who *really* strong—Dimmesdale or Hester? Which one is really behaving like a stereotypical "man"—the man or the woman? Which one is really moral and which one is really immoral? The point, for deconstructors, is not to *reverse* such distinctions but rather to show how they were "always already" unstable to begin with. Thus Dimmesdale, who is called a "good man," knows that he is not an entirely good man, although he is probably not a thoroughly immoral man either. He must pretend to be a good man in the presence of other supposedly good men who are themselves probably flawed in their own secret ways. The categories of moral and immoral thus become destabilized—or, from a deconstructive point of view, were always already unstable from the start. In deconstructive readings of texts, nothing is ever plain, simple, or predictable; anything that seems clear inevitably becomes blurred.

Reader-response approaches to texts have much in common with deconstruction, especially since both approaches lead to the conclusion that there are no single, correct, accurate, or "objective" interpretations. There are only interpretations that have no necessary validity. In approaching the Hawthorne passage, reader-response critics might emphasize the sheer variety of possible responses this passage elicits, depending on the kinds of readers potentially interpreting Hawthorne's words. Puritans of the period might be far more likely than later readers to condemn both Dimmesdale and Hester. Readers of Hawthorne's own day might be more sympathetic to the couple while still sharing many of the same moral values as the Puritans. Readers of our own time might feel great sympathy for the couple and might reject many of the values (including even Christianity) embraced by Puritans and by readers from Hawthorne's day. On an individual level, anyone who has ever felt punished unjustly might sympathize with Hester; anyone who has ever felt hypocritical and weak might relate to Dimmesdale; persons who have freely chosen premarital sex might wonder what all the fuss is about; people who have given birth out of wedlock or been born out of wedlock might respond negatively to the social attitudes the novel depicts. Women who have been abandoned by men might sympathize with Hester. Some feminists might argue that abortion— if it had been available—would have been the easiest solution to Hester's problem, and probably all feminists would reject the social constraints Hester faces. In short, for reader-response critics, there is no "correct" response. There are only various responses that reflect the preferences or experiences of various readers and/or groups of readers.

Dialogical critics, influenced by the ideas of Mikhail Bakhtin (1895-1975), think that the most interesting texts involve interactions between different kinds of voices, whether those are voices of the characters speaking to one another, of the text in dialogue with some other text, the voices of the characters in dialogue with the voice of the narrator, and/or all of these possibilities and others. In this passage, for instance, Dimmesdale is addressing at least three different audiences. These listeners include not only Hester but also his superiors, the assembled crowd, and, most significantly, himself. Everything he says to Hester is influenced by his awareness of all these other audiences. At one point, for instance, he asks, "What can thy silence do for him [i.e., Hester's fellow sinner], except it tempt him—yea, compel him, as it were—to add hypocrisy to sin?" This question is addressed as much to himself as to anyone else. Mr. Wilson, the governor, and the assembled people would think the question demonstrates Dimmesdale's piety; Hester might hear it as evidence of his tormented conscience; and Dimmesdale might understand it as both an ironically hypocritical confession and a condemnation of the very hypocrisy the question mentions. In short, dialogical critics believe that readers must be listening for the ways the words of any text imply and address *multiple* audiences both within and outside the literary work.

Recent Theories and Theorists
New Historicist critics differ from traditional historical critics in various ways. They claim, for instance, that older historical approaches tended to offer simplified versions of particular historical contexts, stressing greater unity, coherence, and agreement than actually ever existed. For example, they often attack a very influential book from the 1940s by E. M. W. Tillyard, titled *The Elizabethan World Picture*, because they think that even the very title of this volume exemplifies typical problems with traditional historical criticism.

According to New Historicists, there is never any single, coherent view of the world at any particular moment in history. Instead, there are multiple, competing, contradictory "world pictures." Similarly, New Historicists would be bothered by the adjective *Elizabethan* in Tillyard's title: they would say it implies that the lives, doings, and values of a society's most powerful people are a culture's most important aspects. Instead, New Historicists emphasize kinds of persons who tended to be neglected by traditional historians. Such persons include women and ethnic, sexual, and religious minorities as well as anyone considered marginal to the dominant (but always potentially unstable) official culture of the time. In approaching the passage from *The Scarlet Letter*, for instance, New Historicists might argue that Hawthorne's text itself partly critiques not only Puritan values of the late 1600s but similar values during his own period. The novel, since it has long been read as a canonical text, may in fact have helped change American values over the lengthy course of its history as a text assigned to students. In fact, it may still be in the process of promoting social change. Hawthorne's book, after all, provides an especially influential example of a strong woman—an example that may even have helped promote the rise of feminism. The book can still be seen as relevant to contemporary social debates, and it was also probably rooted in particular political and cultural debates during its own time and probably contributed to them. The quoted passage, in fact, is all about power (always a key concern of New Historicists). Hawthorne here is concerned with who has power, who might lose it, how to maintain it, and how to perform correctly before others in *order* to maintain it.

Multicultural critics, as the very term implies, see any particular culture as a site of varied and often competing cultures. The component parts of any larger culture might consist of various minority cultures, including cultures rooted in ethnic, racial, religious, sexual, linguistic, geographical, or gender minorities (to mention just a few of the many possibilities). Recently, for instance, the disabled have come to be treated as a distinct minority worthy of attention by literary critics. Often minority statuses overlap with one another: a person might, for instance, be a gay female African American or a disabled Spanish-speaking Orthodox Jew. Multicultural critics might note that the passage from *The Scarlet Letter* implies a very particular culture (white New England Christian and patriarchal Puritan) dominated by a very specific set of inflexible cultural standards. All the characters depicted in the quoted passage are Caucasians with English ancestry; all are living on lands originally possessed by indigenous Americans; most are basically healthy (except for the rapidly weakening Arthur Dimmesdale, who eventually dies from a psychosomatic illness); all are not only Christians but are emphatically identified with a particular (and particularly militant) kind of Christianity; all are members of a theocratic culture that allows for no separation of church and state; and all are presumably heterosexual, since there would have been absolutely no tolerance in Puritan New England for any openly nonheterosexual minorities. Even Hester, for instance, benefits from the fact that she sinned as a straight person rather than as, say, a lesbian or a bisexual.

Postmodernist critics, who agree with deconstructors that there are no stable, objective cultural truths, are therefore suspicious of so-called grand narratives that attempt to impose coherent explanations on the world. Instead, they favor freedom, randomness, improvisation, and the liberty to mix and match one cultural tradition with another or to abandon traditions altogether. Postmodernists might therefore argue that the society depicted in this passage is the opposite of a postmodernist ideal: it is rigidly hierarchical and features one religion imposed on everyone. No true individuality is permitted; New England Puritan society assumes that one truth and one truth only explains everything. Dimmesdale and Hester are oppressed by these inflexible cultural rules. Part of the couple's problem, in fact, is that both Dimmesdale and Hester not only *must* subscribe to their society's values but that both (especially Dimmesdale) *do*, to a large degree, subscribe to those values. To the extent that Hawthorne's text helped question and undermine the kinds of rigid, monolithic assumptions depicted in his text, *The Scarlet Letter* might itself be read, to some extent, as postmodernist before that term had even been coined.

Darwinian critics, influenced by the ideas of Charles Darwin (1809-1882), accept his basic assumption that "natural selection" leads eventually to certain kinds of evolutionary change. These developments are determined by a population's fitness to deal with its environment. According to Darwinians, most human beings, like all other living things, are preprogrammed to reproduce themselves. The humans who do best at passing on their genes are the ones who determine long-range evolutionary trends. Sexual desire is perhaps the most important of all factors contributing to human evolution, and so it would not surprise Darwinian critics that so many works of literature deal—like *The Scarlet Letter*—with sexual desire between young men and women. Darwinians would argue that relations between the sexes are crucial both to life and literature; Dimmesdale, by having sex with Hester and impregnating her even though he and his society consider both behaviors sinful, has demonstrated how exceedingly difficult it is to resist innate, genetically determined impulses, especially sexual impulses. In fact, practically every feature of the quoted passage can be understood in Darwinian terms. The hierarchical structure of New England Puritan society is, arguably, typical of the kind of pecking order common among many kinds of animal societies, in which older males are often dominant and younger males must play by established rules rooted in genes rather than in wholly free choice. Even the way Dimmesdale's complexion and voice react to stress show how difficult it is for the mind to control the body. But Dimmesdale's inability to control his *sexual* urges have resulted in a baby, Pearl. He has, in a Darwinian sense, fulfilled his essential purpose in life by passing on his genes to the next generation. He dies at the end of the novel, but Pearl lives on.

Finally, of all the kinds of criticism surveyed in this essay, **ecological** criticism is one of the most recent but also, one might argue, one of the kinds least relevant *to this particular passage*. Little in the quoted excerpt deals in any obvious way with humans' relationships with nature. But that fact itself is significant: it suggests that this specific section of Hawthorne's novel is mostly concerned with humans' relations with one another. Not all theoretical approaches are necessarily relevant to, or helpful in dealing with, every single literary text. The mere fact that ecological criticism seems relatively unimportant to interpreting these particular paragraphs is itself revealing. To return to the metaphor with which this chapter began, not every single tool will necessarily be needed to perform every particular job of interpretation. At this point in *The Scarlet Letter*, Dimmesdale and Hester find themselves caught up in an environment dominated by other humans. They find themselves distant from the kind of freedoms often associated with a retreat from society into the green world of nature.

The Virtues of Pluralism

Critical pluralism, as an approach to literature, is actually a reasoned justification for *multiple* approaches, operating either independently or in fruitful dialogue. Pluralists believe that literature can be profitably studied from numerous points of view, with no single perspective being necessarily superior to any other. Of course, individual readers may personally prefer particular critical methodologies over alternatives, and pluralists would encourage them to pursue whichever approaches interest them most. But pluralism, by definition, assumes a willingness to acknowledge the potential value of many points of view and many ways of practicing literary criticism. For pluralists, the results of considering multiple perspectives are often far more illuminating than following only a single narrow path.

Note

1. For helpful discussions of critical pluralism as well as useful bibliographical listings, see, for instance, the books by Frederick J. Antczak, James L. Battersby, Gregor McLennan, and Stamos Metzidakis.

Works Cited

Antczak, Frederick J., editor. *Rhetoric and Pluralism: Legacies of Wayne Booth*. Ohio State UP, 1995.

Battersby, James L. *Paradigms Regained: Pluralism and the Practice of Criticism*. U of Pennsylvania P, 1991.

Hawthorne, Nathaniel. *The Scarlet Letter*. Ohio State UP, 1962.

McLennan, Gregor. *Pluralism*. U of Minnesota P, 1995.

Metzidakis, Stamos. *Difference Unbound: The Rise of Pluralism in Literature and Criticism*. Rodopi, 1995.

"Of Connection across Space and Time:" The Scarlet Letter and Jhumpa Lahiri's Unaccustomed Earth

Anupama Arora

> Human nature will not flourish, any more than a potato, if it be planted and replanted, for too long a series of generations, in the same worn-out soil. My children have had other birthplaces, and, so far as their fortunes may be within my control, shall strike their roots into unaccustomed earth.
>
> —Nathaniel Hawthorne, "The Custom-House"

These words from the prefatory chapter, "The Custom-House," of Nathaniel Hawthorne's novel, *The Scarlet Letter* (1850), provide the evocative title of contemporary writer Jhumpa Lahiri's short collection, *Unaccustomed Earth*, and serve as its epigraph. In many interviews, Lahiri has noted that she was rereading *The Scarlet Letter* while working on her stories, and was struck with this passage when she came across it and how it spoke to her own writing project. In these lines, Lahiri sees Hawthorne as offering "an observation and an articulation of America, and what the population of America is: groups of transplanted populations (Leyda 79). It is not surprising that Lahiri, whose oeuvre focuses on Bengali Indian immigrants to the United States and their diasporic children and grandchildren, chose this passage as epigraph to her collection. Like Hawthorne's, moreover, most of Lahiri's stories are set in New England, a milieu with which she is intimately familiar as the adopted locale and home of her immigrant Indian parents, and where she herself grew up. Thus, Lahiri's choice to use words from a canonical American author and a canonical American novel to set up her story collection is a conscious act of embedding herself into the American literary tradition. Through this explicit and direct citation, an intertextual relationship is thus established between Lahiri's stories and Hawthorne's novel. Lahiri claims Hawthorne as a literary ancestor and purposefully reads him as providing a vision of America as a country of foreign transplants who migrate from the old world and create homes in the new, which speaks to her own exploration of the late twentieth century migration of Indian immigrants to the United States.

Lahiri aptly borrows her epigraph from the "Custom House" preface, a semiautobiographical sketch where the narrator (identified with Hawthorne through his employment in the Salem Custom-House) discusses his relationship to his native land, his sense of home and belonging, his relationship to his emigrant ancestors—themes that are central in diasporic writing. Hawthorne remembers the arrival of his ancestors who were some of the earliest immigrants, settlers, to the United States and who have put down roots in the new soil. This imagery of roots and routes, of the history of the United States as one of different waves of immigrants, is what Lahiri is drawn to, as she notes in an interview, "this country is an extraordinary example of so many transplants entering into the soil for so many different reasons" (Leyda 79).

In the preface, Hawthorne writes about the time he returned to Salem, Massachusetts, to work as a surveyor in the Salem Custom-House for three years (1846-1849). Return to Salem brings up memories of the place where he was born and where his ancestors had been some of the earliest settlers and prominent personages of the land. He writes,

> This old town of Salem—my native place, though I have dwelt much away from it, both in boyhood and mature years—possesses, or did possess, a hold on my affections, the force of which I have never realized during my seasons of actual residence here … And, yet, though invariably happiest elsewhere, there is within me a feeling for old Salem, which, in lack of a better phrase, I must be content to call affection. The sentiment is probably assignable to the deep and aged roots which my family has struck into the soil. It is now clearly two centuries and a quarter since the original Briton, the earliest emigrant of my name, made his appearance in the wild and forest-bordered settlement, which has become a city. And here his descendants have

been born and died, and have mingled their earthly substance with the soil. (8)

Like his relationship with his ancestors, Hawthorne's relationship to his native home is marked by ambivalence. He writes about the "figure of that first ancestor," William Hathorne who arrived in New England in 1630, and was a persecutor of the Quakers; and his son, John Hathorne, who was a magistrate involved in the notorious Salem Witch Trials of 1692 (9). This history evokes shame and guilt in his Puritan forefathers, and Hawthorne marks his distance and difference from these rigid and authoritarian ancestors. While he holds, or has held, some affection for Salem, he has been "happiest elsewhere." Hawthorne recognizes, however, that "strong traits of [his ancestors'] nature have intertwined themselves with mine," and that he shares similarities with them (10). This thematic and dynamic resonates throughout Lahiri's stories as various characters seek to negotiate their relationship to the past, and the differing traditions within which they are located, in order to thrive.

Hawthorne writes of feeling like an insider/outsider in Salem, a place that is his native town, and yet a place where he feels he has little in common with the inhabitants from whom he feels alienated and from whom he keeps his identity as a writer secret because he knows he will be adversely judged by the Salem community's standards of masculinity and success in the commercial world. Lahiri echoes Hawthorne's feelings of isolation and alienation, albeit for different reasons. She speaks of feeling estranged in New England, growing up at a time when the South Asian diasporic population in the United States was small. She notes that rereading *The Scarlet Letter* as an adult,

> I was both startled and unspeakably reassured. I felt that a writer who represents everything that I seemed not to be while growing up—an American, a New Englander, whose work is set in the very terrain in which I was raised and from which I felt always estranged—had articulated, almost two centuries ago, the journey and experience of my family, and had also expressed my project as a writer. The sense

of recognition, of connection across space and time, was profound. It was the crossing of a fault line, a handshake in a darkened room.[1]

Rather than distance and difference, she felt an affinity and kinship with this American writer with New England origins, in whose work she found affirmation of her project of writing about the journeys and experiences of migrant populations. In this, Lahiri claims Hawthorne as her literary predecessor and forebear, as a New Englander, an American, and an American writer. Also, as Rajini Srikanth notes, Lahiri's "invocation of [Hawthorne's] sensibility grants credibility to her Bengali characters as being quintessentially American" (55). The use of the geological metaphor of a fault line in the quote is similarly apt for a writer who writes of dislocation and displacement, migration and relocation.

Exploring the Lahiri-Hawthorne connection also provides an invaluable occasion for remembering the forgotten rich, long, and complex history of connections between New England and India or the East Indies as the region was then referred to.[2] In "The Custom-House," Hawthorne gestures briefly to the Salem-East Indies trade in the postrevolutionary era when he discusses Salem's prosperous heyday of international maritime commerce. Surrounded by dilapidated wharfs and crumbling warehouses, he tries to remember the "old town's brighter aspect, when India was a new region, and only Salem knew the way thither" (29). Almost every Salem household had some connection to the trade, and Hawthorne's family was no different. Hawthorne's father (Captain Nathaniel Hathorne) had been an East India captain and sailed to Indian ports in 1796 and 1800. He was first mate on Jacob Crowninshield's ship *America* that brought to the United States from Calcutta, India, its first elephant in 1796; and he was a member of the Salem East India Marine Society (with a library and museum), formed in 1799 by mariners who recognized the import of their maritime endeavors. Hawthorne's in-laws also had East India trade connections. Hawthorne was thus steeped in this history, as he had read his father's logbooks and journals from his voyages to the East and was familiar with the East India museum.[3] When his father died, he left behind, among other things, "an India box and an India punch-bowl and pitcher from Calcutta" (Luedtke 5). This was not exceptional; the East India trade was an important presence in the lives of Salemites, who consumed its goods and objects with ease. While Hawthorne does not delve much into it, Salem played an important role in the United States-India maritime trade; and this trade also exerted much imaginative weight in a newly independent nation, providing the new nation with a sense of national pride through commercial supremacy and entrepreneurial spirit. The East Indies trade made Salem one of the leading urban centers (in 1790, it was the sixth largest city) and richest towns of the new republic.[4] In 1839, Salem adopted a new seal with the images of a palm tree, an East Indian merchant, a ship, and the Latin motto, "Divitas India eusque ad ultmimum sinum" (To the Farthest Port of the Rich East), attesting to the significance of the trade in the identity of the town and the nation (Morison 219).

Lahiri's citation of Hawthorne thus inadvertently also directs attention to this other personal and family history of Hawthorne's—of sea captains and East India trade connections—that is neglected while his Puritan forebears are overemphasized (both by Hawthorne and his biographers). It also illuminates the vast geographical connections of the early republic, not an insular nation but one that was deeply enmeshed in global networks and international maritime commerce.

While Hawthorne speaks of his own immigrant-settler ancestors who had struck roots in the "unaccustomed earth" of the New World, at the time that Hawthorne was writing, a small group of East Indians were beginning to put down roots in New England and assimilating into the local population. In fact, as recently digitized archives have shown, Indians were present in the United States since the seventeenth century.[5] The presence of these earliest East Indians is linked to the British East India Company whose employees brought back servants from India to England, and then to the United States. So, long before Lahiri's Bengali immigrants and diasporics made New England their home, a small group of East Indians—sailors/lascars, servants, merchants—were already present in the same region and elsewhere in the United States. Historian

Rosemarie Zagarri notes, "In fact, Salem might well have been one of most multicultural small towns in the early republic" (14). In her memoir, *When I Lived in Salem, 1822-1866*, a Salemite Caroline Howard King describes a meeting with an Indian man (Ardeshir Cursetji Wadia, from the wealthy Parsi Indian shipbuilding Wadia family that worked with American merchants) in her home (37). Captain Stephen Phillips of Salem (1764-1838) had "a Sikh servant whom he had brought from India on some cruise" who is mentioned in his son's diary (130). Scholars Vijay Prashad and Joan M. Jensen have both also mentioned how, as a result of the Salem-India trade, some East Indian sailors who returned with sea captains worked on the Salem wharves. Jensen writes that, "These men left no history, though some stayed in Salem. They were said to have married Negro women and become part of the black population of Salem" (13). Lahiri's invocation of Hawthorne then has a ripple effect of animating these other hidden histories and global connections of the early national period.

It is important to note that Lahiri is not the first South Asian writer to invoke Hawthorne or *The Scarlet Letter* in her writing. Indian-American novelist Bharati Mukherjee in her novel, *The Holder of the World* (1993) explored the connection between the East Indies and the United States by rewriting *The Scarlet Letter*'s Hester Prynne as Hannah Easton, known as the Salem Bibi (Newman). Hannah is a woman who journeys from Puritan New England to Mughal India in the seventeenth century, and then returns to the United States with an illegitimate child (Pearl Singh) who is the outcome of an affair with an Indian king. This Hannah Easton, it is suggested by Mukherjee, might have been the model for Hawthorne's Hester. Judith Newman notes that, "Mukherjee's project of restoring connections between Hawthorne and India, takes its place in an honorable tradition of filling in the gaps in history, correcting and amplifying the record" (68). Like one of the first prominent contemporary Indian-American woman writers before her, Lahiri too cites Hawthorne and knots her work to a canonical text and writer.

While the focus of this essay is on exploring connections between *The Scarlet Letter* and *Unaccustomed Earth*, Lahiri's stories are replete, textually dense, with allusions to literary traditions, texts and authors; and literary critics (such as Jeffrey Bilbro and Michael Wutz) have commented on this range of references—to Hawthorne's *The Marble Faun*, *The Odyssey*, Thoreau, Emerson, and Greek myth, among others. For Michael Wutz, for instance, who analyzes the ecocritical sensibility of *Unaccustomed Earth*, "Lahiri inscribes herself into various literary and oral traditions about land, migration, and cross-cultural encounters that date back thousands of years" (255).

However, it is to *The Scarlet Letter* that Lahiri's collection tethers itself the most; and in addition to the significance of the epigraph from "The Custom-House" to understanding Lahiri's project, there are frequent echoes of *The Scarlet Letter* in the nine stories of the collection. Thematic concerns that are central in Hawthorne's preface and novel—such as secrecy, isolation, shame, the individual's relationship with community, the struggle between conformity and rebellion and between desire and guilt—find expression variously in Lahiri's stories of diasporic Indians. Thus, Lahiri appropriates thematic concerns of Hawthorne's novel to articulate her own vision of the South Asian American diaspora.

The title story, "Unaccustomed Earth," revolves around an immigrant Indian father's short visit to his diasporic daughter, Ruma's, new house, and the complicated feelings this visit evokes in the daughter. Ruma is married to a white American man, Adam, has a three-old son, Akash, and is pregnant with a second child. The father's passion for gardening provides the subplot and main trope of the story. The father represents the immigrant who has uprooted himself from India and rerooted himself in the United States, his "adopted land" (7). Ruma remembers how her father was a resilient and successful gardener who would "toil in unfriendly soil, coaxing ... things [for her mother] from the ground," a metaphor for nurturing their marriage (16). When he sees Ruma's neglected garden, which also mirrors the daughter's melancholic state of mind, he starts watering the plants and sows new flowers and shrubs, a way of cultivating his relationship with his daughter and caring for her; he even starts teaching his grandson how to garden just as he imparts other lessons to him (such as teaching him how to count in Bengali). In the story, Ruma misunderstands her father when he mentions the "nursery." While he is talking about the plant nursery where he stopped to pick up plants for her garden, she thinks he is talking about the nursery school that Akash will soon attend (41). A plant nursery and a school nursery are similar places—places where plants or children are cared for so that they can grow and flourish. The father, who has successfully rerooted himself in new soil, wants to pass on the lessons of adaptation and survival to successive generations. Like the autobiographical narrator of "The Custom-House," this immigrant father's "children have had other birthplaces" and have struck "their roots into [the] unaccustomed earth" of the new land (Hawthorne 12). However, as the story shows, the children struggle to ground themselves. Ruma herself is struggling to find her bearings after her mother's death and her move to a new city. Her old friendships don't endure or provide sustenance to her after the move since "the roots did not go deep" (35); and she is unable to root herself in the unaccustomed earth of Seattle, where she moved from Brooklyn.

This planting metaphor of rooting, uprooting, rerooting is an evocative and fitting one to write about diasporic populations. The word *diaspora* derives from the Greek *dia*, (through) and *speirein* (to scatter). The word conjures up the image of spores dispersing and scattering to settle somewhere, some successfully rooting to become new plants with new seeds. In "Unaccustomed Earth," Akash and his future sibling, the third-generation biracial children, like and unlike their parents and grandparents, will have "other birthplaces" and stake their claim to these. But, just like the flowers, vegetables, and shrubs that Ruma's father plants will die if they don't get appropriate water, sun, and care, it is not a given that the new generations will naturally thrive in the new soil.

In this cautiousness, Lahiri modifies Hawthorne's optimism about assuming that the transplantation will be successful and that the new generations will naturally and automatically thrive in new soil. While Lahiri finds affirmation in Hawthorne's articulation of the United States as a "diaspora space" (Brah 208), she also says in an interview that some transplants don't "thrive and flourish" (Leyda 79). This is evident in the three "Hema and Kaushik" stories that conclude the collection where both the diasporic characters are drifters who lack destination or direction. Kaushik especially struggles to set down roots anywhere; though born in the United States, he moved to India at the age of seven when his parents decided to go back, only to return to the United States six years later as a teenager. After his mother dies of cancer two years after their move, his fragile sense of home and belonging further dissolves. The "colossal upheavals he experienced as a boy" have led Kaushik never to "trust the places he's lived, never turned to them for refuge;" and, working as a photojournalist, he is "happiest to be outside," often spending time in war-torn and conflict zones (Lahiri 309). He feels like a "refugee" as he "drifts across the globe without making meaningful ties" (306). Min Hyoung Song comments that these stories "twist the meaning of Hawthorne's hopeful comments about the advantages of, and the need for, migration by highlighting how a loss of rootedness can leave one rootless" (158-59). Ambreen Hai echoes Song as she notes, "Unlike Hawthorne whose narrator optimistically rejects 'tired soil' for new earth, Lahiri suggests that individuals and families too get tired, damaged, and wrenched apart if they must continually reroot, that there is much pain in rerooting" (198). We see this psychic damage in "A Choice of Accommodations" where Amit, a second-generation Indian American, is haunted as an adult by his adolescent feelings of betrayal, abandonment, and desertion by his parents who had enrolled him in a boarding school in Massachusetts when he was in ninth grade and returned to India themselves (89). Like Kaushik, Amit struggles with feelings of displacement in the United States, although his story has a somewhat happier ending than Kaushik's, who dies in the 2004 tsunami off the coast of Thailand.

Commenting on Lahiri's choice of epigraph, Susan Koshy writes that, "Hawthorne's anticipatory vision of diasporic renewal and paternal hope of generational flourishing are refracted in Lahiri's transnational feminist retelling of the affective pathways and crossways of naturalization" (356). Thus, for instance, Lahiri exposes how the immigrant wives who accompany their husbands as they seek professional opportunities in the United States, and the diasporic children (especially the daughters), are at the receiving end of the diasporic exhortation to preserve cultural identity and reproduce and maintain cultural continuity, to ensure generational succession. In this context, it is also relevant to note Stefan Helmreich's discussion of the etymological roots of the term "*diaspora*,

> The original meaning of diaspora summons up the image of scattered seeds and ... in Judeo-Christian ... cosmology, seeds are metaphorical for the male "substance" that is traced in genealogical histories. The word "sperm" is metaphorically linked to diaspora. It comes from the same stem [in Greek meaning to sow or scatter] and is defined by the OED as "the generative substance or seed of male animals." Diaspora, in its traditional sense, thus refers us to a system of kinship reckoned through men and suggests the questions of legitimacy in paternity that patriarchy generates. (qtd. in Gopinath 5)

This reflection exposes the patriarchal underpinning of the term diaspora. Instead of imagining a diasporic subjectivity that focuses on father-son or male-male relationships or patrilineality, Lahiri's stories often focus on wives and daughters and "convey the discrepant gendered burdens of diasporic inheritance" (Koshy 357). In "Hell-Heaven," the loneliness of the immigrant wife is emphasized; in "Nobody's Business," "Unaccustomed Earth," and "Only Goodness," we see how the daughters feel the pressure to marry partners from the Bengali Indian community arranged for them, and feel obliged to please their parents and meet their spoken and sometimes unspoken demands. As these women struggle, the stories interrupt the hope and optimism of generational succession implied in the epigraph.

Other thematic concerns of *The Scarlet Letter* are echoed everywhere in "Unaccustomed Earth."Different characters in the story feel guilt and shame on various occasions. Ruma's father remembers the shame he felt for abandoning his parents in India when he left for the United States and settled there. Ruma feels guilty that she doesn't want her father to stay with her: "She knew her father did not need taking care of, and yet this very fact caused her to feel guilty; in India, there would have been no question of his not moving in with her" (6). The father especially feels guilty of keeping a secret from his daughter so as to not upset her, that he has met a woman, Mrs. Bagchi, during his travels who has become somewhat of a traveling companion and with whom he has developed an emotional connection. The postcard that he was going to mail to Mrs. Bagchi, discovered by the daughter, can be read as the *scarlet letter* since it speaks to her father's guilty secret, even though he isn't committing adultery as his wife is no longer alive. The father wonders if this was how his "children had felt in the past, covertly conducting relationships back when it was something he and his wife had forbidden, something that would have devastated them" (19).

The theme of adultery – or socially unsanctioned desires—is present in other stories in the collection too as characters seek to escape loneliness or rebel or navigate the constraints or demands imposed on them. In "Going Ashore" (the third story in the "Hema and Kaushik triptych), the Indian-American Hema has two affairs—a decade-long liaison with a married man, Julian, and a second short-lived affair with Kaushik (a family friend from her childhood) even though she is engaged to another man. In "Nobody's Business," Sang entertains calls by suitable Indian men arranged by her parents in the hope that Sang will marry one of them, while she is in love and carrying out a secret affair with an Egyptian man. The story "Hell-Heaven" resonates richly with Hawthornian themes. The story is narrated by Usha, a second-generation diasporic, who recalls the time from her childhood when a Bengali man, Pranab, entered their lives in Boston and became a part of the family. Married to an unresponsive and busy man, Usha's lonely mother falls in love with Pranab, a man who was closer to her in age and who spends more time with her than her own husband, although this love is never professed or consummated. Pranab ends up marrying an American woman, Deborah, and then divorcing her twenty-three years into their marriage, after committing adultery with a married Bengali woman.

While not villainous, the description of Usha's father resonates with the character of Chillingworth—aloof, unfeeling, impassive, "My father ... had married my mother to placate his parents ... He was wedded to his work, his research, and he existed in a shell that neither my mother nor I could penetrate. Conversation was a chore for him" (65). In contrast, Pranab argues passionately with Usha's mother in "playful combat," eats with a "reckless appetite," and listens to her "stories with interest" (65).

The story also highlights how the first-generation immigrants are Puritanical in their rigid rules as they try to cling to the old way of life. The Bengali community, for instance, responds to Pranab and Deborah's mixed-race marriage with unease; when the couple stops coming to Bengali gatherings, the narrator observes that, "Their absences were attributed, by my parents and their circle, to Deborah, and it was universally agreed that she had stripped Pranab Kaku not only of his origins but his independence. She was the enemy, he was her prey, and their example was invoked as a warning, and as vindication, that mixed marriages were a doomed enterprise" (75). Just like Hester who is censured by Puritan women in *The Scarlet Letter*, Deborah is ostracized by Bengali immigrant women who treat her like an outcast. Even Pranab's situation parallels Hester's as his parents "disown" him when he marries a non-Bengali woman.

"Nobody's Business" also features a triangulated relationship that invokes *The Scarlet Letter*. It revolves around Sang, a single Indian-American woman, who is involved in a secretive relationship with Farouk, an Egyptian man. Paul, her white American housemate, gets increasingly obsessed with Sang's love life, and in revealing to Sang that Farouk is a two-timing cheater. Like Hester, Sang is unconventional, and associated with the ideals of passion, self-expression, deviance, and rebellion as opposed to authority, conformity, and restraint. Like Hester, many of Lahiri's female characters try to navigate their way through a patriarchal world that tries to constantly curtail their agency and surveil and control their independence and sexuality. Sang feels the judgment—like Hester and the autobiographical narrator of "The Custom-House"—of her parents and the extended community as she refuses to live by their rules and be a kind of poster child for success as defined by them by being single at thirty, studying philosophy instead of physics, dropping out of Harvard after a year. Ironically, while she dissents and rebels against their desires and demands, she ends up in a self-destructive relationship with another man where she conforms to the role of a caretaker girlfriend who cooks and cleans. We also see these contradictions in Hester as she defies the community but also accepts guilt, humbles herself, and sacrifices her pride. We hear echoes of Chillingworth's obsession to expose Dimmesdale as the sinner in Paul's fixation in exposing the truth about Farouk to Sang. Like Chillingworth and Dimmesdale, both Paul and Farouk also sexualize and fantasize about Sang. They are cruel and self-absorbed men, involvement with who is devastating to Sang in the end. Thus, Lahiri's intertextuality returns us to reflecting on Hawthorne's novel, as much as it provides a lens to think through her stories.

Through her intertextual move, Lahiri inserts herself in a tradition and as a contemporary of Hawthorne's, to be read alongside him as an American writer in her own right, and not in any hierarchical manner as beneath him. Like some other recent American authors, Lahiri is invested in pushing open the borders of American literature beyond Euro-American referents and sensibility. Her acute awareness that readers are not accustomed to imagining her and Hawthorne together as American authors makes her choice of epigraph especially deliberate. She says in an interview, "I think that, on an average syllabus, my books would probably not be taught alongside Hawthorne's. Now maybe someone would because I've invoked him in my work. But say, I hadn't written *Unaccustomed Earth*, it's highly doubtful that *The Namesake* and *The Scarlet Letter* would be taught in the same class. Why would they? There's nothing in common, one would think" (Leyda 80).Lahiri wants to claim the commonality of their projects, rather than difference, as American writers; and many literary critics have commented on Lahiri's inclination to emphasize universal values or sentiments. If Hawthorne wrote of his Puritan settler ancestors in seventeenth-century New England, Lahiri writes of the arrival and settlement of new migrants in the same region a century or so later, suggesting that migration and transplantation are centuries-old phenomena. Her act of invoking Hawthorne thus also nudges and encourages an unearthing of a host of other forgotten and buried histories of multicultural and multiracial United States.

Notes

1. See https://www.theguardian.com/books/2013/aug/31/naccustomed-earth-lahiri-book-club.

2. See Anupama Arora and Rajender Kaur. See also Anapuma Arora.

3. Jee Yoon Lee makes an argument that Hawthorne's contact with oriental objects housed in the East India Marine Museum was what helped him to "imagine Hester and Salem as nineteenth-century representations of the Orient" (950). Lee suggests that Hawthorne's "literary imagination is powerfully grounded in the material objects from the Orient" (952).

4. Historian Dane Anthony Morrison concurs that for a brief period, Salem had a remarkable influence on American life. "Its exploits shaped national character, and did so at a critical moment. [...] At a time when tariffs made up the bulk of all federal revenues, Salem's commerce [...] contributed 5 per cent to the national treasury" (109). Susan Bean similarly contends that, "In the first decades after Independence, this commerce [along the Eastern seaboard] played a significant role in American life. The trade generated federal tax revenues, helped relieve the war debt, and raised capital to build up nascent industries" (11).

5. East Indians were often sold into slavery and exploited as indentured servants. See Paul Heinegg for advertisements for East Indian runaway slaves. See also Francis C. Assisi and Elizabeth F. Pothen's award-winning journalism on the earliest South Asians in the United States, in which they track the earliest South Asians to Virginia in 1624.

Works Cited

Arora, Anupama. "'The Wonders of India So Near Our Front Doors:' Consuming India, Imagining America," *TOPIA: Canadian Journal of Cultural Studies*, vol. 37, May 2017, pp. 111-35.

_____, and Rajender Kaur. *India in the American Imaginary 1780s-1880s.* Palgrave, 2017.

Assisi, Francis C. "First Indian-American Identified: Mary Fisher, Born 1680 in Maryland." https://indiacurrents.com/indian-slaves-in-colonial-america/.

_____. "Indian Slaves in Colonial America." May 16, 2007. https://www.indiacurrents.com/articles/2007/05/16/indian-slaves-in-colonial-america.

_____, and Elizabeth Pothen. "South Asians in Colonial America." *SPAN*, May/June 2007, pp. 6-7. issuu.com/spanmagazine/docs/200705-06-c.

Bean, Susan. *Yankee India: American Commercial and Cultural Encounters with India in the Age of Sail, 1784-1860.* Peabody Essex Museum, 2001.

Bilbro, Jeffrey. "Lahiri's Hawthornian Roots: Art and Tradition in 'Hema and Kaushik.'"

Brah, Avtar. *Cartographies of Diaspora.* Routledge, 1996.

Gopinath, Gayatri. *Impossible Desires: Queer Diasporas and South Asian Public Cultures.* Duke UP, 2005.

Hai, Ambreen. "Re-rooting Families: The Alter/Natal as the central dynamic of Jhumpa Lahiri's *Unaccustomed Earth*." *Naming Jhumpa Lahiri: Canons and Controversies.* Edited by Lavina Dhingra and Floyd Cheung. Lexington, 2012, pp. 181-209.

Hawthorne, Nathaniel. *The Centenary Edition of the Works of Nathaniel Hawthorne.* Edited by William Charvat et al. Ohio State UP, 1962-1997. 23 vols.

Heinegg, Paul. www.freeafricanamericans.com/East_Indians.htm.

Jensen, Joan M. *Passage from India: Asian Indian Immigrants in North America.* Yale UP, 1988.

King, Caroline Howard. *When I Lived in Salem, 1822-1866.* Stephen Daye, 1937.

Koshy, Susan. "Neoliberal Family Matters." *American Literary History* vol. 25, no. 2, 2013, pp. 344-380.

Lahiri, Jhumpa. *Unaccustomed Earth.* Knopf, 2008.

Lee, Jee Yoon. "'The Rude Contact of Some Actual Circumstance': Hawthorne and Salem's East India Marine Museum," *ELH*, vol. 73, no. 4, Winter 2006, pp. 949-73.

Leyda, Julia. "An Interview with Jhumpa Lahiri." *Contemporary Women's Writing 5.1*, January 2011, pp. 66-83.

Luedtke, Luther S. *Nathaniel Hawthorne and the Romance of the Orient.* Indiana UP, 1989.

Morison, Samuel Eliot. *The Maritime History of Massachusetts 1783-1860.* Houghton Mifflin. Riverside Press Cambridge, 1921.

Morrison, Dane Anthony. "Salem as Citizen of the World." Edited by Dane Anthony Morrison and Nancy Lusignan Schultz. *Salem: Place, Myth, and Memory.* Northeastern UP, 2004, pp. 107-27.

Newman, Judie. "Spaces In-Between: Hester Prynne as the Salem Bibi in Bharati Mukherjee's *The Holder of the World.*" *Journal of Literary Studies*, vol. 13, no. 1/2, 1997, pp. 62-91.

Phillips, James Duncan. April 1940. Essex Institute—Historical Collections, Vol. LXXVI, No. 2.

Prashad, Vijay. *The Karma of Brown Folk.* U of Minnesota P, 2000.

Song, Min Hyoung. *The Children of 1965: On Writing, and Not Writing, as an Asian American.* Duke UP, 2013.

Srikanth, Rajini. "Lahiri's Brand of Desirable Difference in *Unaccustomed Earth.*" In *Naming Jhumpa Lahiri: Canons and Controversies.* Edited by Lavina Dinghra and Floyd Cheung. Lexington, 2012.

Wutz, Michael. "The Archaeology of the Colonial: Un-earthing Jhumpa Lahiri's *Unaccustomed Earth. Studies in American Fiction*, vol. 42, no. 2, Fall 2015, pp. 243-68.

Zagarri, Rosemarie. "The Significance of the 'Global Turn' for the Early American Republic: Globalization in the Age of Nation-Building." *Journal of the Early Republic*, vol. 31, no. 1, 2011, pp. 1-37.

Puritans and Transcendentalists: The Scarlet Letter in New England Culture_____

Brian Yothers

For students of literature, two figures always hover over colonial and nineteenth-century New England: the stern yet erudite Puritan minister of the seventeenth century and the brilliant if erratic transcendentalist visionary of the nineteenth. Nathaniel Hawthorne, who thanks to both *The Scarlet Letter* and his many widely taught short stories set in early New England is perhaps more closely associated with New England literature in the popular imagination than anyone, showed considerable ambivalence toward both figures, even as he was closely linked to both tendencies through his family history and personal and professional attachments.

Anyone who has taught the first half of the standard American Literature survey (beginnings to 1865 is a typical formulation) has discovered that many students find it easy to confuse the nineteenth-century novelist Nathaniel Hawthorne with his seventeenth-century characters. When I have taught the survey and have asked at the beginning of the class for students to identify a Puritan writer, Hawthorne has been identified as such more frequently than any writer who actually lived in the seventeenth century or who was actually an adherent of Puritan theology. This issue arises for two reasons: first, Hawthorne's own intense reflections on his Puritan ancestors can really make it seem that he is among their contemporaries, and second, Hawthorne's connections with his own century are often underplayed in classroom discussions at the introductory level, even as they have become increasingly important in the scholarship.

One major strand in American literary scholarship, extending from Perry Miller in the 1940s through Sacvan Bercovitch at the end of the twentieth century and the beginning of the twenty-first, has focused on the genealogy of nineteenth-century American literary culture as the intellectual offspring of early colonial New England. Miller argued in his classic essay "From Edwards to Emerson" that the brilliant eighteenth-century theologian most famous today for his fearsome sermon "Sinners in the Hands of an Angry God" was in fact a crucial forebear for American transcendentalists looking to find divinity in nature, via Edwards's extension of typological interpretation of the Bible to the natural world. Bercovitch made the ties even tighter in his broadly influential *The Puritan Origins of the American Self* and *The American Jeremiad*, where he suggested that the form of the Puritan sermon would prove determinative for not just the aesthetic, but also the ideological form that nineteenth-century American literature would take, suggesting that both the Puritans and their descendants developed literary forms that both expressed dissent and contained it. He connected the tendency most directly to Hawthorne in his landmark study *The Office of the Scarlet Letter.* Michael J. Colacurcio has pointed in particular to the ways in which Hawthorne functions as a self-conscious recorder of this genealogy, functioning not just as a teller of stories set in New England, but as a composer of alternative histories of the development of colonial, revolutionary, and early national New England.

In the following pages, rather than starting with the setting of *The Scarlet Letter* in colonial New England and considering the resonances of the story for nineteenth-century readers, an approach with a venerable history in American literary studies, this chapter will explore how critical issues that shaped Hawthorne's sensibility in the nineteenth century play out on a seventeenth-century stage. When we understand *The Scarlet Letter* as a work of fiction that spans the seventeenth and nineteenth centuries in its treatment of artistic, religious, and philosophical ideals and has ample appreciation for and criticism of both eras, we truly read Hawthorne well.

Hawthorne the Nineteenth-Century Intellectual

For a man so readily identified with an earlier century, Hawthorne boasted an especially rich set of intellectual connections in his own. Hawthorne spent a significant amount of time at the start of the 1840s at Brook Farm, one of the nineteenth-century United States' great utopian experiments, and his time there shaped one of his major novels, *The Blithedale Romance*, explicitly, and perhaps all of his novels to one degree or another. Hawthorne was closely connected to many of the most prominent literary, philosophical, and political figures of his time: poet Henry Wadsworth Longfellow and President Franklin Pierce from Bowdoin College; Ralph Waldo Emerson and Henry David Thoreau from his time as a resident of Concord in the Old Manse, which he and his wife Sophia Peabody Hawthorne rented from Emerson; George Ripley, Bronson Alcott, and Margaret Fuller from Brook Farm; Elizabeth Peabody through his marriage to her sister Sophia; and Herman Melville after their meeting in Western Massachusetts in 1850.

Hawthorne's relationship to the literary transcendentalism that framed his own period was complex. He appears to have shared a great deal of the moral seriousness and the belief in the moral efficacy of art and philosophy that characterized contemporaries like Emerson and Fuller, and he shared a great deal of their enthusiasm for British and German Romanticism and their love of the natural world, but he also seems to have distrusted their sense of themselves as cut off from and more advanced than their contemporaries. He also seems to have found the transcendentalist critique of tradition to contain the potential for overreach. Notably, in "The Celestial Railroad," Hawthorne connects Ralph Waldo Emerson's optimistic sense of human possibility with the uncritical faith in technological progress that could characterize precisely those aspects of nineteenth-century American culture that Emerson would be most likely to criticize as excessively materialistic. The story is a retelling of John Bunyan's *Pilgrim's Progress* that envisions a train replacing the hard work of Christian pilgrimage and connects this technologically enabled sloth with a kind of moral sloth enabled by transcendental flights of elevation. In one of the most biting critiques of transcendentalism in the story, Hawthorne presents the transcendentalist figure in the story, Mr. Smooth-it-away, as being positively diabolical:

> And then did my excellent friend, Mr. Smooth-it-away, laugh outright; in the midst of which cachinnation, a smoke-wreath issued from his mouth and nostrils; while a twinkle of lurid flame darted out of either eye, proving indubitably that his heart was all of a red blaze.

The impudent Fiend! To deny the fires of Tophet when he felt its fiery tortures raging within his breast! (X.206)

"The Celestial Railroad" offers sharp criticism of Hawthorne's own time period, both in its material aspects (the railroad) and in influential modes of thought, like transcendentalism, that both attracted and repelled him. Although the passage above is one of the more forceful critiques of transcendentalism that Hawthorne wrote, it is also characteristic of his consistent suspicion of what he regarded as a too-facile approach on their part to questions of suffering and moral evil.

In his ambivalence toward transcendentalism, Hawthorne resembled no one so much as one of his contemporaries who was most intimately connected to the central intellectual figure in the transcendentalist movement: Ralph Waldo Emerson's second wife, Lidian Jackson Emerson (so named after her marriage because Emerson found the aesthetic qualities of the name *Lidian* preferable to the aesthetic qualities of *Lydia*). In her short piece "Transcendental Bible," tongue firmly in cheek, Lidian Emerson wrote a series of transcendental commandments:

> Loathe and shun the sick. They are in bad taste, and may untune us for writing the poem floating through our mind.
>
> Scorn the infirm of character and omit no opportunity of insulting and exposing them. They ought not to be infirm and should be punished by contempt and avoidance.
>
> Despise the unintellectual, and make them feel that you do by not noticing their remark and question lest they presume to intrude into your conversation.
>
> Abhor those who commit certain crimes because they indicate stupidity, want of intellect which is the one thing needful.
>
> Justify those who commit certain other crimes. Their commission is consistent with the possession of intellect. We should not judge the intellectual as common men. It is mean enough to wish to put a great mind into the strait-jacket of morality.
>
> It is mean and weak to seek for sympathy; it is mean and weak to give it. Great souls are self-sustained and stand every erect, saying

only to the prostrate sufferer, "Get up, and stop your complaining."
(381-82)

Lidian Emerson here associates transcendentalism with a kind of intellectual cruelty. Those who believe they have a special insight into the universe can fail to empathize with those who lack this insight, and their pursuit of a transcendent truth means that they have abandoned the need to show compassion to their fellow human beings. Lidian Emerson's remarks show that as exhilarating as transcendentalist reverence for nature and devotion to self-improvement could be, both tendencies had a dark side.

In this sense, Hawthorne's portrait of the Puritan minister John Wilson can seem to offer a corrective to the coldness and priggishness that transcendentalism and Puritanism could share. Notably, when Wilson responds to Roger Chillingworth's suggestion that analyzing Pearl's character might make it possible to identify her father (an act of cruelty on Chillingworth's part, given that Pearl's father, Arthur Dimmesdale, was present), Wilson's words are not just a manifestation of conventional religious aversion to secular scientific inquiry. Wilson begins by declining Chillingworth's challenge on the grounds that "it would be sinful, in such a question, to follow the clew of profane philosophy"—a conventional instance of devout obscurantism—but he proceeds to a truly moving conclusion. The primary reason that Wilson wants to preserve the "mystery" of Pearl's origins is that "Thereby, every good Christian man hath a father's title to show kindness to the poor deserted babe" (116). This statement is adduced in the novel as an example of Wilson's personal kindly nature, but it is also in keeping with Puritan social ethics as expressed in John Winthrop's "A Model of Christian Charity," in which Winthrop argues that the settlers of the Massachusetts Bay Colony should be bound together by mutual love and that every member of the colony should feel compelled to contribute to the well-being of those in need. If much of *The Scarlet Letter* seems to be a critique of the illiberal aspects of seventeenth-century communal moralism from the standpoint of a liberated nineteenth century, there is also a significant insight into the ways in which excessive individualism can be damaging.

Hawthorne's literary friendships may shed still more light on his treatment of both his transcendentalist contemporaries and his Puritan forebears. As a student at Bowdoin College in Maine, Hawthorne formed a friendship with a New England literary figure whose status would surpass his own during his lifetime, even as Hawthorne's reputation would gradually eclipse that of his friend after both had died. Henry Wadsworth Longfellow was the most famous poet in New England during his lifetime, and he had few if any rivals in the entirety of the English-speaking world. Notably, although Longfellow was not himself a transcendentalist, he shared important elements of transcendentalist thought through his religious liberalism, his devotion to nature, and his interest in German Romantic thought. Longfellow also shared important aspects of Hawthorne's interest the Puritan heritage of New England, and his long poem *The Courtship of Miles Standish* can easily be read as a companion piece of sorts to Hawthorne's New England fiction. In Longfellow's poem, as in Hawthorne's novel, there is a tension between the potentially heartless principles of the Puritan leadership and the human connections that both Hawthorne and Longfellow associate with domestic life.

In a curious reversal of the relationship with Longfellow, Hawthorne became friends with a man whose posthumous literary reputation would become even more substantial than Hawthorne's own: Herman Melville. Melville's review of Hawthorne's short stories from *Mosses from an Old Manse* in "Hawthorne and His Mosses" is extraordinarily revelatory of the relationship between Hawthorne's investment in his own century and his investment in the past. In one of the most frequently quoted passages in "Hawthorne and His Mosses," Melville reflected quite explicitly on Hawthorne's relationship to the Calvinist theology that shaped New England Puritanism:

> For spite of all the Indian-Summer sunlight on the hither side of
> Hawthorne's soul, the other side—like the dark half of the physical

sphere—is shrouded in a blackness, ten times black. But this darkness but gives more effect to the ever-moving dawn that forever advances through it, and circumnavigates his world. Whether Hawthorne has simply availed himself of this mystical blackness as a means to the wondrous effects he makes it to produce in his lights and shades, or whether there really lurks in him, perhaps unknown to himself, a touch of Puritanic gloom—this, I cannot altogether tell. Certain it is, however, that this great power of blackness in him derives its force from its appeals to that Calvinistic sense of Innate Depravity and Original Sin, from whose visitations, in one form or another, no deeply thinking mind is always and wholly free. (243)

In a way, Melville was claiming Hawthorne for a differing sort of literary Romanticism than the transcendentalism associated with Ralph Waldo Emerson. Hawthorne, Melville implied, was alive to the "power of blackness" that Melville associated with Puritan religious thought, and thus was capable of depths of insight and sympathy that could elude many of Hawthorne's and Melville's contemporaries. If Hawthorne's connections with Brook Farm, Margaret Fuller, Ralph Waldo Emerson, and transcendentalism could in some respects make him a very characteristic nineteenth-century intellectual, Melville understood that in some respects, Hawthorne also had strong intellectual connections to the Puritanism he ambivalently critiqued throughout his fiction, and it was precisely because of these connections that he was able to give expression to both the "Indian-Summer sunlight" of transcendental reverence for nature and "Puritanic gloom" in his work.

Hawthorne as Heir to the Puritans
So how does Hawthorne's broader struggle with his transcendentalist-inflected present and the Puritan past play out in *The Scarlet Letter*? The tension between past and present works its way through the introductory "Custom-House" sketch and the story of Hester Prynne and her tortured love quadrangle itself. In "The Custom-House," Hawthorne reflects explicitly on the ways in which his vocation as a novelist would not have been valued by his Puritan forebears, giving

voice to the way in which his contemporaries in the nineteenth century understood the seventeenth century:

"What is he?" murmurs one gray shadow of my forefathers to another. "A writer of story-books! What kind of business in life,—what mode of glorifying God, or being serviceable to mankind in his day and generation,—may that be? Why, the degenerate fellow may as well have been a fiddler!" (10)

Hawthorne imagines his ancestors responding to the apparent frivolity of a literary vocation with scorn, seeing it as neither sufficiently spiritual ("glorifying God") nor adequately practical ("serviceable to mankind") to be of any merit at all.

This ambivalence about literature might seem to be one of the areas in which transcendentalists were most distant from their Puritan ancestors: Emerson, Fuller, and Thoreau all expressed their high opinion of literature routinely. And yet they also tended to focus their praise of literature to that which could be thought of as comprising myth or scripture. Thus Hawthorne, as a mere storyteller, could seem as frivolous to the literary intellectuals of his nineteenth-century present as he would to the theocratic intellectuals of his seventeenth-century past.

Hester Prynne, meanwhile, seems to give voice to a nineteenth-century revolt against the past, speaking back against the sort of ancestors whose disapproving gaze Hawthorne imagines in "The Custom-House." She reasons boldly on the flaws in the Puritan understanding, not just of the relationship between the sexes, but of human relations in general, and imagines a world in which human relationships can be established on a more rational basis:

The world's law was no law for her mind. It was an age in which the human intellect, newly emancipated, had taken a more active and a wider range than for many centuries before. Men of the sword had overthrown noblemen and kings. Men bolder than these had overthrown and rearranged—not actually, but in the sphere of theory, which was their most real abode—the whole system of ancient prejudice, wherewith was linked much of ancient principle. Hester

Prynne imbibed this spirit. She assumed a freedom of speculation, then common enough on the other side of the Atlantic, but which our forefathers, had they known of it, would have held to be a deadlier crime than that stigmatized by the scarlet letter. (164)

As Hawthorne's reflection on the crises of authority in the seventeenth century shows, what complicates matters is the degree to which the Puritans themselves were revolutionaries and the degree to which Hawthorne acknowledges this fact in *The Scarlet Letter*, and indeed throughout his body of work. Hawthorne frequently reminds his readers of the Puritans' status as rebels and regicides. In earlier stories like "The Gray Champion," from *Twice-Told Tales*, he also calls attention to the Puritans' regicidal history in England, noting that New England's early generations included members who had gone so far as to behead a king. Later in the same decade in which *The Scarlet Letter* was published, Henry David Thoreau wrote a speech entitled "A Plea for Captain John Brown" that defined Puritanism in a way that could make Hester's rebelliousness seem as thoroughly Puritan as any of her other qualities. For Thoreau, John Brown, the antislavery revolutionary executed for his raid on Harper's Ferry, was both a Puritan and a transcendentalist in the highest sense of both terms. If Puritans could be remembered in the nineteenth century as exemplars of a past intolerance, this cultural memory could equally represent them as exemplars of a moral courage and fortitude that had since been abandoned. Hester's pursuit of an ideal that challenged those of the surrounding society marks her as much as a Puritan as a transcendentalist.

A further complicating factor is the way in which Puritans themselves could be social visionaries, and an important way into *The Scarlet Letter* is provided by the sermons that served to make up the main body of Puritan literature when it became canonized as the foundational body of work for understanding the United States in the middle of the twentieth century. When John Winthrop, a Puritan leader who is explicitly mentioned in *The Scarlet Letter*, delivered a sermon entitled "A Model of Christian Charity" that outlined what a Puritan commonwealth should look like, he emphasized the idea that the community should be built around expressions of mutual love:

> Thirdly, nothing yields more pleasure and content to the soul than when it finds that which it may love fervently; for to love and live beloved is the soul's paradise both here and in heaven. In the State of wedlock there be many comforts to learn out of the troubles of that condition; but let such as have tried the most, say if there be any sweetness in that condition comparable to the exercise of mutual love. (Winthrop 7)

Notably, Winthrop's communal ideal for the Massachusetts Bay Colony provided precisely the sort of human sympathy and interdependence that Lidian Jackson Emerson criticized nineteenth-century transcendentalism for lacking.

If communal relationships could mark a contrast between Puritans and transcendentalists, the relationship between humans and the natural world could, as critics going back at least to Perry Miller have noted, bring the two traditions together. For example, John Winthrop recorded in his journals that John Wilson, having observed a mouse improbably kill a snake, could conclude that this event constituted a message from God that the Puritan mission in New England was bound to prosper, as the mouse could stand in for the Puritans and the snake could stand for the devil (Winthrop 72).

This interest in the connections between the natural and supernatural worlds ties the Puritans and the transcendentalists together. In one of the climactic scenes in the relationship between Arthur Dimmesdale and Hester and their daughter Pearl, the three of them stand together on a scaffold in the midst of Salem in the middle of the night, and the sky is illuminated by a meteor. Hawthorne's narrator comments:

> It was indeed a majestic idea, that the destiny of nations should be revealed, in these awful hieroglyphics, on the cope of heaven. A scroll so wide might not be deemed too expansive for Providence to write a people's doom upon. The belief was a favorite one with our forefathers, as betokening that their infant commonwealth was under

a celestial guidance of peculiar intimacy and strictness. But what shall we say, when an individual discovers a revelation, addressed to himself alone, on that vast sheet of record! In such a case, it could only be the symptom of a highly disordered mental state, when a man, rendered morbidly self-contemplative by long, intense, and secret pain, had extended his egotism over the whole expanse of nature, until the firmament itself should appear no more than a fitting page for his soul's history and fate. (155)

A reader who is familiar with Puritan typology and transcendentalist symbolism will readily recognize that this moment is typical of both movements: both transcendentalists and Puritans found nature to be suffused with meaning, and for both groups this belief could offer profound comfort and spiritual sustenance. At the same time, Hawthorne saw that in both Puritanism and transcendentalism, this tendency to read nature as the source of direct communication from the divine could easily subside into a destructive egotism. In a passage like the one above, Hawthorne finds that the continuities between Puritanism and transcendentalism are as powerful as the differences.

Hawthorne and the Gender Politics of Puritanism and Transcendentalism

One way that the gender politics of *The Scarlet Letter* might be illuminated by the struggle between the seventeenth and nineteenth centuries in Hawthorne's work becomes apparent when we compare the work of the seventeenth-century Puritan poet Anne Bradstreet to that of the nineteenth-century American Romantic Margaret Fuller. Hawthorne knew Fuller and was highly ambivalent in his response to her. Fuller was among the most erudite Americans, male or female, of her generation, and she shared with transcendentalists like Emerson and Thoreau and seventeenth-century Puritan ministers a devotion to ideals that transcended human pleasures and desires. As editor of *The Dial*, the leading transcendentalist journal, Fuller sought to show the interconnections of the full range of world religions, and her highly cerebral work had as its ultimate goal a redefining of human relationships that could be morally and intellectually uplifting for both men and women. Fuller explicitly imagined a woman who could be a prophet of a new dispensation in gender relations in her classic feminist essay *Woman in the Nineteenth Century*:

> Meanwhile, not a few believe, and men themselves have expressed the opinion, that the time is come when Eurydice is to call for an Orpheus, rather than Orpheus for Eurydice: that the idea of Man, however imperfectly brought out, has been far more so than that of Woman, that she, the other half of the same thought, the other chamber of the heart of life, needs now to take her turn in the full pulsation, and that improvement in the daughters will best aid in the reformation of the sons of this age. (Fuller 12)

We know that Hawthorne admired Fuller deeply, even as he worried that transcendentalism's emphasis on an individual intellectual and spiritual quest could loosen the bonds of community.

Anne Bradstreet would have been a near contemporary of the fictional Hester Prynne had Hester existed. Like Hester, Bradstreet was married to an erudite minister; unlike Hester, Bradstreet had found a marital relationship with a man she truly loved. Bradstreet's poetry can strike us as curiously modern, and indeed as suggestive of the kind of relationship between men and women that Hester Prynne envisions in *The Scarlet Letter.*

> If ever two were one, then surely we.
> If ever man were loved by wife, then thee;
> If ever wife was happy in a man,
> Compare with me, ye women, if you can.
> I prize thy love more than whole mines of gold
> Or all the riches that the East doth hold.
> My love is such that rivers cannot quench,
> Nor ought but love from thee, give recompense.
> Thy love is such I can no way repay,
> The heavens reward thee manifold, I pray.
> Then while we live, in love let's so persevere
> That when we live no more, we may live ever. (225)

Bradstreet is writing about her husband, the Puritan minister Simon Bradstreet, in this poem, yet there are qualities here that are reminiscent of the world of mutual respect between the sexes that both the fictional Hester Prynne and Hawthorne's real-world contemporary Margaret Fuller desire. The female speaker in this poem is desiring as well as desired, and she imagines herself and her husband persevering together, in a mutually supportive relationship like that which Hester hopes for with Dimmesdale when she suggests that they run away together, and like that which Margaret Fuller imagines as constituting the ideal for marriage in *Woman in the Nineteenth Century*. When considering how Hawthorne negotiates between his transcendentalist contemporaries and Puritan forebears, it is worth keeping these sorts of curious correlations in mind.

Still more important than Bradstreet for understanding the linkages between seventeenth-century New England and nineteenth-century reform movements is a figure that Hawthorne mentions explicitly in *The Scarlet Letter*, Ann Hutchinson. Several times in Hester Prynne's story, she is explicitly compared to the most controversial woman in early New England literary history: when Hester is first introduced, the narrator refers to a rose bush that "had sprung up under the footsteps of the sainted Ann Hutchinson as she entered the prison-door" (48), and much later, the narrator suggests that Hester "might have come down to us in history, hand in hand with Ann Hutchinson, as the foundress of a religious sect" (165).

Unlike Hester Prynne, Hutchinson had not been condemned for adultery, but rather for the fact that she had advocated a doctrine, antinomianism, that had suggested that humans could have a radically individual relation to God, and she had promulgated this doctrine as a woman in a highly patriarchal society (Baym 7-8). In some ways, however, the two cases are comparable: Hester's relationship to Dimmesdale, at least after Pearl's birth, was informed by her willingness to make her own moral judgments, and she, like Ann Hutchinson, is morally and intellectually more powerful than many of the men in her life. Hawthorne's narrator's ambivalence about Hester, her story, and her reasoning, has, as many critics have suggested, a great deal to do with Hawthorne's mix of admiration and anxiety in the face of powerful women like the fictional Hester and the real-life Ann Hutchinson in the seventeenth century and Margaret Fuller in his own time. We might suspect that it also has to do with Hawthorne's complicated relationship to individualism and communalism: Hawthorne recognized that community, as represented by his Puritan ancestors, could be both nurturing and stifling, and individualism, as represented by both seventeenth-century antinomians and nineteenth-century transcendentalists, could discard the positive as well as the negative aspects of community.

Considering Hawthorne's context carefully as we reflect on *The Scarlet Letter* might lead us to the conclusion that Hawthorne's ambivalences are neither just those of a man who is worried about losing a connection to the past through an exuberantly forward-looking presence nor just those of a man who wishes to resist the dead hand of the past. Rather, Hawthorne, like his contemporaries, seems to see profound analogies between past and present in New England, and he seems to raise questions about New England's future precisely where the Puritan past and the transcendentalist present meet. For Hawthorne, Hester can be at once a Puritan and a transcendentalist, at once a representative of the seventeenth century and a premonition of the nineteenth, and she can inspire both admiration and concern.

Insofar as Hester maintains a profound connection with her contemporaries that does not allow her to condemn them either as reprobates in the manner of a Puritan minister or as small minds in the vein of a transcendentalist sage, she is a figure to be admired. This admiration extends to her ability to transcend the narrowness of her time in her thought, but it becomes tinged with concern when she seems in danger of losing contact with her contemporaries altogether.

In *The Scarlet Letter*, then, the moral and intellectual strengths and weaknesses of the seventeenth-century Puritans and their nineteenth-century transcendentalist descendants often run on parallel tracks: Hawthorne seems drawn to the intellectual and moral rigor of both groups, even as he finds a spiritual arrogance that he does not admire among both. Meanwhile, the gender politics of *The Scarlet Letter* are complicated by both the visionary aspects of Puritan and transcendentalist understandings of sexuality and by the ways in which both movements can reassert patriarchal authority. If Hester herself accumulates as many meanings as the letter that she wears over the course of Hawthorne's story, this multiplicity of meaning mirrors a similar complexity in the Puritan and transcendentalist movements she ambivalently inhabits and foreshadows.

Works Cited

Baym, Nina. *The Scarlet Letter: A Reading.* Hall, 1986.

Bercovitch, Sacvan. *The American Jeremiad.* U of Wisconsin P, 1978.

_____. *The Office of the Scarlet Letter.* Johns Hopkins UP, 1991.

_____. *The Puritan Origins of the American Self.* Yale UP, 1975.

Bradstreet, Anne. *The Works of Anne Bradstreet.* Harvard UP, 1967.

Colacurcio, Michael J. *The Province of Piety: Moral History in Hawthorne's Earlier Tales.* Harvard UP, 1984.

Emerson, Lidian Jackson. "Transcendental Bible." In *Transcendentalism: A Reader.* Edited by Joel Myerson. Oxford UP, 2000.

Fuller, Margaret. *Woman in the Nineteenth Century. 1845.* Norton Critical Edition. Edited by Larry J. Reynolds. Norton, 1998.

Hawthorne, Nathaniel. *The Centenary Edition of the Works of Nathaniel Hawthorne.* Edited by William Charvat et al. Ohio State UP, 1962-1997. 23 vols.

Melville, Herman. *The Piazza Tales and Other Prose Pieces, 1839–1860.* Edited by Harrison Hayford, Alma A. MacDougall, and G. Thomas Tanselle. Northwestern UP and The Newberry Library, 1987.

Miller, Perry. *Errand into the Wilderness.* Harvard UP, 1956.

Thoreau, Henry David. "A Plea for Captain John Brown." In *Thoreau: Political Writings.* Edited by Nancy L. Rosenblum. Cambridge UP, 1996. pp. 137-58.

Winthrop, John. *The Journal of John Winthrop, 1630-1649.* Edited by Richard S. Dunn and Laetitia Yeandell. Harvard UP, 1996.

CRITICAL
READINGS

"Absolutely American": Hawthorne's Postcolonial and Neocolonial Masterplot

Jane Zwart

> The best of it was that the thing was absolutely American; it belonged
> to the soil, to the air; it came out of the very heart of New England.
> —Henry James, *Nathaniel Hawthorne*

Decade after decade, students assigned *The Scarlet Letter* face the same temptation. The book does not tempt them to adultery (or, at least, not often). But readers are tempted, almost invariably, to skip "The Custom-House," the long essay "introductory to" (3) the story of Hester Prynne and the letter she wears on her breast. John Carlos Rowe's claim that, in *The Scarlet Letter*, "literature becomes the proper 'custom-house' through which cultural [...] goods circulate" (95) will probably not reduce, significantly, the number of students who decide to skip "The Custom-House." Nevertheless, Rowe's analogy is perfect. Hawthorne does indeed understand literature as an import-export business where, the more stories an author can "imprin[t]" (27) with his own name, the richer the nation he narrates. Rowe goes on: "For Hawthorne, 'American literature' will have to be simultaneously national and transnational" (95). The ambition of *The Scarlet Letter* extends even further. It does not settle for being "simultaneously national and transnational." Rather, this text works to absorb the transnational within the national. Its ambition is to extract elements of other peoples and other nations and to repackage them, folding them into its own American story.

Put otherwise, *The Scarlet Letter* practices an American exceptionalism that is both absorptive and selective. On one hand, Hawthorne's romance enacts an absorptive nationalism: his narrative will allow nothing touching the States' horizon to remain alien to it. On the other hand, *The Scarlet Letter* refuses to permit America's counternarratives easy entry; it is selective. It requires, in fact, that everything at the national horizon—its imperial ancestors, the tribes beyond its frontiers—be made over before it fits them into the American narrative.

Authoring America

The complicating factor here is history. For, as Amritjit Singh and Peter Schmidt observe, "The U.S. may be understood to be the world's first postcolonial *and* neocolonial country" (5, their italics). That is, our national story begins with a layered colonialism, in which English citizens settling North America subjugate and displace indigenous tribes, but, in turn, find themselves oppressed by the British Empire. The next chapter of the story is a familiar one: Britain's colonies turn anticolonial, and they succeed in throwing off imperial England. The chapter after that one, though, proves messier, largely because the colonies have to reckon with their updated role. No longer colonized, they are colonizers by default— unless they can forge a new nation whose natives they are (or are on the way to becoming).

Any nation, as Homi K. Bhabha maintains, is constituted by narration. "The ambivalent, antagonistic perspective of nation as narration," he writes, "will establish the cultural boundaries of the nation so that they may be acknowledged as 'containing' thresholds of meaning that must be crossed, erased, and translated in the process of cultural production" (*Nation* 4). Put otherwise, a nation is the stories people tell about it, and, like all stories, its composition means deciding what to let in and what to leave out. Its composition also means defining boundaries and borders. But in the case of a nation, the story keeps changing. A nation as narration, for example, can pull in the characters hovering at its edges, taming their counternarratives by revising them and then working the tame version into its telling. By the same token, a nation as narration can deport characters. It can amend its setting, too, pushing the frontiers of its earlier renditions outward as it annexes new territories or pulling them inward as its imperial reach declines.

We can see the work of nation-making, therefore, in national literatures. Timothy Brennan makes precisely this point in his essay "The National Longing for Form." He asserts: "It was the *novel* that historically accompanied the rise of nations by objectifying the 'one, yet many' of national life, [...] by mimicking the structure of the nation, a clearly bordered jumble of languages and styles" (49, his italics). The novel, though, does not necessarily stop at "mimicking the structure of a nation"; it can also take part in actually structuring the nation. That, at least, was the judgment of Horace Scudder, one of Hawthorne's literary contemporaries. According to Richard Brodhead, Scudder pressed educators to emphasize classic American literature (including *The Scarlet Letter*) in their curricula because of its function as "the central agency of acculturation: the channel through which [the national] ethos is disseminated, and above all the means by which outsiders are brought inside it" (60). Yet Scudder's understanding that American literature "is literally that which Americanizes" (60) needs broadening. Yes, American literature can acculturate its readers. But American literature can withhold or enact the acculturation of the figures at its margins, too.

Imperial Forebears

Not all scholars, admittedly, read *The Scarlet Letter* as a force of American acculturation. Lawrence Buell, for one, reads it as a cultural debtor. In framing his argument, Buell points up what Hawthorne's romance owes to the Scottish novel *Adam Blair* and where it alludes to Sir Walter Scott and Andrew Marvell. "*The Scarlet Letter*'s quiet affiliation with these texts," Buell claims, "helps establish *its* story not just as a Puritan tale but also as part and parcel of Euro-diasporic collective memory stretching back to the Middle Ages" (74-76, his italics). The adjective *Euro-diasporic* as Buell uses it here describes a diffusion of European peoples and their stories to new lands, and no doubt he is right to insist that Hawthorne borrows against a whole genealogy of writers on the other side of the Atlantic.

What Buell overlooks is that *The Scarlet Letter* is not shy about its diasporic entanglements. Nor are all its allusions to the literature of the Old World "quiet affiliations." Rather, the novel advertises several of its links to European literature and history outright. In "The Custom-House," for instance, Hawthorne lumps himself in with Robert Burns and Geoffrey Chaucer, observing that "each

[…] was a Custom-House officer in his day, as well as I" (26). He mentions, too, a colleague always eager to chitchat about Napoleon or Shakespeare (27). In addition, Hawthorne's romance does not skirt the mention of Hester's "native village, in Old England" (58). It gives Arthur Dimmesdale a British birthplace and a Geneva cloak. And a gossipy Bostonian tells the undercover Roger Chillingworth his own backstory by way of explaining that Hester, the woman atop a scaffold with her "sin-born infant" (63), "was the wife of a certain learned man, English by birth, but who had long dwelt in Amsterdam" (62). In short, *The Scarlet Letter* adds its central characters' and intrusive narrator's individual connections with Europe to what Buell calls a "Euro-diasporic collective memory." In citing its European pretexts, though, Hawthorne's fiction does not disqualify itself from inaugurating an American literary tradition. On the contrary, *The Scarlet Letter* can take part in constructing a nation as narration *because* it cites the pretexts that it then revises and absorbs.

Still, the question of whether *The Scarlet Letter*'s pretexts prevent or enable it to Americanize the story it tells depends upon a bigger question: the question of how Hawthorne's novel relates to the myth of American exceptionalism. At its most basic, American exceptionalism names a belief that the United States is, among other nations, original, unique, inimitable. And *The Scarlet Letter* has become a tricky scripture with regard to American exceptionalism. Lawrence Buell blames the interpreters of Hawthorne's masterplot for having misconstrued it as a myth of American origin, as the story of a national genesis without precedents. To whatever extent *The Scarlet Letter* is conscious of the myth of American origin at all, Buell says, it debunks it. He depicts a Hawthorne immune to the exceptionalist fantasy that the New World was new and that the Old World was moot. All of which is true, as far as it goes.

But American exceptionalism comes in a number of different packages, and one of its brands, instead of relying upon a myth of origin, relies upon the myth of the melting pot. This myth regards America not as a new-sprung act of creation, pastless and perfect. Rather, this second brand of American exceptionalism regards

America as the destined crucible for other peoples and cultures, along with their pasts and stories. In this myth, America proves able to accommodate all of them—and bound to transform them: breaking them down, refining them, and, of course, adding them to its national alloy. It is under the sway of this myth that *The Scarlet Letter* Americanizes itself.

Indeed, Hawthorne's novel constructs a nation as narration that is uniquely equipped to revise and absorb its counternarratives—including its pretexts, among them European literature and British history. Take, for example, the passage describing the festivities for the Massachusetts Bay Colony's newly elected governor. The text is at first sardonic, caricaturing the Puritans as doleful even in celebration. Then, however, the narrator pivots, and what follows deserves to be quoted at length:

> But we perhaps exaggerate the gray or sable tinge, which undoubtedly characterized the mood and manner of the age. The persons now in the market-place of Boston had not been born to an inheritance of Puritanic gloom. They were native Englishmen. [...] Had they followed their hereditary taste, the New England settlers would have illustrated all events of public importance by bonfires, banquets, pageantries, and processions. Nor would it have been impracticable, in the observance of majestic ceremonies, to combine mirthful recreation with solemnity, and give, as it were, a grotesque and brilliant embroidery to the great robe of state, which a nation, at such festivals puts on. [...] The father and founders of the commonwealth— the statesman, the priest, and the soldier—deemed it a duty then to assume the outward state and majesty, which, in accordance with antique style, was looked upon as the proper garb of public or social eminence. All came forth, to move in procession before the people's eye, and thus impart a needed dignity to the simple framework of a government so newly constructed. (230-31)

This account, at first gloss, seems to define New England as a *mere* diasporic outpost of the British Empire. Most basically, it dubs the Puritans "native Englishmen" and distinguishes between the nation (Britain) and the commonwealth (the American colonies). What's more, the colony's election festivities come across as the watered-down (if buttoned-up) echo of English holiday-making, and its efforts at pomp and circumstance sound derivative and drab by comparison—and not in comparison to "a royal coronation" but rather to a more lowly "Lord Mayor's show" (230-31).

What looks like a hapless and dim repetition of the British Empire, however, is a more deliberate transformation. The "fathers and founders of the commonwealth" are not putting on second-rate versions of the imperial regalia; rather, the text dresses them up in a spirit of anticolonial mimicry. Mimicry, as postcolonial theorists understand it, numbers among the ways in which colonized people challenge their colonizers' power. The idea is this: consciously or not, colonized populations almost inevitably mimic their colonizers—but, because the imitation is always imperfect, it undermines the colonial power, edging toward mockery. Bhabha fleshes out this concept: "The excess of slippage produced by the *ambivalence* of mimicry (almost the same, *but not quite*) does not merely 'rupture' [colonial] discourse, but becomes transformed into an uncertainty which fixes the colonial subject as a 'partial' presence" (*Location* 123, his italics). Imperial Britain's stance toward New England's settlers is, of course, the shallowest layer of the colonialism enacted in North America; it does not even begin to compare to the colonial oppression of indigenous tribes.

Nevertheless, mimicry of the British Empire by the colonial Americans takes hold here. For example, when the officials of the colonial commonwealth "assume the outward state and majesty" of imperial England, they reveal its style as outdated. The finery that the empire "puts on" for state occasions is revealed to be just a costume—and an "antique" costume at that, in serious need of revision. *The Scarlet Letter*, then, takes the British counternarrative (which would deny the States' authority while also performing its own sovereignty) and changes it through mimicry. In the American reenactment, England's ceremony looks pretentious and outdated instead of imposing and venerable. Yet, once transformed, the British narrative can become a source of America's "needed dignity," which is "almost the same, *but not quite*" as English pageantry. Put otherwise: the British narrative as rewritten by mimicry helps the commonwealth begin to fill in their nation's new and "simple framework," thereby beginning its own mythology.

Hawthorne's prose, to sum up, wedges Europe's cosmopolitanism into its crucible. Even so, to melt down what it inherits from the European diaspora will not suffice to forge American exceptionalism.

Indigenous Tribes

The Scarlet Letter's brand of American exceptionalism requires "some diversity of hue" (232) that European cosmopolitanism cannot provide. So Hawthorne turns—as the Puritans once did—to Native Americans. More specifically, as Renée Bergland remarks, he turns both to the "real, substantial Indians in town" and also to a more "spectral, [...] internalized Indianness"(157). *The Scarlet Letter*, though, uses its "substantial" and "spectral" Indians to Americanize itself in very different ways. Where its Indians "are real"—and potentially actual characters—the narrative keeps them on its periphery. But where its indigenous figures are "spectral," the novel uses metaphor to absorb select "Indian characteristics" into the American character.

For an example of "real" Indians consigned to the text's periphery, we could simply glance back at the account of the election festivities. Requiring "some diversity of hue" to enliven "the sad gray, brown, or black of the English emigrants," the narrative conjures up "a party of Indians [who]—in their savage finery [...]—*stood apart*" (232, italics mine). In other instances, Native Americans serve *The Scarlet Letter* only as context. The Pequod War hovers in the background, lending Governor Bellingham's armor its shine (105-06). Meteors are taken to "prefigur[e] Indian warfare" (154). Boston's surrounding tribes also give the Apostle John Eliot converts and, by extension, provide Arthur Dimmesdale with a clerical errand that takes him across the frontier the novel defines (182-83). And so on.

Even when its Indians do not function as context, though, Hawthorne refuses to let them number among its characters. Take the man who escorts Hester's long-absent husband into Boston (60). At first, he commands Hester's attention as she stands on the scaffold, but the text is quick to deny him, explaining that "the red men were not so infrequent visitors of the English settlements, that one of them would have attracted any notice from Hester Prynne, at such a time" (60). So the Indian turns out to be a red herring, as it were, and Hester's attention quickly shifts to the white man standing beside him. Sacvan Bercovitch, given this scene, accuses Hawthorne of "a high literary variation on an imperial rhetoric" that "deprives [...] Indians of both nature and civilization" (29). The text bears Bercovitch's indictment out: even when *The Scarlet Letter* costumes its Indian figures with "curiously embroidered deer-skin robes, wampum-belts, red and yellow ochre, and feathers" (232), it also decorates them with stereotypical adjectives, such as "savage" (61), "untutored" (120), and "wild" (199), thereby consigning them to the narrative's margins.

Yet, as scholars have noted, presumed indigenous traits do make their way to the narrative's center. They arrive at this center, however, only inasmuch as *The Scarlet Letter* pours them, hastily refined, into its "white" characters. Philip J. Deloria, in his book *Playing Indian*, forefronts this operation's crudeness. "Nathaniel Hawthorne's *Scarlet Letter*," he alleges, equates an "instinctual 'blood consciousness' with an 'animal wildness' coded as Indian" (3). Deloria, then, sees Hawthorne as using Indianness as the shorthand for transgressive behaviors, especially those born out of passion. Laura Doyle upholds that critique, but she also thinks through the consequences of "cod[ing]" transgression "as Indian." Specifically, she argues that, throughout *The Scarlet Letter*, "the Indian's freedom or 'wildness' gets absorbed into the stories of white characters, in a racial sleight of hand that enhances, ironically, the nativeness of the whites' free interiors" (262). Doyle recognizes here the novel's pattern of deracinating Indians—scrubbing them of their ethnic and cultural particularity—so that white characters can internalize a sanitized version of their "freedom" and Americanize it, thereby making a case for their own "nativeness."

Mita Banerjee, for her part, unpacks how *The Scarlet Letter*'s "racial sleight of hand" works. Pointing to a phenomenon she calls "ethnic ventriloquism," Banerjee writes, "The perfection of ethnic ventriloquism is that it reconciles an ethnic voice with a white body: it is this split which ethnicizes a white system which remains itself" (170). The analogy is unmistakable: unseen, an "ethnic" people throws out their voice while a "white body" lip syncs. The illusion is of course imperfect, and sometimes deliberately so—as when the white voice drowns out something inconvenient the ethnic voice utters. But, those alterations notwithstanding, Banerjee says, American literature annexes the ethnic voice, muting and sampling it as the nation's exceptionalist narrative requires.

Despite her critique of "the white system which remains itself," Banerjee sees "ethnic ventriloquism" in classic American texts as complicated, especially because "what preceded American self-definition against the Indian was American self-definition *as* Indian" (11, her italics). Banerjee holds, in other words, that New England's first settlers took themselves for its natives. For the British colonial, North America's indigenous peoples were not people. Nor were they American. They were prototypes or archetypes, extras or allegorical figures, and from their midst would emerge the occasional threat, the exceptional sidekick.

That said, not all New Englanders justified their "nativeness" through "ethnic ventriloquism," and most of the primary characters in *The Scarlet Letter* prove incapable of that "racial sleight of hand." For example, despite Leslie A. Fiedler's famously labeling Pearl's mother "the wildest Indian of them all!" (519), Hester always distinguishes what belongs to the marketplace from "what happens to us in the forest" (240). Put otherwise: she cannot integrate Indianness into Americanness. She has, instead, to choose between America and what lies at its horizons, the Indian wilderness on one side and a transatlantic cosmopolitanism on the other. Chillingworth, too, fails to Americanize native culture for *The Scarlet Letter*. Granted, he does first appear "in a strange disarray of civilized and savage costume" (60), and he does add native remedies to his European pharmacology. But Chillingworth never manages to sanitize and coopt what he borrows from indigenous tribes. Actually, the novel leaves open the opposite possibility: that the Indians have corrupted and coopted him. Note, for instance, that he comes under suspicion as an individual who may have "gone native" (127)—that is, become "contaminat[ed] by absorption into native life and custom" (Ashcroft, et al. 115). As for Dimmesdale, his sojourn over the frontier to visit John Eliot, the apostle to the Indians, only leaves him "look[ing] pale" (223). Where Bergland contends, then, that "each of [*The Scarlet Letter*'s] main characters is, at the very least, described as internalizing Indian consciousness" (157), the novel itself suggests that its characters "internali[ze] Indian consciousness" not "at the very least," but at the very most.

Pearl alone possesses the knack of Americanizing the Indian. So when Bergland concludes that *The Scarlet Letter* "constructs a white America with a blood-red Indian legacy at its heart" (158), she is right. But without Pearl, the "blood-red [...] legacy at [America's] heart" would only appear on the text's surface, whether as local color (posing Indians at the edge of the marketplace) or as Hester's "richness of complexion" (53).

Born with "a certain depth of hue, which she never lost" (90), Pearl does inherit a "richness of complexion" from her mother. She is, in fact, as Sophie Bell quips, "many shades of red" (1). But Pearl, unlike Hester, also proves able to revise and absorb the Indian archetype—to enact "ethnic ventriloquism." She begins by deracinating "the wild Indian." She "look[s him] in the face; and he gr[ows] conscious of a nature wilder than his own" (244). In the next sentence, Hawthorne credits Pearl with "native audacity" (244), and it is audacious, to be sure, that the misbegotten American child, not the indigenous man, earns the adjective "native." But this is ethnic ventriloquism at work: the text effaces the Indian, who becomes "spectral" compared to the unruly Pearl, and she magnifies and manages his "wildness," coopting it for her "native" self, as well as her "native" land.

The Scarlet Letter tasks Pearl with Americanizing its indigenous peoples and cultures in other instances as well, and Sophie Bell deftly traces many of them. Yet she also reads "the novel's final removal of Pearl" from its American setting as evidence that "Hawthorne's mischievous red-faced child [...] is never interpellated into colonial society" (17). The novel, though, doesn't "remov[e]" Pearl; on the contrary, it gives her a passport. The last pages of the book report that Pearl "bec[omes] the richest heiress of her day, in the New World," with "a very considerable amount of property both here [in America] and in England" (261). That Pearl is not an heiress of note in England but is "the richest [...] of her day, in the New World" binds her to America, as do the letters she addresses there. To be sure, those letters bear "armorial seals [...] of bearings unknown to English heraldry" (262), but the limits of English heraldry have, by the novel's end, been well established. What matters is that Pearl puts those "armorial seals"—not to mention her story—in the possession of her mother and her motherland.

All told, Pearl, who converts an Indian wildness into American currency, becomes an expatriate, and as an expatriate, she continues to funnel a needed "diversity of hue" into America's crucible. And even before the novel sends her abroad, Pearl draws to herself—and contributes to America's absorptive exceptionalism—not only an "Indian presence," but a global presence. As we will see.

Transnational Others

Just as *The Scarlet Letter* conjures Indianness and then either pushes it to the periphery or absorbs a deracinated version of it, so it Americanizes or marginalizes the rest of the world at its horizon. Specifically, the novel treats the "real, substantial" Africans within its borders much as it does the "real, substantial Indians" at its frontier. It sidelines them. In the meantime, when it comes to the absorption of other peoples and cultures—those who happen to be oceans away—the novel cribs from imperialism. With one crucial difference: instead of annexing these Others literally (as the British Empire did), *The Scarlet Letter* annexes them metaphorically.

As for the African peoples he pushes to *The Scarlet Letter*'s periphery, Hawthorne does acknowledge their existence. Already in "The Custom-House," for instance, he casually mentions "vessels [...] from Africa or South America—or [...] on the verge of their departure thitherward" (6) but never mentions the ship from Africa's inevitable cargo. He also lays out a geography that puts the black Americans living in Salem on its outermost edge. Salem's "long and lazy street," according to Hawthorne, "has 'Gallows Hill' and 'New Guinea' at one end, and a view of the alms-house at the other" (8). "'New Guinea,'" as Michael Sokolow explains, "was a familiar phrase commonly used to refer to black neighborhoods in [Northern] cities." But Salem, he goes on, "had no 'New Guinea' to speak of" (204), and Sokolow deduces that, "Like most of his white townsfolk, Hawthorne was almost totally unacquainted with Salem's black community" (205). In this case, then, marginalizing those of African descent comes easily to the novelist.

The antebellum novel finds slaves harder to overlook, as scholars have remarked. Teresa Goddu, for one, explores *The Scarlet Letter*'s perspective on slavery, alleging that the narrative affiliates both Hester and Pearl with images of bondage (65). But Laura Hanft Korobkin rightly complicates Goddu's reading. Korobkin grants that the text does bear traces of the Africanist presence, as defined by Toni Morrison (204), who writes that classic American literature is rife with a "sometimes allegorical, sometimes metaphorical, but always choked representation" of ethnically African peoples (17). *The Scarlet Letter* ultimately focuses, though, insists Korobkin, on Hawthorne's refusal, even symbolically, to "merge [its white characters'] situation with that of slaves" (205). Her primary evidence for this claim is the narrative's key historical anomaly: Hester does not, in punishment for her crime, receive a whipping. "In designing Hester's punishment," Korobkin writes, "Hawthorne eliminated whatever would have suggested a resemblance between her situation and that of the slave" (195). Thus, the figure of the slave—like the free black living in Salem—remains on the narrative's outskirts.

Nonetheless, *The Scarlet Letter* does fold into its construct of America repackaged imports from other lands, peoples, and cultures—and slavery was a linchpin of the States' transatlantic trade. Again, "The Custom-House" proves relevant. Hawthorne there observes that his name is no longer "blazoned abroad on title-pages" but instead "imprinted, with a stencil and black paint, on pepper-bags, and baskets of annatto, and cigar-boxes, and bales of all kinds of dutiable merchandise" (27). Given this passage, Goddu promptly points out that "the commodities upon which

Hawthorne's name is imprinted [...] are from Salem's trade with Africa, the East Indies, South America, and the Caribbean" (62) and asserts that "Hawthorne was economically embedded within a commercial marketplace connected to the slave economy" (50). *The Scarlet Letter* offers nothing to rebut that claim; instead it avoids the question altogether. Throughout, the novel tends to concentrate on the big picture of exchange across cultures and between nations— and to blink at the fine-grained realities of imperialism, painstakingly ignoring American slavery.

Yet, even as *The Scarlet Letter* refuses to bear witness to slavery, it countenances other spoils of imperialism—and it Americanizes them eagerly, just as it readily coopts the European diaspora and Indians' nativeness.

For instance, Wilfried Raussert traces *The Scarlet Letter*'s orientalism, beginning with the narrator's description of Hester as "ha[ving] in her nature a rich, voluptuous, Oriental characteristic" (83). Orientalism of this sort is, according to Edward Said, the West's way of "dealing with [the Orient] by making statements about it, authorizing views of it, describing it, by teaching it, settling it, ruling over it" (3). And *The Scarlet Letter* does "authoriz[e]" a version of the East by singling out one "Oriental characteristic": "a taste for the gorgeously beautiful" (83). At the same time, the novel metaphorically "settle[s] and rul[es] over" the Orient by bestowing its assumed "characteristic" on Hester. Yet Raussert does not point up this presumption on *The Scarlet Letter*'s part; rather, he suggests that its strain of orientalism "let[s Hawthorne] infuse his critique of Puritan patriarchy [...] with the inclusion of difference" (63).The text's presumption is unmistakable, though: it uses Hester to Americanize "a rich, voluptuous, Oriental characteristic," and it grants the so-called Orient no agency. Hawthorne's prose does not, for instance, label Hester herself as "Oriental," overwriting her Americanness. Instead, it gives "her nature" possession of an "Oriental characteristic." "She has" it; it does not have her. *The Scarlet Letter*'s orientalism, in other words, simply infuses the American narrative with what it imagines to be the flavor of the Other.

And the same strain of exceptionalism that infuses the text with orientalism also absorbs a very different source of flavor: a party of "rough-looking desperadoes, with sun-blackened faces, and an immensity of beard" (232). Plainly stated, Hawthorne portrays this rowdy crew as the next thing to pirates; they represent the "Age of Discovery"'s full-scale transnational plunder. In its own plunder, naturally, *The Scarlet Letter* is subtler than these "desperadoes."

Consider the scene in which "one of these seafaring men [is] so smitten with Pearl's aspect, that he attempt[s] to lay hands on her, with the purpose to snatch a kiss" (245). The girl evades him, and once bested, he is an inordinately good sport. He throws her a gold chain from his own costume, which "Pearl immediately twine[s …] around her neck and waist, with such happy skill, that, once seen there, it bec[omes] a part of her, and it [is] difficult to imagine her without it" (245). This episode, whatever other purposes it serves, is an allegory for Americanization. The shipmaster cannot capture Pearl, but she can captivate him. What's more, the American girl takes the much-traveled captain's gold chain—the symbol of his global fortunes—and transforms it, making it "a part of her." Symbolically, then, she takes possession of the sailor's transnational acquisitions.

The text of Hawthorne's romance does the same thing: it makes transnational exchange its own. In the words of Gillian Brown, "Hawthorne [...] develops an account of American nationalism in which national identification continually operates in tandem with resistances to it" (122). As already discussed, these points of resistance to American nationalism take shape, particularly, in the counternarratives of the peoples and cultures at its horizon. But *The Scarlet Letter*, when it does not marginalize them, perpetually revises and claims these Others' stories for its own. In the end, therefore, it is no easier to imagine Hawthorne's romance apart from what it has absorbed—from the European diaspora, from indigenous tribes, and from its transnational horizon—than it is to imagine Pearl without a gold chain "twined [...] around her neck and waist, with such happy skill."

The one remaining question, perhaps, is what we should call Nathaniel Hawthorne's "happy skill": forgery or mimicry, smelting or alchemy, plagiarism or translation? All of the above, probably, and then some. Hawthorne stands behind the plot of an absorptive American exceptionalism.

In fact, he stands behind what may be the States' postcolonial and neocolonial masterplot. For, even as "the U.S. may be understood to be the world's first postcolonial *and* neocolonial country," so this classic American novel narrates a nation through the methods of both postcolonial resistance and neocolonial absorption. *The Scarlet Letter* remakes and then usurps the British narrative through anticolonial mimicry, after all, but this romance also practices a neocolonial annexation of other peoples' stories. The term "neocolonialism," it is true, does not come into circulation until 1965, at which time Kwame Nkrumah uses it to name the ways in which "international monetary bodies, [...] multinational corporations and cartels and a variety of educational and cultural institutions" exert a "more insidious" control over postcolonial nations than old-fashioned, unsubtle colonialism did (Ashcroft, et al. 162-63). But that no one named neocolonialism until 1965 does not disprove *The Scarlet Letter*'s literary neocolonialism. On the contrary, the book is an early prodigy of the United States' absorptive exceptionalism. It incorporates indigeneity. It Americanizes the Orient and the pirate. And it prophesies what the United States has since become.

Works Cited

Ashcroft, Bill, et al. *Postcolonial Studies: The Key Concepts.* Routledge, 1998.

Banerjee, Mita. *Ethnic Ventriloquism: Literary Minstrelsy in Nineteenth-Century American Literature.* Universitätsverlag, 2008.

Bell, Sophie. "Misreading *The Scarlet Letter*: Race, Sentimental Pedagogy, and Antebellum Indian Literacy." *Studies in American Fiction*, vol. 42, no. 1, 2015, pp. 1-27.

Bercovitch, Sacvan. *The Office of* The Scarlet Letter. Johns Hopkins UP, 1991.

Bergland, Renée. *The National Uncanny: Indian Ghosts and American Subjects*. UP of New England, 2000.

Bhabha, Homi K. *The Location of Culture*. Routledge, 1994.

_____, editor. *Nation and Narration*. Routledge, 1990.

Brennan, Timothy. "The National Longing for Form." *Nation and Narration*. Edited by Homi K. Bhabha. Routledge, 1990, pp. 44-70.

Brodhead, Richard. *The School of Hawthorne*. Oxford UP, 1986.

Brown, Gillian. "Hawthorne's American History." *The Cambridge Companion to Nathaniel Hawthorne*. Edited by Richard H. Millington. Cambridge UP, 2004, pp. 121-42.

Buell, Lawrence. "Hawthorne and the Problem of 'American' Fiction: The Example of *The Scarlet Letter*." *Hawthorne and the Real: Bicentennial Essays*. Edited by Millicent Bell. Ohio State UP, 2005. 70-87.

Deloria, Philip J. *Playing Indian*. Yale UP, 1998.

Doyle, Laura. "'A' for Atlantic: The Colonizing Force of Hawthorne's *The Scarlet Letter*." *American Literature*, vol. 79, no. 2, 2007, pp. 243-73.

Fiedler, Leslie A. *Love and Death in the American Novel*. 1960. Meridian, 1962.

Goddu, Teresa. "Letters Turned to Gold: Hawthorne, Authorship, and Slavery." *Studies in American Fiction*, vol. 29, no. 1, 2001, pp. 49-76.

Hawthorne, Nathaniel. *The Scarlet Letter*. 1850. Ohio State UP, 1962.

James, Henry. *Nathaniel Hawthorne*. Harper, 1879.

Korobkin, Laura Hanft. "The Scarlet Letter of the Law: Hawthorne and Criminal Justice." *Novel: A Forum on Fiction*, vol. 30, no. 2, 1997, pp. 193-217.

Morrison, Toni. *Playing in the Dark: Whiteness and the Literary Imagination*. Vintage, 1993.

Raussert, Wilfried. "Orientalism, Othering, and Critique of the Nation in Hawthorne's *The Scarlet Letter*." *Of Fatherlands and Motherlands: Gender and Nation in the Americas*. Edited by Sebastian Thies, et al. Wissenschaftlicher Verlag Trier, 2015, pp. 61-74.

Rowe, John Carlos. "Nathaniel Hawthorne and Transnationality." *Hawthorne and the Real: Bicentennial Essays*. Edited by Millicent Bell. Ohio State UP, 2005, pp. 88-106.

Said, Edward. *Orientalism: Western Conceptions of the Orient*. 1978. Penguin, 1991.

Singh, Amritjit, and Peter Schmidt, editors. *Postcolonial Theory and the United States: Race, Ethnicity, and Literature*. UP of Mississippi, 2000.

Sokolow, Michael. "'New Guinea at One End, and a View of the Alms-House at the Other': The Decline of Black Salem, 1850-1920." *The New England Quarterly*, vol. 71, no. 2, 1998, pp. 204-28.

Autobiography and Romance in Hawthorne's "The Custom-House": Literary Creation and the Second Story

John Wenke

> There was always a prophetic instinct, a low whisper in my ear, that,
> within no long period, and whenever a new change of custom should
> be essential to my good, a change would come.
>
> —Nathaniel Hawthorne, "The Custom-House"

Toward a True Narrative Relation

At the outset of "The Custom-House: Introductory to 'The Scarlet
Letter'" Nathaniel Hawthorne repeatedly describes the act of
writing as a form of "talk" (3) and contends that this conversational
medium establishes the optimal foundation for his preferred relation
to his readers. [1] He describes a dramatically immediate, reciprocal
liaison that nevertheless has circumscribed limits and falls well
short of providing those "confidential depths of revelation as could
fittingly be addressed, only and exclusively, to the one heart and
mind of perfect sympathy" (3). What allows "the speaker [to] stand
in some true relation with his audience" is a qualified, carefully
modulated familiarity that balances competing claims of revelation
and retention: "[W]e may prate of the circumstances that lie around
us, and even of ourself, but still keep the inmost Me behind its
veil" (4). Such are the conditions, Hawthorne avers, that permit an
author to "be autobiographical, without violating either the reader's
rights or his own" (4). As Stephen Railton observes, "The ideal
of understanding forms the author and his or her audience into a
community more intimately bound together than even the minister
and his congregation" (116).

Given such concern with moral rights and degrees of mutuality,
it may seem strange, disconcerting, and paradoxical that Hawthorne
immediately lies. He claims that his "true reason" for writing this
autobiographical sketch describing his 1846-49 appointment as chief

executive officer of the Salem Custom-House is to offer "proofs of the authenticity of a narrative therein contained" (4). The assertion that Hawthorne derived archival evidence of Hester Prynne's life from a manuscript compiled by his official ancestor, surveyor Jonathan Pue, is no more true than his assertion that he is not so much author as "editor, or very little more" of *The Scarlet Letter* (4). Surveyor Pue did exist, having taken office in 1752, almost a century before Hawthorne's tenure, but he did not leave a manuscript for his successor to preserve for the scrutiny of anyone willing to call. In fact, the indirect, though cumulative, sources of *The Scarlet Letter* emerged slowly through the numerous tales that Hawthorne wrote in the decade and a half following his 1825 graduation from Bowdoin College. This body of work includes the pieces intended for a late 1820s unpublished collection entitled "Seven Tales of My Native Land" and the great short stories published in magazines and gift books throughout the 1830s. Such tales as "Alice Doane's Appeal" (1835), "Young Goodman Brown" (1835), "The Minister's Black Veil" (1836), and "Endicott and the Red Cross" (1838) concentrate on depicting the moral history of the theocratic Puritan Plantation Religious.[2] The first published anticipation of Hester Prynne herself appears in "Endicott and the Red Cross." For relatively minor social and religious transgressions, the tyrannical John Endicott favors public punishment and ridicule "for the space of one hour noonday" (435). More egregious perpetrators may suffer lifelong, emblematic afflictions:

> There was likewise a young woman with no mean share of beauty, whose doom it was to wear the letter A on the breast of her gown in the eyes of all the world and her own children. And even her own children knew what that initial signified. Sporting with her infamy, the lost and desperate creature had embroidered the fatal token in scarlet cloth, with golden thread, and the nicest art of needle-work so that the capital A might have been thought to mean Admirable, or any thing rather than Adulterous. (435)

In a notebook entry from late 1844 or early 1845, Hawthorne reflects briefly on the possibility of developing a more lengthy treatment of an unnamed scarlet sinner: "The life of a woman, who, by the old colony law, was condemned to wear the letter A, sewed on her garment, in token of her having committed Adultery" (*American Notebooks* 107).

Even if Hawthorne's ostensible reasons for writing "The Custom-House" are not literally true, he nevertheless remains deeply preoccupied with the matter of his story's authenticity—and not merely in its outline, as he insists, but in its substance and moral weight. In attempting to establish a "true relation" with his audience, Hawthorne also aspires to create the means, or the aesthetic medium, through which author and reader can enlist the prosaic, often topical, genre of the nineteenth-century sketch as an induction into moral and experiential complexities associated with the past as dramatized within the genre of the historical romance.[3] Hawthorne's essential purpose is to take the airy, ethereal workings of the imagination and infuse them with the heft of deeply felt experience, to take the inventions of the fancy and make them seem real and true. In "The Custom-House" sketch, the elemental problem Hawthorne grapples with concerns the debilitating impact of sterile, present-day actualities on his creative psyche and the ways in which these impediments deny access to the life of the mind and the imagined historical past.

In an early story well known to scholars but seldom reprinted in anthologies, Hawthorne directly engages this foundational problem—the relationship between an author-narrator and his contemporary readers, especially as it dramatizes the performative difficulty of bringing the reconstructed past to life for an audience accustomed to the facile present. In the form published in 1835 "Alice Doane's Appeal" likely contains a truncated, heavily redacted version of a longer tale—now lost—that was originally designed for inclusion in "Seven Tales of My Native Land." The narrator of the story is a projected version of Hawthorne's authorial self, whimsically conceived as a young writer on a walk with "two young ladies" (266) not to customary recreational haunts but, mordantly enough, to Salem's Gallows Hill, "the high place where our fathers set up their shame, to the mournful gaze of generations far remote.

The dust of martyrs was beneath our feet" (267). Supplied with a clutch of manuscript leaves, the narrator intends to read from his historical narrative with the purpose of displacing the niceties of contemporary Salem and replacing them with the terrors that roiled the all-too-easily forgotten past. After lamenting the dearth of historical consciousness on the part of "a people of the present . . .[who] have no heartfelt interest in the olden time" (267), the narrator reads his lady friends a lurid tale of murder, wizardry, perverted love, hellish hate, and a most macabre scene of resurrected specters spilling from graves—all culminating with the "universal madness" of the witchcraft hysteria (278). The narrator strives with all the power of his art to bring the past to life, to dramatize the overwhelming horror of convicted witches about to endure public execution at the hands of "a guilty and miserable band; villains who had thus avenged themselves on their enemies, and viler wretches, whose cowardice had destroyed their friends" (279). The narrator builds to a rhetorical and dramatic crescendo that climaxes with the appearance on horseback of Satan's "good friend, Cotton Mather, proud of his well won dignity, as the representative of all the hateful features of his time" (279). In the process of telling his story, the narrator moves back and forth between reading his phantasmagoric tale and describing his attentive female listeners. In a moment of metafictional self-analysis, the narrator contends, "By this fantastic piece of description. . . I intended to throw a ghostly glimmer round the reader, so that his imagination might view the town through a medium that should take off its every day aspect, and make it a proper theatre for so wild a scene as the final one" (274).

In "Alice Doane's Appeal" Hawthorne engages the very materials that dominate "The Custom-House"—how author and audience might evade the soul-deadening impress of contemporary life's "every day aspect" (274) and what aesthetic conditions must obtain before the romance writer can successfully compose a powerful work of historical fiction that reaches readers and communicates the moral truth of the past. The narrator of "Alice Doane's Appeal" attempts to conflate past scene and present place and thus depicts with a sense of experiential immediacy the emotional extremity of the execution scene that took place on "the hill-top, where we stood. I plunged into my imagination for a blacker horror, and a deeper woe, and pictured the scaffold—" (279). But suddenly, here and now, the narrator is interrupted by his success. He has deeply touched his female auditors, striking through their surface sensibilities and shocking their emotional core: "But here my companions seized an arm on each side; their nerves were trembling; and sweeter victory still, I had reached the seldom trodden places of their hearts, and found the well-spring of their tears" (279-80). In this short masterwork, the narrator exercises his powers and brings the forgotten past to the present, concluding his reconstructive literary performance with a statement of self-congratulatory recompense: "And now the past had done all it could" (280).

Hawthorne's problem in "The Custom-House" is not so much to bring the past to the present as it is to bring the present—through the agency of the narrator and his relationship to his reader—into the past. In "The Custom-House" the author himself aspires to become disentangled from the contemporary malaise, especially the comfort of fool's gold, the enervating effects of governmental dependency, and the languor afflicting his artistic powers. At stake is Hawthorne's liberation from the stultifying torpor that attended his three-year tenure in the Port of Salem and his rediscovery of the rich creative possibilities of aesthetic self-actualization. As we shall see, by leaving behind the sphere of present-day actualities, by figuratively suffering a figurative form of political decapitation, Hawthorne reconstitutes himself as one capable of dramatizing the entangled, nuanced world of the remote historical past. He not only offers a sketch of his time as a political appointee and the (fictive) account of how he came to possess the (fictive) archival sources of Hester's tale, but more importantly he propounds his fullest explanation of those attributes and elements that inform, shape, and liberate his artistic powers. Hawthorne finds a way to leave the contemporary domain of custom, thereby regaining his ability to create, thereby investing the imagined past with a greater degree of moral value than anything in the vaporous, ephemeral present.

To effect his transit from present to past, from sketch to romance, Hawthorne must dramatize the complexities associated with the following issues: his natal affiliation with the soil of Salem; his ambiguous relationship with his infamous, ancestral blood kindred; his account of experiencing sharp pain as he unwittingly brings Hester's tattered *A*—that enticing "mystic symbol" (31)—to his breast; and, most significantly, the transformative agency associated with the "neutral territory" (36). Essentially, this chapter explores how and why Hawthorne adapts his experiences as a Custom-House officer to the cause of writing himself into becoming the expansive, transhistorical first-person narrator of *The Scarlet Letter*. In finding himself "a citizen of somewhere else" (44) he establishes the aesthetic medium whereby the reader—this "kind, and apprehensive, though not the closest friend" (4)—can enter the past with him.

The Problem Present

To counteract his portrait of a contemporary Salem languishing in decay, Hawthorne considers the divided nature of his social and genealogical attachment to his home town. How do "the deep and aged roots which [his] family has struck into the soil" (8) affect him not only as their current representative but also as a returning political appointee—one who no longer functions as a literary artist? He must reach into, and make peace with, his family's heritage as well as the literal and figurative soil out of which his progenitors emerged and into which they returned. In asserting the extreme notion that his genealogical connection to his ancestral home has conferred on him an inescapable ontological and chemical bond, Hawthorne notes that his forbearers have "mingled their earthy substance with the soil; until no small portion of it must necessarily be akin to the mortal frame wherewith . . . I walk the streets" (9). He thus accepts his relation to Salem as "the mere sensuous sympathy of dust for dust" (9). Nevertheless, the ties that bind self to place embody those very qualities that define and animate his authorial identity. His experience of "sensuous sympathy" evokes that foundational quality of empathy that allows him to participate in a shared humanity, even as this sense of sympathy "induces a sort of home-feeling with the past, which I scarcely claim in reference to the present phase of the town" (9). This "home-feeling with the past" inevitably brings Hawthorne to consider his infamous Puritan ancestors—William Hathorne (ca. 1606-1681), the righteous scourge of Quakers and Indians, and his son John Hathorne (1641-1717), the unrepentant hanging judge of the Salem witch trials. On the one hand, Hawthorne positions himself in opposition to his ancestors' crimes against humanity, especially those terrible excesses perpetrated in the name of Puritan piety, even taking "shame upon himself for their sakes" in hopes of expiating any curse that might have been levied on posterity (10). On the other hand, the historical world of the Puritans provides the well-spring of materials that shapes and sustains his literary career, even though he sardonically—and as a form of muted self-congratulation—gives voice to the ghostly disdain that his great-grandfathers would allegedly heap on him for being nothing more than "[a] writer of story-books! . . . Why the degenerate fellow might as well have been a fiddler" (10).

Hawthorne's return to Salem with a good government salary impedes rather than fosters the progress of his literary life and he finds himself not only creatively dormant, but psychologically oppressed by the weight of his (very light) official duties and the vitiating atmosphere of dullness and redundancy. In the Custom-House, the past seems little more than the repository of old jokes told and retold, of "frozen witticisms . . . [that] were thawed out, and came bubbling with laughter" from the lips of his wizened associates (15). The sketch of the venerable Inspector epitomizes the moral vacancy of the problem present. The Inspector "possessed no power of thought, no depth of feeling, no troublesome sensibilities" (17). A paradigmatic portrait of the amoral materiality afflicting the world of custom, the Inspector has "no soul, no heart, no mind" (18). At best, he recollects with relish the satisfying experience of dinners long departed. An antidote to the Inspector's overwhelming identification with materiality can be found in the Collector, General Miller. On the one hand, the Collector prefigures elements later associated with Hester—"[w]eight, solidity, firmness" along with "stubborn and ponderous endurance. . . of integrity . . . and of benevolence" (21-22).[4] A man of "innate kindliness," the Collector reflects the positive qualities of an active inner life (22). As Hawthorne observes, "It might be, that he lived a more real life within his thoughts, than amid the unappropriate environment of the Collector's office" (23). The Inspector and the Collector represent distinct, inimical responses to the realm of material actuality. The Inspector *is* the Custom-House personified—dull, unimaginative, spiritless. By contrast, the Collector retreats into a rich interior world where memories play out on the reflecting screen of his still vigorous consciousness. "[A]s much out of place as an old sword" the Collector witnesses scenes from his martial past that are "all alive before his intellectual sense" (23).

Unlike the Collector, Hawthorne cannot find "repose" (20) in witnessing the protean play of mind. He is not a meditative mystic but an artist, a writer of sketches and tales, a maker of forms. Caught within the materialistic miasma of contemporary Salem, he finds himself detached from his artistry. As this sketch makes clear, the resources that shape Hawthorne's creativity depend on his ability to recover a procreant relation to the past. Even though he intrepidly asserts that "it lay at my option to recall whatever was valuable in the past"(26)—that is, his vocational dedication to writing stories about the moral history of Puritan New England—he cannot reenact these energies without "a new change of custom" (26). An inherent conflict obtains between the oppressive demands of everyday life and the exalted enticements of artistic self-actualization, the isolated, though privileged, office of literary creation. "The Custom-House" dramatizes the paralyzing consequences of this impasse. It is not until Hawthorne moves away from the first-floor bustle of everyday tedium and ascends into the dusty, quiet, secluded, unfinished second story that he happens upon a prospective solution to the problem present.

"A Neutral Territory, Somewhere between the Real World and Fairy-land"

Hawthorne's series of lies regarding archival materials left behind by the late Surveyor Pue are best viewed as self-enabling fictions that establish the framework wherein Hawthorne seeks to reclaim his vocational identity as a literary artist. The envelope that he putatively finds advances the supporting illusion of documentary authenticity, especially through those alleged "traces of Mr. Pue's mental part" (30) that detail the Ur-story of Hester Prynne's tribulations. In attempting to make these fictions seem real, Hawthorne expands his narrative reach beyond the boundaries of custom. He begins to reconnect with a slowly emergent authorial and historical past. He becomes, at first, an ostensible interpreter of "a certain affair of fine red cloth, much worn and faded" (31). In his uninformed misreading of Hester's tattered letter, Hawthorne indicates how the interpretive process unfolds through an oscillating display of dialectically charged possibilities. In advancing his misinformed speculations, Hawthorne delineates his own distance from the hidden truth of the past: "[T]he capital letter A . . . had been intended, there could be no doubt, as an ornamental article of dress; but how it was to be worn, or what rank, honor, and dignity, in by-past times, were signified by it, was a riddle which . . . I saw little hope of solving" (31). At this moment, Hawthorne remains circumscribed within his myopic perspective as Surveyor of Customs. In the second story, one flight removed from the drudgery of contemporary affairs, he is enticed, attracted, and allured, but he languishes in an uncomprehending state of hermeneutical premonition. His feelings draw him toward the historical past, which is to say toward his own currently defunct vocational identify as a fiction-making artificer, but he can only perceive the strange object as latently possessing "some deep meaning . . . worthy of interpretation, and which, as it were, streamed forth from the mystic symbol, subtly communicating itself to my sensibilities, but evading the analysis of my mind" (31). He has yet to become the awakened authorial self released from the suffocating present and operating as a discerning, transhistorical narrative voice.

The key moment of transfer that impels Hawthorne's artistic awakening occurs when he touches the *A* to his chest. Such intimate physical contact with Hester's now-ragged letter excites and inflames his inchoate "sensibilities": "It seemed to me,—the reader may smile, but must not doubt my word,—it seemed to me, then, that I experienced a sensation not altogether physical, yet almost so, as of burning heat; and as if the letter were not of red cloth, but red-hot iron" (32). Hawthorne twice uses similes—"as of" and "as if"—to create the fictive semblance—indeed, the "sensation"—of actual experience. He thus provides an accurate prefiguration of how extreme emotional suffering in *The Scarlet Letter* inflicts physical pain—Arthur Dimmesdale's hand over his heart being the clearest example—while at the same time dramatizing the need for Hawthorne as sketch writer and soon-to-be romance writer to *feel* the pain that the *A* inflicts, to have his "sensibilities" engaged as a prelude to feeling *sympathy* for the letter's sinful victim. In *The Scarlet Letter*, human sympathy is not only the source of communal bonding. It also creates the possibility for empathetic mutuality, psychological rehabilitation, and spiritual redemption. Throughout the narrative, the obverse of sympathy—unmitigated harsh judgment and unrelenting vengeance—imposes a systemic hardening of individual and communal sensibilities. In the case of Roger Chillingworth, such a condition leads to a debilitating form of dehumanization, a self-imposed degree of villainy tantamount to damnation. The fact that a benighted Hawthorne in the second story experiences a sharp semblance of pain establishes in him an empathetic quality that will later balance, and leaven, his recurrent judgmental assessments regarding the destructive consequences of Hester's adultery. As narrator of *The Scarlet Letter*, Hawthorne is often unflinchingly condemnatory. In remarking on how during the first scaffold scene Hester's beauty when holding her child falsely evokes "the image of Divine Maternity," he writes: "Here, there was the taint of deepest sin in the most sacred quality of human life, working such effect, that the world was only the darker for this woman's beauty, and the more lost for the infant that she had borne" (56). Later, however, the same narrator frequently celebrates Hester's compassionate qualities. Indeed she was "quick to acknowledge her sisterhood with the race of man, whenever benefits were to be conferred. . . . Hester's nature showed itself warm and rich; a well-spring of human tenderness, unfailing to very real demand, and inexhaustible by the largest" (160-61). The narrator's recurrent assertions of sympathy for Hester's plight mitigate his recurrent harsh judgments in condemning her transgressions, especially when he depicts Hester as less the solitary reprobate among a community of pious Puritan Elect than the scapegoated personification of a universalized condition of shared human sinfulness.

In "The Custom-House" the point at which Hawthorne feels "as if" he is scorched by "red hot iron" (32) is the point at which he commits himself to finding out what the *A* means and turning it into a story. Indeed, upon discovering "the groundwork of a tale," he dramatizes a stunning scene when a voice out of the dead past speaks directly to a voice in the emergent present (33). He feels "as if the ancient Surveyor. . . had met me in the deserted chamber of the Custom-House" (33). When Hawthorne reports Pue's spoken words, however, he does not include a qualifying simile. Instead, he presents their interaction as an unfolding conversation. Hawthorne illustrates the scene with dramatic directness. The "ghostly" Surveyor appears as an "obscurely seen, but majestic, figure," who exhorts Hawthorne "[w]ith his own ghostly voice. . . as my official ancestor,—to bring his mouldy and moth-eaten lucubrations before the public. 'Do this,' said the ghost of Mr. Surveyor Pue" (33). In answering the ghost with "I will," Hawthorne animates his figural progenitor from the departed past and briefly displaces the enervating impress of present-day Salem (34). It is the inherent attribute of the romance form to extend the sphere of experiential possibility to include the strange, the bizarre, the liminal, the spectral, and the supernatural, thus expanding the range of what is possible or plausible.

Hawthorne's business with Surveyor Pue and his putative archival trove is provocative and anticipatory, operating as a prospectus, or prolegomenon, to transfigurations yet to be realized. When Hawthorne descends from the second story, he is literally right back where he started. Still locked in place, still enmeshed in present time, he is restrained by the mental detritus so characteristic of his relation to the domain of custom. Nevertheless, in now carrying within him the "groundwork of a tale," a necessary point of aesthetic departure, he has a foundation on which to build, even though his "imagination was a tarnished mirror. It would not reflect, or only with miserable dimness, the figures with which I did my best to people it" (34). Paradoxically, at this precise moment of "wretched numbness" (35), Hawthorne depicts more clearly and fully than anywhere else in his work his aesthetic theory regarding the transformational agency of the romance genre. His creative "torpor" afflicts him, he observes, even late at night when he sits "in the deserted parlour, lighted only by the glimmering coal-fire and the moon" (35). Approximately seventeen years before, in a great early tale, Hawthorne associates the cold, silvery moonlight with the power of the imagination. In "My Kinsman, Major Molineux" young, confused Robin sits at night on a church step in an inhospitable city, awaiting the impending, mysterious rendezvous with his father's cousin, Robin's ostensible guide and surrogate father. The narrator writes, "[T]he moon, 'creating, like the imaginative power, a beautiful strangeness in familiar objects,' gave something of romance to a scene, that might not have possessed it in the light of day" (221). Hawthorne uses moonlight to reflect the powerful medium of imaginative transformation. It is a light that takes everyday objects and re-presents them in spiritualized ways. In "The Custom-House" Hawthorne once again redacts material from his early tales of Colonial America, reconceiving the moonlight as reflecting the power of "the imaginative faculty": "Moonlight, in a familiar room, falling so white upon the carpet, and showing all its figures so distinctly,—making every object so minutely visible, yet so unlike a morning or noontide visibility,—is a medium the most suitable for a romance-writer to get acquainted with his illusive guests" (35). The cold light of the moon invests commonplace objects "with a quality of strangeness and remoteness" (35). Moonlight symbolizes the power of the procreant imagination, especially its ability to convert everyday objects into strange and beautiful forms: "Thus, therefore, the floor of our familiar room has become a neutral territory, somewhere between the real world and fairy-land, where the Actual and the Imaginary may meet, and each imbue itself with the nature of the other. Ghosts might enter here, without affrighting us" (36). This scenic tour de force is not complete without the qualifying light of "[t]he somewhat dim coal-fire" that suffuses "the cold spirituality of the moonbeams" with a "warmer light" that "communicates . . . a heart and sensibilities of human tenderness to the forms which fancy summons up" (36). Here Hawthorne celebrates the synergistic fusion of the "Actual" and the "Imaginary" that resides at the heart of the romance genre. He synthesizes the cold light of the imagination with "coal-fire" warmth and thus allows objects of the intellect to assume the appearance of life and human sensation.

"I Am a Citizen of Somewhere Else"

Even though he develops this arresting scene, Hawthorne remains trapped within the sphere of custom: he "cannot dream strange things, and make them look like truth" (36). He still suffers from the tyranny of the Actual, his creative life suspended by "the enervating magic of place" (38). Ironically, Hawthorne's liberation from the soul-sapping present is a consequence of those very political forces that seduced him with a soft patronage job in the first place. Hawthorne's escape from the overbearing domain of custom derives, oddly enough, not from action but inaction. He does not quit his position with a departing cry of "non servium." Rather, after President James K. Polk loses his reelection bid in 1848 his successor, Whig Zachary Taylor, fires Hawthorne in the summer of 1849. In describing his figurative decapitation, especially his surprise when he discovers, "My own head was the first that fell!" (41), Hawthorne affects a tone of bemused stoicism that belies his agitated, futile attempts to retain his position and salary.[5] Hawthorne taps into his deep reserve of genial, sometimes sardonic wit to describe the emotional impact of this disconcerting point of passage: "The moment when a man's head drops off is seldom or never, I am inclined to think, precisely the most agreeable of his life" (41). His recurrent evocation of decapitation metaphors not only associates the Whig opposition

---

with the avenging anarchists of the French Revolution, but more importantly he reflects how the figurative political execution of a dependent, essentially useless, hack appointee under the spoils system brings with it an opportunity for artistic liberation. Having taken up pen and page, having again become "a literary man" (43), Hawthorne retreats very happily into "the gloom of these sunless fantasies" that becomes the inscribed substance of *The Scarlet Letter* (43). As he approaches the end of the sketch and the beginning of his narrative, Hawthorne reports that the once oppressive sphere of custom has been displaced by a sense of unreality. The power of the present is dissipating:

> Soon, likewise, my old native town will loom upon me through the haze of memory, a mist brooding over and around it; as if it were no portion of the real earth, but an overgrown village in cloud-land, with only imaginary inhabitants to people its wooden houses, and walk its homely lanes . . . . Henceforth, it ceases to be a reality of my life. I am a citizen of somewhere else. (44)

By the end of "The Custom-House" Hawthorne has become "a citizen" of the world of his art, this "neutral territory" that fuses the ethereal energies of artistic invention with the appearance of experiential actuality. At the outset of "The Prison-Door" chapter of *The Scarlet Letter*, the narrator makes clear that he is far removed from "cloud-land" Salem circa 1850. He has left behind the enervating present and now resides as a narrating voice within the past world of Boston in 1642, where the narrator's originating purpose is to accentuate the harsh circumstances and inescapable necessities afflicting Massachusetts Bay Colony. Indeed, "[t]he founders of his new colony"—this oppressive theocratic society— almost immediately jettisoned any utopic pretentions and responded to the "practical necessities" of mortality and human depravity (47). Following the 1630 death of Isaac Johnson, "a portion of the virgin soil" served as a cemetery. Out of the now troubled earth grows not only a tangle of "unsightly vegetation" but also the "black flower of civilized society," a prison" (48). These respective consequences of death and transgression, Hawthorne's imagery suggests, cannot be dissociated from the inescapable organic continuum that links past, present, and future. Such natural, organic entities, however, also supply a hopeful dialectical counterpoint to the ineluctable signatures of a fallen world:

> But, on one side of the portal, and rooted almost on the threshold, was a wild rose bush covered, in this month of June, with its delicate gems, which might be imagined to offer their fragrance and fragile beauty to the prisoner as he went in, and to the condemned criminal as he came forth to his doom, in token that the deep heart of nature could pity and be kind to him" (48).

Indeed, with the adulterous Hester Prynne about to exit the prison carrying her sin-born daughter, the narrator positions himself, like the wild rose bush, "directly on the threshold of our narrative" (48). Standing here, on the solid groundwork of this historicized scene, the narrator insists that "we could hardly do otherwise than to pluck one of its flowers and present it to the reader" (48). For this significant transaction to occur, the narrator would not only have to be standing outside the prison in June 1642, but the reader must also be imagined as standing there as well. Having made a transit into the past, Hawthorne has brought the reader with him. By receiving "some sweet moral blossom" (48) the reader has not only left behind the commonplace world of custom and now partakes in the sympathy that flows from "the deep heart of Nature," but also receives a literal and figurative warrant to join the narrator as an interpretive, speculative, and empathetic presence. With moral blossom in hand, the reader assumes his or her place in the reconstituted past and prepares to serve as the narrator's companionate audience.

Notes

1. "The Custom-House" constitutes an integral part of *The Scarlet Letter*. The reader will find all citations to Hawthorne's sketch (including the epigraph above) within *The Scarlet Letter*.

2. In his magisterial study, Michael J. Colacurcio offers the following premise:"[N]early all of the tales we have long regarded as the most powerful and significant of Hawthorne's early productions do indeed

function as moral history. Often, though not always, that history involves the imaginative re-enactment of some pitfall of the Puritan piety. Characteristically, it is a matter of freeing the moral actuality of the past from its popular or political use in the present. The history is arguably at once evidently fictional and arguably deconstructive" (34-35). Also see Michael Davitt Bell for a discerning exploration of the evolution of the historical romance in New England.

3.   Milton R. Stern considers some ideological implications relating to the aesthetic categories of the sketch and romance as these genres were understood in Hawthorne's day: "The functions of romance, tale, novel, and sketch were defined implicitly and explicitly in terms of Americanness and manliness. . . . The Romance, like its shorter counterpart, the tale, was ostensibly a matter for feminine sensibility: it was ethereal, imaginary, and . . .perhaps luxurious . . . . The novel, like its shorter counterpart, the sketch, was ostensibly more suited to the manly taste" (72-73). For a study of the evolution of the American Romance in the nineteenth century as well as an account of modern critical attempts to define and explain the possibilities and limitations of this genre, see Emily Miller Budick.

4.   When Hawthorne was three chapters from finishing *The Scarlet Letter*, he suspended composition to write "The Custom-House." When delineating imagistic affinities between the Collector and Hester, Hawthorne was drawing on materials already written. As a genetic matter, these attributes of Hester's character inform Hawthorne's depiction of General Miller, not the other way around.

5.   See Edwin Haviland Miller's lively account of Hawthorne's effort to retain his patronage job in the face of strenuous partisan opposition: "As soon as Hawthorne learned of the campaign to unseat him, he set the wheels turning for a full-scale counteroffensive which in the next few months would involve political figures as influential as Daniel Webster and newspapers of both parties in Salem, Boston, Philadelphia, Baltimore, New York, and probably elsewhere" (267 and 267-70).

Works Cited

Bell, Michael Davitt. *Hawthorne and the Historical Romance of New England*. Princeton UP, 1971.

Budick, Emily Miller. *Nineteenth-Century American Romance: Genre and the Construction of Democratic Culture*. Twayne, 1996.

Colacurcio, Michael J. *The Province of Piety: Moral History in Hawthorne's Early Tales*. Duke UP, 1995.

Hawthorne, Nathaniel. "Alice Doane's Appeal." *The Snow-Image and Uncollected Tales*. Edited by William Charvat, et al. *The Centenary Edition of the Works of Nathaniel Hawthorne*, vol. 11, Ohio State UP, 1974. pp. 266-80.

_____. *The American Notebooks by Nathaniel Hawthorne*. Edited by Randall Stewart. Yale UP, 1932.

_____. "Endicott and the Red Cross." *Twice-Told Tales*. Edited by William Charvat, et al. *The Centenary Edition of the Works of Nathaniel Hawthorne*, vol. 9, Ohio State UP, 1974. pp. 433-41.

_____. "My Kinsman, Major Molineux." *The Snow-Image and Uncollected Tales*. Edited by William Charvat, et al. *The Centenary Edition of the Works of Nathaniel Hawthorne*, vol. 11, Ohio State UP, 1974. pp. 208-31.

_____. *The Scarlet Letter*. Edited by William Charvat, et al. *The Centenary Edition of the Works of Nathaniel Hawthorne*, vol. 1, Ohio State UP, 1962.

Miller, Edwin Haviland. *Salem Is My Dwelling Place: A Life of Nathaniel Hawthorne*. U of Iowa P, 1991.

Railton, Stephen. *Authorship and Audience: Literary Performance in the American Renaissance*. Princeton UP, 1991.

Stern, Milton R. *Contexts for Hawthorne:* The Marble Faun *and the Politics of Openness and Closure in American Literature*. U of Illinois P, 1991.

Hawthorne's Removal from the Salem Custom House and the Thematics of Public Exposure in *The Scarlet Letter*_____

Jonathan A. Cook

As an allegedly timeless literary classic, *The Scarlet Letter* is often considered a universal tale of guilt, sorrow, revelation, and redemption transpiring within the repressive realm of early colonial Boston. But, as Hawthorne indicates in his extended introduction to the narrative, the romance was actually composed in the context of a major personal crisis of Hawthorne's life resulting from his controversial firing from his job as surveyor at the Salem Custom House in June and July 1849, an emotional and financial trauma augmented by the death of his mother at the end of July. By examining the humiliating ordeal that Hawthorne, a famously shy individual, experienced when accused and then exposed for wrongdoing at his government job, we can gain deeper insight into "The Custom-House" introduction and *The Scarlet Letter* proper as alternately discursive and narrative means for representing a thematics of public exposure that Hawthorne suffered at this time. While Hawthorne had previously written in his tales and sketches about the dynamics of sin and redemption in both Puritan and contemporary New England, this personal involvement in a drama of public shaming gave him the creative impetus and firsthand experience to create his first mature full-length work of fiction.

For many contemporary readers, "The Custom-House" conveys the impression of Hawthorne as a mild-mannered humorist whose three-year stint in the Salem Custom House constituted a kind of spiritual imprisonment within the confines of a government sinecure on the decaying wharves of his ancestral hometown; moreover, his ejection from his post as a result of the spoils system was a providential intervention that restored his fiction writing powers, even as the archives of the Custom House itself provided him with a subject for his new romance. But such an impression belies the dramatic history of Hawthorne's dismissal, which became a focus of national attention as Hawthorne fought to retain his job but suffered an ignominious removal following a climactic act of exposure of apparent wrongdoing (Nevins; Cortissoz ch. 5; Nissenbaum). The ultimate cause of Hawthorne's dismissal was the election of the Whig Mexican War hero, Zachary Taylor, to the presidency in November 1848 and his inauguration in March 1849, leading to the possibility for many Democratic-appointed officials that they might have their jobs terminated as part of the reassignment of government jobs under the spoils system. In a June 5, 1849, letter to Henry Wadsworth Longfellow, Hawthorne thus expressed anger at the cabal of Salem Whigs whom he called "political bloodhounds" and who were apparently plotting to remove him from office (*Letters* 269); but when Hawthorne actually obtained notice of his removal as surveyor of the Salem Custom House three days later, he was at first stoically ready to leave his position, envisaging a return to the fiction writing that had been curtailed by the uninspired routine and ennui of the sleepy Salem Custom House. However, when Hawthorne soon learned that his dismissal was being justified by charges of malfeasance rather than being a routine rotation of political office, he quickly reversed course and began a campaign to defend his job while enlisting the support of sympathetic Whigs.

As Hawthorne quickly discovered, the main instigator behind his firing was the head of the Salem Whigs, Charles W. Upham, a former Unitarian minister whom Hawthorne had known as a friendly acquaintance over the previous two decades, especially in the minister's capacity as a fellow historian of Salem witchcraft as well as other aspects of the New England colonial past (Cook). As the month of June progressed, Hawthorne was increasingly enraged by the manner in which Upham seemed to be orchestrating a series of invented charges against him after previously assuring him that his job was secure. In the formal charges adduced by the Salem Whigs and published in an unsigned letter to the Whig *Boston Atlas* on June 16 (likely written by Upham), Hawthorne thus stood accused of political activism and corruption, both of which allegedly belied his claim to being a nonpartisan literary man who happened to be a Democrat. Claiming that Hawthorne had displaced a Whig when he obtained his Custom House position in 1846, the writer insisted that Hawthorne had in fact been active as a Democrat in a variety of areas, including marching in a political torchlight parade, serving on a Democratic town committee and as a delegate at a Democratic state convention in Worcester, writing political articles for Democratic publications, and—perhaps most damning—paying the four Democratic inspectors under his supervision more than the Whig inspectors. Hawthorne replied to these charges on June 18 in a letter to his Whig friend George Hillard, published in the Whig *Boston Daily Advertiser*, denying the trumped-up charges of Democratic political activity while claiming that the issue of a salary differential for the inspectors, the result of extra work being assigned to the four Democratic inspectors, was determined by his immediate superior, the Whig deputy collector, Ephraim Miller, son of the long-time Whig collector, General James Miller, a hero of the War of 1812, now retired and succeeded by his son.

By mid-June, newspapers in Salem and Boston were echoing with discussions of Hawthorne's case while the author himself commissioned Hillard and his Whig brother-in-law Horace Mann to enlist support for him among powerful Whigs at the state and federal level—a list that would eventually include such well-known figures as Charles Sumner, Rufus Choate, Abbott Lawrence, George Ticknor, Edward Everett, and Daniel Webster. In the meantime, Hawthorne's case spread as a topic of discussion outside the state of Massachusetts as fellow Democrats came to his defense. For example, the Democratic *Albany Atlas* noted on June 17, 1849: "Hawthorne removed! Can it be possible? If every other Democratic incumbent of office had been swept by the board, we should still have looked to see an exception made in the case of the gentle Elia [pseudonym of the English essayist Charles Lamb] of our American literature. . . . The man who would knowingly commit such an act would broil a hummingbird, and break a harp to pieces to make the fire" (Cortissoz 87). So, too, William Cullen Bryant editorialized in the Democratic *New York Post* on June 22, 1849: "The removal of Mr. Hawthorne from the Custom House at Salem was a flagrant case of political proscription. . . . His removal was an act of wanton and unmitigated oppression" (Cortissoz 88).

By the end of June, Hawthorne and his wife, Sophia, thought that the tide had turned in his favor and that he had successfully fought against the charges of malfeasance while defending himself as an honest and efficient government employee despite his party affiliation. Yet Hawthorne was in for a rude awakening when the Salem Whigs under the direction of Upham sought to counter the national campaign in Hawthorne's favor by insisting that the issue was a local matter and that serious grounds for Hawthorne's firing remained intact and were even worse than what was previously charged against him. Thus in a detailed letter, or "Memorial," dated July 6 and addressed to the secretary of the treasury, William Meredith, the Salem Whig committee sought to end the possibility of Hawthorne's reinstatement by exposing a scheme of "corruption, fraud and iniquity" (Nevins 117) in order to clear the way for the appointment of his Whig replacement. After a detailed recital of the political background to the current situation, the writer, Charles W. Upham, enumerated the new, most serious charges against Hawthorne by pointing out a differentiated pay scale for Democratic and Whig Inspectors averaging about $130, half of which was demanded as kickbacks to support the party:

> Were the procedure sifted to the bottom, it would be found, we doubt not, one of the most flagrant instances of political financiering and official extortion and corruption yet developed. The democratic inspectors were required to pay back, ostensibly and professedly for the support of "the party," at least one-half of the proceeds of the extra jobs, or, in other words one-half of the excess of their receipts over those of the whig inspectors. That is, what rightfully belong to the whig inspectors, their legitimate share was withheld from them and appropriated, or supposed to be appropriated, to the party purposes of their opponents. (Nevins 117)

The writer added that a further "assessment" was required from Democratic inspectors for the support of the local Democratic newspaper, the *Salem Advertiser*: "The editor, under the sanction of Mr. Hawthorne, claimed from the democratic inspectors, for the support of his paper, an assessment, so much beyond all reason, that three of their number, conferring together, declined to pay it, and proposed a smaller sum" (Nevins 117).The writer noted that when threatened with dismissal in a note signed by Hawthorne, two of them agreed to the assessment while the third did not and was duly punished by having extra work withheld.

After citing these seemingly damning facts, the writer paradoxically went on to state his belief that Hawthorne did not likely know of them but was being used as a tool of other Democratic operators in the Salem Custom House; thus, he was more fool than knave: "His entire ignorance, previous to his appointment, of matters of business, his inexperience of the stratagems of political managers, and the very slight interest which his thoughts could take in such things, have made him less conscious of the part he has performed, than almost any other man would have been" (Nevins 118). Thus, Hawthorne's friends "ought to be thankful that Mr. Hawthorne is withdrawn and delivered" from the corrupt Custom House so that he could get back to being "one of the most amiable and elegant writers of America" (Nevins 119). As a result of the more devastating charges in the Memorial, Hawthorne was finally dismissed from his post on July 24 and a Whig replacement (Allen Putnam) named, although Hawthorne still hoped to defend his honor in an appearance before the Senate in Washington, a wish that was never fulfilled. Thus, in an August 8 letter to his brother-in-law, Horace Mann, Hawthorne explained the circumstances behind the most damning charges in order to maintain his innocence while still noting his suspicion that "there really was an operation to squeeze an assessment out of the recusant inspectors" (*Letters* 292). And while he recognized that his government position was now irretrievably lost, he expressed the wish to publicly defend his honor:"My purpose is simply to make such a defense to the Senate as will ensure the rejection of my successor, and thus satisfy the public that I was removed on false or insufficient grounds" (*Letters* 292). We will never know how complicit Hawthorne was with the shady practices of his fellow Democrats in the Salem Custom House, but he clearly wanted to clear his name in this shameful scandal.

Hawthorne's "Custom-House" essay prefacing *The Scarlet Letter* provided him with a means to satirically reexamine his experience as a government-appointed custom house inspector, to provide the reader with a glimpse into the actual operation of the Salem Custom House, and to introduce the means whereby he came to the knowledge of the scarlet letter and began writing its history. But "The Custom-House" clearly seeks to relieve the sense of anger, frustration, mortification, and shame that Hawthorne likely felt as a result of his month-long ordeal in getting fired from the Salem Custom House by the opposing political party of Whigs led by its local leader, Charles W. Upham. Although Hawthorne deliberately strikes a genial tone in "The Custom-House," the pain of public humiliation that he felt during his prolonged dismissal from office was evident at several points in his essay, beginning with his reference to the image of the American eagle over the entrance to the Custom House, which ill-tempered bird is all too "apt to fling off her nestlings with a scratch of her claw, and a dab of her beak, or a rankling wound from her barbed arrows" (5). So, too, Hawthorne later plays upon the emasculatory metaphor of his "decapitation" from office, a term that he did not originate but one that was particularly appropriate for the very public and ruthless nature of his removal by the rival political party, which, unlike the more forgiving Democrats, was inclined "ignominiously to kick the head which they have just struck off" (41).

Contrary to his previous defense of his position as surveyor in the Salem Custom House because he allegedly belonged to a nonpartisan sacred fraternity of writers and artists, Hawthorne now makes fun of himself as a lowly storyteller whose illustrious and public-minded Puritan ancestors would be ashamed to acknowledge him. "No aim, that I have ever cherished, would they recognize as laudable; no success of mine—if my life, beyond its domestic scope, had ever been brightened by success—would they deem otherwise than worthless, if not positively disgraceful. 'What is he?' murmurs one gray shadow of my forefathers to the other. 'A writer of story-books!'" (10). Such an act of seriocomic mortification and humility shows that he would not spare himself in the larger satirical portrait he paints of the sleepy and inactive Salem Custom House and its antiquated occupants, as embodied most grotesquely in the description of the ancient permanent inspector whose vacuous life revolved around the recollection of past meals—a pungent caricature of one of Hawthorne's Whig enemies (Lease). Moreover, contrary to his concerted attempt to keep his position as surveyor, Hawthorne now conveys the idea that his job exerted a numbing and oppressive hold on him, stifling his imagination and threatening to damage his character and terminate his career as a writer. Possibly alluding to the scandal over illegal payments detailed in the Memorial that got him fired, Hawthorne now implies that being on a government salary might in fact involve one in a Faustian bargain: "Who touches it should look well to himself, or he may find the bargain to go hard against him, involving, if not his soul, yet many of its better attributes" (39).

One of the most suggestive moments in "The Custom-House" preface occurs when Hawthorne discusses the mesmerizing effect that the discovery of the antiquated scarlet letter had on him when he found it among piles of old documents in the second story of the Salem Custom House. As he notes his fascination with the capital letter *A* once worn by Hester Prynne, "My eyes fastened themselves upon the old scarlet letter, and would not be turned aside. Certainly there was some deep meaning in it, most worthy of interpretation, and which, as it were, streamed forth from the mystic symbol, subtly communicating itself to my sensibilities but evading the analysis of my mind" (31). Hawthorne's reaction here suggests his intuitive awareness of the *A* as a punitive symbol of sin and shame, a recognition culturally embedded in the first page of the New England Primer introducing the first letter of the alphabet while teaching "In Adam's fall, we sinned all." But apart from the larger recognition of the letter as a symbol of original sin, Hawthorne's reaction to the letter also suggests his sense of participation in the punitive purpose of the letter. For while debating the ultimate meaning of the strange letter, Hawthorne instinctively put it against his chest and had a very marked reaction: "it seemed to me, then, that I experienced a sensation not altogether physical, yet almost so, as of burning heat; and as if the letter were not of red cloth, but red-hot iron. I shuddered, and involuntarily let it fall upon the floor" (32). Like his protagonist Arthur Dimmesdale, Hawthorne has both proleptically and psychosomatically inscribed the burning "brand" of the scarlet letter on his chest.

Hawthorne's visceral sensation of the alleged heat emitted by the letter anticipates our impending witness in the novel proper to the cloth letter as Hester Prynne's legally enforced badge of shame for adultery; but the author's strong personal reaction to the letter is also suggestive in this context of his own personal history of being fired from the Salem Custom House for alleged misdeeds in his capacity as surveyor. Hawthorne seeks to undercut the violence of his reaction to the letter by invoking the reader's skepticism ("the reader may smile but must not doubt my word"), but his placing the *A* on his own chest, his sense of its painful heat, and his letting it fall to the floor all palpably suggest the recent ordeal of shame and humiliation he himself had undergone when getting fired from his job. For beyond its general application to him as a generic son of Adam and as a more direct descendent of seventeenth-century Puritan patriarchs who persecuted Quakers and witches, the *A* of the letter might also suggest the traumatic letter written by Charles W. Upham in the form of a Memorial to the treasury secretary, William Meredith, in early July containing the explosive charges that led to his final dismissal. And if Hawthorne was obviously not susceptible to the same carnal transgression figured by the red letter, he nevertheless stood accused by Upham and the Salem Whigs of financial crimes in the form of, illegal kickbacks and "assessments" on Democratic inspectors' salaries. Hence the act of placing the burning *A* on his chest conceivably figures Hawthorne's repressed feelings of shame at his public exposure, if not a sense of actual guilt over the practices of the Salem Custom House where he sought to honestly perform his duties but was apparently surrounded by partisan wire-pulling and peculation.

When we move from the introductory "Custom-House" sketch to the novel proper, we see that the thematics of public exposure immediately assume a prominent place in the development of the narrative, for Hawthorne almost certainly used his own experience of prolonged exposure to the public eye during the scandal of his removal as a displaced means of inspiration for a tale set two centuries earlier. The story would thus involve a trio of characters who are all involved in alternately displaying (Hester Prynne), concealing (Arthur Dimmesdale), or detecting (Roger Chillingsworth) the sin and crime of adultery that has led to the birth of Hester's child, Pearl—a collective study of the psychology of shame, hypocrisy, and repression in which Hawthorne specialized as a writer (Rust; Harris; Adamson). Thus, the first three chapters of the novel depict Hester's emergence from the Boston prison while wearing the embroidered badge of her shame to public exposure on a scaffold in the marketplace designed for the punishment of malefactors. With her babe in arm, Hester undergoes the humiliating ordeal of public shaming before the crowd of her fellow townspeople on an elevated scaffold that "was held, in the old time, to be as effectual an agent in the promotion of good citizenship, as ever was the guillotine among the terrorist in France" (55)—a comparison that evokes the metaphor of decapitation that Hawthorne had used only a few pages earlier in "The Custom-House" for his own public humiliation and emasculation.

Hester's prolonged public exposure in Chapter 3 leads to her recognition by her newly arrived husband, Roger Chillingsworth, who signals Hester to keep his identity a secret, while the leading colonial authorities—Reverend Wilson and Governor Bellingham— exhort Hester's pastor, Arthur Dimmesdale, to make her reveal the name of the father of her child, and the pastor undertakes this task while claiming that such a confession would actually be beneficial to her fellow sinner: "Heaven hath granted thee an open ignominy, that thereby thou mayest work out an open triumph over the evil within thee, and the sorrow without. Take heed how thou deniest to him—who, perchance, hath not the courage to grasp it for himself— the bitter, but wholesome, cup that is now presented to thy lips"

(67). The reader will realize, from the eloquence of his remarks on how the hidden sinner would benefit from Hester's naming him, that Dimmesdale is the likely guilty party who lacks the moral strength to make his own confession—an act that historically would lead to removal from office, exile, or even death (Baughman).

Despite their obviously different degrees and kinds of guilt, Hester's public shaming in front of the whole community of Puritan Boston for the potentially capital crime of adultery is comparable to Hawthorne's own extended public shaming in the Whig newspapers of Salem and Boston in June 1849 for malfeasance as surveyor of the Salem Custom House. Just as Hester faces exposure to the whole community of early colonial Boston, the audience for the controversy over Hawthorne's firing had attained a broad scope by the time of his final dismissal and involved many leading New England political figures and opinion makers. And just as Hawthorne remained silent with regard to any potential Democratic collaborators (such as his friend Zachariah Burchmore) in the allegedly corrupt schemes at the Salem Custom House, Hester refused to name her partner in crime. So too, after her initial public shaming, Hester's decision to remain in Salem to raise her young daughter because it was the scene of her criminal trespass may remind us of Hawthorne's own sense of irrational attachment to Salem because of the sins of his persecuting Puritan ancestors, and his desire to atone for them, as expressed near the beginning of his "Custom-House" essay.

In the novel's unfolding history of secret sin and public atonement, the characters of Chillingworth and Dimmesdale become inextricably entwined when the former becomes the doctor (or "leech") to the ailing minister and moves in with him in order ostensibly to better serve his patient. As we soon discover, however, Chillingsworth's mask of benevolent care for Dimmesdale and his selection of medicinal remedies all seem aimed at ascertaining the guilt of the minister and then punishing him by keeping him a dependent and self-torturing invalid after Dimmesdale's sin becomes evident to him. Chillingsworth's treatment of the minister would seem to combine the roles of both physician and spiritual counselor, a position that enables him to explore like a thief for Dimmesdale's secret history of sexual sin; on such occasions Chillingsworth "strove to go deep into his patient's bosom, delving among his principles, prying into his recollection, and probing everything with a cautious touch, like a treasure-seeker in a dark cavern. Few secrets can escape an investigator, who has opportunity and license to undertake such a quest, and skill to follow it up" (124).

As the narrator notes, the more Chillingsworth investigates Dimmesdale's life for hints of his guilt, the more he transforms himself into a diabolical figure revealing to the public "something ugly and evil in his face, which they had not previously noticed" (88). By indulging his own secret desire for vengeance against the man who had violated his masculine honor—even though Chillingsworth earlier recognized he was unsuited to be a husband for Hester—Chillingsworth thus greedily pursued his goal of Dimmesdale's guilt, which puts his own spiritual fate at risk: "He now dug into the poor clergyman's heart, like a miner searching for gold; or, rather, like a sexton delving into a grave, possibly in quest of a jewel that had been buried on the dead man's bosom, but likely to find nothing save mortality and corruption. Alas for his own soul, if these were what he sought!" (129). Instead of forgiving injuries and allowing God to avenge wrongdoing as Christian doctrine taught, Chillingsworth assumes a divine prerogative to violate the sanctity of Dimmesdale's person and soul in what amounts to an example of the "unpardonable sin" dramatized elsewhere in Hawthorne's fiction. This sin is symbolically consummated when Chillingsworth attains visual confirmation of Dimmesdale's guilt when the minister is sleeping in his chair and the former "thrust aside the vestment" to examine the bare chest, apparently finding a visible indication of Dimmesdale's guilt in what is hinted to be a self-inflicted stigma of the scarlet letter. Chillingsworth's "ghastly rapture" (138) here conveys a hint of displaced sexual violation of his housemate, just as the leech's facial expression during the "moment of his ecstasy" shows "how Satan comports himself, when a precious human soul is lost to heaven, and won into his kingdom" (138).

The narrator's extended description of Dimmesdale's victimization by Chillingsworth, as the leech probes for the

---

minister's guilt and finally discovers it in a perverse and self-debasing ecstasy, is again suggestive of Hawthorne's ordeal of exposure during the crisis of his removal from his job at the Salem Custom House. More specifically, the scenes between Dimmesdale and Chillingsworth evoke the relationship between the author and the head of the Salem Whigs, Charles W. Upham, who was largely responsible for methodically gathering and repeatedly articulating the charges against Hawthorne justifying his removal, all while claiming to be Hawthorne's advocate for another job in government service and pretending to act in his interests. Thus, Chillingsworth's early probings into Dimmesdale's life for traces of his guilt are comparable to Upham's initial set of accusations against Hawthorne as an engaged partisan who exploited his government office for party purposes. As we have seen, Hawthorne was able to refute many of the charges that Upham publicly presented in mid-June 1849 and thought that this might be enough to turn the tide against his removal. But Upham's aggressive investigation of some of the malcontent inspectors within the Salem Custom House turned up the stories of salary kickbacks and "assessments" on Democratic employees, as recorded in the definitive Memorial submitted to the Secretary of the Treasury. And just as Chillingsworth had his triumphant moment of confirmation of Dimmesdale's guilt, Upham attained his own triumphant exposure of Hawthorne's secret sins of kickbacks and "assessments" in the Memorial letter that confirmed the Whig case against him. This is not to imply that Hawthorne felt the same tortured and deep-seated guilt as Dimmesdale, for Hawthorne clearly thought of himself as largely innocent, or perhaps naively acquiescent in serving the interests of his political party (Nissenbaum). Yet by figuratively depicting Chillingsworth as a greedy treasure seeker and thief, Hawthorne is conceivably reapplying Upham's charges of financial misdeeds to his demonic literary counterpart in the novel.

In addition, the implied evil and diabolism that emerges in Chillingsworth's characterization during his sustained investigation and ensuing violation of Dimmesdale's soul is also comparable to repeated characterizations of Charles W. Upham by Hawthorne, his wife Sophia, and others as an unholy, manipulative, hypocritical, and evil-minded man whose identity as a former minister and sometime literary friend of Hawthorne's was now grotesquely ironic. Thus, after citing an example of Upham's apparent dishonesty, Sophia Hawthorne wrote her father on June 10 that the former minister "had perjured his soul" and "had proved himself a liar and a most consummate hypocrite; for he has always professed himself the warmest friend" (Lathrop 96). And after Hawthorne had finally lost his position in the Custom House, Sophia wrote her mother: "But there is no language to describe him. He is, my husband says, the most satisfactory villain that ever was, for at every point he is consummate. The Government had decided to reinstate Mr. Hawthorne before Mr. U's arrival at Washington, and his representations changed the purpose" (Lathrop 100-01). Hawthorne would in fact further elaborate on Upham's apparent transformation into a demonic inquisitor and hypocrite by extensively caricaturing him in the person of the villainous Judge Pyncheon in his next novel, *The House of the Seven Gables* (Cook).

In conversation with Chillingsworth, Dimmesdale rationalizes his need to hide his secret guilt until the Last Judgment, claiming that there can be "no power, short of Divine mercy, to disclose, whether by uttered words, or by type or emblem, the secrets that may be buried with a human heart. The heart, making itself guilty of such secrets, must perforce hold them, until the day when all hidden things shall be revealed" (131). Dimmesdale thus sees any revelation of guilt as an impediment to effectuating any further good in the world, and he in fact gains in eloquence as a minister by means of his tortured conscience, which gives him insight into the hearts of his parishioners. Dimmesdale makes an initial trial effort at public confession one spring night seven years after Hester's initial exposure on the town scaffold by himself mounting the scaffold in therapeutic imitation of her public shaming, where he is eventually joined by Hester and Pearl following Hester's late-night visit to the house of the deceased Governor Winthrop. Yet the scene is interrupted by Chillingsworth's unwelcome appearance, an event soon leading to Hester's finally revealing to Dimmesdale the physician's identity as her revenge-seeking husband during a subsequent tryst in the forest. It is during this extended meeting—the first sign of intimacy we witness between the former lovers—that Hester's shares a daring plan to flee Boston with the minister and their child. Dimmesdale's agreement to the plan shows him succumbing to a deadly temptation that brings him to the brink of damnation, and which is only averted by a mysterious final act of divine grace surrounding his Election Day sermon (Abel).

Dimmesdale's cathartic and redemptive confession comes immediately after the Election Day sermon in which he provides his fellow citizens a final demonstration of his moral and rhetorical powers as a minister in a glorious vision of their political future; yet the sermon is the prelude to his confession, for he now publicly joins Hester and Pearl on the scaffold while alluding to the scene of Hester's initial public shaming, during which he neglected to expose his own complicit sin. Speaking of himself in the third person, he notes that while Hester wore the visible token of her sin, her guilty associate's "brand of sin and infamy" (255) was hidden for seven years. In order to confirm his guilt, Dimmesdale now claims that he has visible proof of his judgment by God on his physical person: "With a convulsive motion, he tore away the ministerial band from before his breast. It was revealed! But it were irreverent to describe that revelation. For an instant the gaze of the horror-stricken multitude was concentrated on the ghastly miracle; while the minister stood with a flush of triumph on his face, as one who, in the crisis of acutest pain, had won a victory. Then, down he sank upon the scaffold!" (255).

The immodest audacity of Dimmesdale's sensational action, showing his stigma as a sign of guilty solidarity with Hester's letter, is a form of self-punishment in keeping with the monkish physical punishments such as flagellation he had earlier practiced on himself. Yet the whole scene is rendered problematic when the narrator claims that it would be "irreverent" to describe what the crowd actually saw on Dimmesdale's chest, a sight taking the oxymoronic form of a "ghastly miracle" to the crowd. Is the narrator claiming that Dimmesdale's revelation requires the reader to look the other way out of pity for the minister? Would a description of Dimmesdale's hidden stigma be a sinful violation of the privacy of his inmost soul? Or is the narrator hinting that the stigma is tainted with Catholic-style superstitions? Whatever the case, the narrator is ironically denying the reader actual ocular proof of Dimmesdale's corporeal scarlet letter, in contrast to Hester's seven years of visibly displaying, and even elaborately embellishing, her letter. Moreover, the scene is rendering the actual existence of Dimmesdale's guilty stigma terminally ambiguous.

This ambiguity is only enhanced at the beginning of the next chapter—the last chapter of the novel—when different groups of spectators have different reports of what actually happened on the scaffold, one (the "majority") testifying to seeing the scarlet letter on Dimmesdale's breast while adducing different theories about its provenance, with another group of "highly respectable witnesses" (259) denying any mark on his breast, and claiming that his words and actions were intended to convey a Calvinistic parable of the utter sinfulness of even the most meritorious person, with Hester used as a mere prop. Such a radical disparity of reports may remind us of the psychological experiments in which different spectators interpret a crime scene in completely different ways depending on the limits of their visual focus, susceptibility to inattention blindness, or personal bias. Thus, the narrator implies that his more positive interpretation of Dimmesdale's alleged confession could be traced to "that stubborn fidelity with which a man's friends—and especially a clergyman's—will sometimes uphold his character; when proofs clear as the mid-day sunshine on the scarlet letter, establish him a false and sin-stained creature of the dust" (260).

If we compare the scene of the "revelation" of Dimmesdale's scarlet letter to Hawthorne's own disgraced dismissal from the Salem Custom House, we may find some suggestive parallels. For the Memorial written by Charles W. Upham and presented to the Secretary of the Treasury in early July 1849 was adduced as a final proof of Hawthorne's engagement in unethical practices that required his immediate removal; yet despite providing seemingly incontrovertible proof of Hawthorne's guilt, the Memorial still stated that as a writer of fiction and a political novice, Hawthorne was likely unaware of the full meaning of the corrupt practices in which he allegedly participated. Like Dimmesdale, Hawthorne was thus paradoxically both guilty and innocent, depending on one's perspective. Moreover, the actual "scarlet letter" proving Hawthorne's guilt, the letter of Charles W. Upham (among other things) exposing Hawthorne's "assessments" on his Custom House employees, was never published but only known to the government, the Salem Whigs, and those like Hawthorne with access to the document through Whig friends. And like Dimmesdale's public supporters, Hawthorne's many high-placed Democratic and Whig friends upheld his character when he was under attack for corrupt practices in the Salem Custom House.

On the other hand, the upstanding Whig "friends" in Salem who were willing to support a sinful former minister, Charles W. Upham, as leader of the slanderous witch hunt against Hawthorne could also be cited as confirmation of the narrator's assertion here. Unlike Dimmesdale, whose death coincides with the exposure and confession of his sin, Hawthorne obviously survived his public disgrace and removal from a government sinecure; indeed, it breathed new life into his literary career, as the writing of *The Scarlet Letter* and *The House of the Seven Gables* attests. But, like Dimmesdale and Hester, who had planned to flee Puritan Boston with their child, Pearl, for a freer life elsewhere, Hawthorne and his wife and children soon decamped from the hated town of Salem in May 1850, immediately following publication of *The Scarlet Letter*, never to live there again.

The circumstances of Hawthorne's removal from the Salem Custom House were thus clearly instrumental, both literally and figuratively, in the novel that made him famous and helped launch the major phase of his writing career. From his mortifying public exposure in the national press for his alleged political sins, and the ambiguous guilt that ultimately cost him his job, he acquired the knowledge of public shaming and exposure by his native community that gave him many of the insights he needed to write *The Scarlet Letter*. Hawthorne's designated moral for the novel—a plea to unabashedly acknowledge one's moral failings—could thus apply as much to the author as to his sin-stained characters, and as much to mid-nineteenth-century America as to seventeenth-century Boston: "Be true !Be true! Be true! Show freely to the world, if not your worst, yet some trait whereby the worst may be inferred" (260).

Works Cited

Abel, Darrel. "Hawthorne's Dimmesdale: Fugitive from Wrath." *Nineteenth-Century Fiction*, vol. 11, Sept. 1956, pp. 81-105.

Adamson, Joseph. "'Guardian of the Inmost Me': Hawthorne and Shame."In *Scenes of Shame: Psychoanalysis, Shame, and Writing.* Edited by Joseph Adamson and Hillary Clark. State University of New York P, 1999.

Baughman, Ernest. "Public Confession and *The Scarlet Letter.*" *New England Quarterly*, 40, 1967, pp. 532-50.

Cook, Jonathan A. "'The Most Satisfactory Villain That Ever Was': Charles W. Upham and *The House of the Seven Gables.*" *New England Quarterly*, vol. 88, June 2015, pp. 252-85.

Cortissoz, Paul."The Political Life of Nathaniel Hawthorne." Dissertation, New York University, 1955.

Harris, Kenneth Marc. *Hypocrisy and Self-Deception in Hawthorne's Fiction.* UP of Virginia, 1988.

Hawthorne, Nathaniel. *The Centenary Edition of the Works of Nathaniel Hawthorne.* Edited by William Charvat et al. Ohio State UP, 1962-1997. 23 vols.

Lathrop, Rose Hawthorne. *Memories of Hawthorne.* Houghton Mifflin, 1897.

Lease, Benjamin. "Hawthorne and 'A Certain Venerable Personage': New Light on 'The Custom-House."*Jahrbuch fürAmerikastudien.* vol. 15, 1970, pp. 201-07.

Nevins, Winfield S. "Nathaniel Hawthorne's Removal from the Salem Custom House." *Essex Institute Historical Collections*, vol. 53, April 1917, pp. 97-132.

Nissenbaum, Stephen. "The Firing of Nathaniel Hawthorne." *Essex Institute Historical Collections*, vol. 114, April 1978, pp. 57-86.

Rust, Richard D. "'Take Shame' and 'Be True': Hawthorne and his Characters in *The Scarlet Letter*." In *Critical Essays on Hawthorne's "The Scarlet Letter."* Edited by David B. Kesterson. Hall, 1988.

Dark Romanticism, American Ascetism: The Transatlantic Contexts of *The Scarlet Letter*____

Brad Bannon

"That some remnant of Puritan asceticism should be found in the writings of a novelist from Concord, in Massachusetts, would seem natural to an English reader," Anthony Trollope observes in the September 1879 issue of *The North American Review*, "though I doubt there be much of the flavor of the Mayflower left at present to pervade the literary parterres of Boston" (206). Trollope's statement here, though it would have been a fine opening line for his essay on "The Genius of Nathaniel Hawthorne," actually concludes four paragraphs of a more general introduction before Trollope turns to a closer treatment of Hawthorne's fiction. "It is not sufficient for us to have a good thing and to enjoy it without knowing something of its nature, and inquiring how it has been produced," he writes at the outset, "how far it is perfect, how far deficient, how it might have been improved, how it might have been marred" (203). The nature of Hawthorne, however, strikes Trollope as quite peculiar: "There never surely was a powerful, active, continually effective mind less round, more lop-sided than that of NATHANIEL HAWTHORNE . . . we could not have obtained that weird, mysterious, thrilling charm with which he has awed and delighted us had he not allowed his mind to revel in one direction, so as to lose its fair proportions" (204).

Nevertheless, according to Trollope, that thrilling weirdness and mysteriousness does not emanate from the author's self-acknowledged past. If it had, "readers both in England and the States would have accepted it without surprise. It is, however, altogether different, though ascetic enough" (206). But why should Trollope make so much of insisting that the strange quality of Hawthorne's fiction has nothing to do with Puritanism? Just months after the first publication of *The Scarlet Letter*, Herman Melville had wondered aloud in an anonymous review of *Mosses from an Old Manse*

"Whether Hawthorne has simply availed himself of this mystical blackness as a means to the wondrous effects he makes it to produce in his lights and shades; or whether there really lurks in him, perhaps unknown to himself, a touch of Puritanic gloom," before concluding, "certain it is . . . that this great power of blackness in him derives its force from its appeal to that Calvinistic sense of Innate Depravity and Original Sin, from whose visitations, in some shape or other, no deeply thinking mind is always and wholly free" (243). Nor did Hawthorne dispute this account. Writing to Evert Duyckinck in the same month as Melville's anonymous review appeared, he acknowledged that "next to deserving his praise, it is good to have beguiled or bewitched such a man into praising me more than I deserve" (16: 32). Five days prior to this, Henry Wadsworth Longfellow, who would later become the only American poet honored with a bust in Westminster Abbey, had also sent Hawthorne a copy of the review along with this endorsement: "I have rarely seen a more appreciative and sympathizing critic: and though I do not endorse all he says about others, I do endorse all he says about you" (3: 266).

Given these circumstances, Trollope's rejection of Hawthorne as having "a touch of Puritanic gloom" about him is both an illustration of the way in which an Englishman steeped in Victorian culture would differ from the American Romantics in his apprehension and estimation of Hawthorne's work, as well as an index of Hawthorne's transformation from a provincial American author to a transatlantic bestseller—a transformation at the center of which stands the publication of *The Scarlet Letter*. By 1879, the stakes were also to some extent personal: Trollope was a friend of Julian Hawthorne's, who had been moving in London's literary circles since he had arrived in 1874. Having received a much friendlier reception to his writings in England than in the United States, the younger Hawthorne had relocated to Twickenham to make his fortune. As Gary Scharnhorst writes in his biography of Hawthorne's only son, "he became a habitué of the salons of George Eliot, T. H. Huxley, and the publisher Nicholas Trübner, where he met Bret Harte, Anthony Trollope, and his father's old friend, Richard Monckton Milnes

(Lord Houghton)" (74). Though Julian's attempts to break into the literary marketplace were ultimately unsuccessful, and his financial circumstances grew increasingly dire, he largely maintained the appearance of an English gentleman—and, as Scharnhurst notes, "Although his father had worked at menial jobs at Brook Farm and the Boston and Salem Custom Houses, Julian was too stubborn or too proud to work for a salary" (77). Trollope would have had time to form his own impression of Julian Hawthorne in the five years that he knew him before publishing "The Genius of Nathaniel Hawthorne," and though the extent to which his sense of Hawthorne would have been influenced by Julian during this time cannot be known, their views are unmistakably similar.

Indeed, in the first volume of his biography of his father, *Nathaniel Hawthorne and His Wife*, Julian mounted a sustained defense against the notion that his father was in any sense an heir of the Puritan tradition. First describing Hawthorne's ancestors as "active, practical men," who were "sea-captains, farmers, soldiers, magistrates," Julian acknowledges his father's heritage—and his own—while simultaneously disavowing its reach into a world in which the word *Puritan* has become a slur:

> True, they were Puritans, and doubtless were more or less under dominion to the terrible Puritan conscience, but it is hardly reasonable to suppose that this was the only one of their traits which they bequeathed to their successor. On the contrary, one would incline to think that this legacy, in its transmission to a legatee of such enlightened and unprejudiced understanding, would have been relieved of its peculiarly virulent and tyrannical character, and become an object rather of intellectual or imaginative curiosity than of moral awe. The fact that it figures largely in Hawthorne's stories certainly can scarcely be said to weaken this hypothesis; the pleasurable exercise of the imagination lies in its relieving us from the pressure of our realities, not in repeating and dallying with them. (*HW* 1: 83-84)

Julian's reasons for advancing this view of his father also lead us back to Melville again. Around the time that Julian published this biography (the preface to the first edition is dated July 1884), he also met with Melville in New York, and the description of the encounter that he provides in his second biography of his father, *Hawthorne and His Circle*, makes it clear that he had never forgotten (and perhaps never forgiven) Melville for the influential portrayal of his father as possessed of a mysterious "Puritanic gloom."

Recalling that Melville would often come to visit with his Newfoundland dog and tell stories "about the South Sea Island and the whale fishery" when the Hawthorne family lived in Lenox, Massachusetts, Julian goes on to level at Melville the very charge of Puritanism that it seems he felt had been unfairly laid against his father: "Through all his wild and reckless adventures, of which a small part only got into his fascinating books, he had been unable to rid himself of a Puritan conscience; he afterwards tried to loosen its grip by studying German metaphysics, but in vain" (*HC* 32-33). Of additional note is Julian's adoption of the popular German metaphysics critique, which had been used by critics of Samuel Taylor Coleridge to dismiss his later prose works as unnecessarily abstruse, particularly in England. Nevertheless, works like *Biographia Literaria*, *The Friend*, and *Aids to Reflection* were of great importance to the American Romantics, especially the latter work, which enjoyed a kind of second life in the United States when it was published in 1829 with an introductory essay by James Marsh, a Congregationalist adherent of Coleridge and German metaphysics who was then serving as president of the University of Vermont.

In Julian's retelling, however, it is only Melville who inherits this divided tradition of Puritan conscience and metaphysical obsession, and whatever it is that Melville believes he sees in Hawthorne is no more than his own reflection. "His later writings were incomprehensible," Julian writes, both highlighting Melville's lack of popular success in the aftermath of *Moby-Dick* and ignoring his father's unfinished romances—unaware of the unfinished *Billy Budd* manuscript and surely not expecting the critical reappraisal of Melville's work in the 1920s. Likewise, for Julian it is Melville, not Hawthorne, who carries with him a dark secret: " . . . he told me, during our talk, that he was convinced that there was some secret in my father's life which had never been revealed, and which accounted for the gloomy passages in his books. It was characteristic in him to imagine so; there were many secrets untold in his own career" (*HC* 33). In this sense, what Julian's reading of the relationship between Hawthorne and Melville proposed was a kind of alternate literary history in which Melville is the brooding intellect who fails to live up to his potential while Hawthorne is able to break free of his ancestral prejudices and avoid the pitfalls of German metaphysics to become the witty, urbane, almost British author of *The Scarlet Letter*. Likewise, if Poe, Hawthorne, and Melville are thought of together in this schema as the Dark Romantics, it is primarily in their choice of the gothic genre and not in any credence they give to the notion of primordial darkness. For so far as Julian was concerned, while Poe and Melville may have viewed the Puritan mind with "moral awe," to Hawthorne it could only be an "intellectual or imaginative curiosity" (*HW* 1 83). Most crucially, this conception of Hawthorne makes available to the reader a cosmopolitan author in the tradition of Washington Irving: a sophisticated skeptic not unlike the narrator of "The Legend of Sleepy Hollow," who holds the Puritan tradition up for derision rather than for serious reckoning. To those who wish to read Hawthorne not as a provincial American author on the world stage, but as a world author whose most celebrated work explores New England's Puritan history as a way to critique it, this conception is surely attractive—yet to British readers and critics of the late nineteenth century (as well as to Julian Hawthorne, who hoped to endear himself to a British audience) it offered something even more important: a trajectory of American identity that renounces its Puritanism and recovers its British sensibility, or perhaps reveals itself to have been in possession of it all along, albeit in the form of a quiet intellectual resistance. Put another way, it allows one to acknowledge *The Scarlet Letter* as a work of genius without attributing its achievement or originality to the influence of Puritanism in New England *per se*.

Notwithstanding this, the novel was undeniably American, and perhaps even regional. In the same year as Trollope's essay was published, Henry James, who had resided in England since 1869 and would eventually become a British citizen, recalled the excitement surrounding the publication of *The Scarlet Letter*, both on account of its recognition as the first American novel that without question stood among the best in English literature, as well one that had done so with material wholly particular to its native land:

> In fact, the publication of *The Scarlet Letter* was in the United States a literary event of the first importance. The book was the finest piece of imaginative writing yet put forth in the country. There was a consciousness of this in the welcome that was given it—a satisfaction in the idea of America having produced a novel that belonged to literature, and to the forefront of it. Something might at last be sent to Europe as exquisite in quality as anything that had been received, and the best of it was that the thing was absolutely American; it belonged to the soil, to the air; it came out of the very heart of New England. (111)

Yet for all that, James is consistent with Trollope and Julian Hawthorne when it comes to the question of whether there is attributable to Hawthorne any of the moral severity that so invests his most celebrated novel. "Puritanism in a word, is there," James concludes, "not only objectively, as Hawthorne tried to place it there, but subjectively as well. Not, I mean, in his judgment of his characters, in any harshness of prejudice, or in the obtrusion of a moral lesson; but in the very quality of his own vision, in the tone of the picture, in a certain coldness and exclusiveness of treatment." Here, though James initially seems to acknowledge an element of Puritanism that is both a matter of the novel's historical material as well as an index of the author's own nature, he is actually finessing the point, suggesting that although *The Scarlet Letter* is perhaps the highest manifestation of Hawthorne's Puritan aesthetic, it is nevertheless an artistic tone or characteristic rather than a system of belief, and wholly distinct from anything resembling the stern moral worldview of his ancestors. To James, the moral admonishment in the book's final chapter—"Be true! Be true! Be true! Show freely to the world, if not your worst, yet some trait whereby the worst may be inferred!" (1: 260)—can only be another convention furnished

---

by the narrator in his re-creation of Surveyor Pue's narrative, and should not be taken as Hawthorne own pronouncement.

Trollope takes a similar tack, describing Hawthorne as grim in style and expression, but not in earnest: "Hawthorne is severe, but his severity is never of a nature to form laws for life. His is a mixture of romance and austerity, quite as far removed from the realities of Puritanism as it is from the sentimentalism of poetry." In answer, then, to Melville's question of whether Hawthorne is puritanical himself without necessarily being aware of it, or whether he has simply harnessed the power of the Puritan medium in order to produce a particular effect, Trollope holds the latter view. In the wonderful passage that follows, he even explains how it is that this aesthetic of moral gloom works its magic upon the reader. "Prometheus chained, with the bird at his liver, had wherewithal to console himself in the magnificence of his thoughts," Trollope counsels, "And so in the world of melancholy romance, of agony more realistic than melancholy, to which Hawthorne brings his readers, there is compensation to the reader in the feeling that, in having submitted himself to such sublime affliction, he has proved himself capable of sublimity. The bird that feeds upon your vitals would not have gorged himself with common flesh" (206). Most remarkable about Trollope's assessment is that he credits Hawthorne with the expressive power of ancient myth at the same time as he portrays the pleasure derived from his work as a kind of solipsism: entering Hawthorne's world allows us to imagine that our ruminations on human suffering and moral guilt lend us significance and wisdom. The satisfaction of Hawthorne's asceticism, Trollope tells us, lies in the pleasing sense of ourselves as heroic enough to suffer the way that Hester does throughout the novel rather than in the consideration of any moral law. Likewise, the narrator's seeming acquiescence to Hester's fate is actually satire. Though Hawthorne treats Hester "in a spirit of assumed hardness," this is merely "a streak of that satire with which Hawthorne always speaks of the peculiar institutions of that country" (210). Of course by this point, the nationalist underpinnings of Trollope's reading have become all too evident.

Confronted with a powerfully original work of American literature that did not unambiguously denounce the Puritans, Trollope and other readers found ways to read *The Scarlet Letter* as if it were written by Washington Irving. For surely no author of Hawthorne's refinement, wit, and intelligence could *really* believe in any of the main tenets of a cruel and outdated theology like Calvinism, and certain it was that the Puritans left only a legacy to be mocked and derided rather than regarded with a sense of historical awe and moral uncertainty. America's most successful and renowned author had demonstrated this in "The Legend of Sleepy Hollow" with his characterization of Ichabod Crane, the itinerant, malnourished, and pedantic schoolteacher who abuses his students and covets the hand of the well-born Katrina Van Tassel not out of true affection, but out of a desire to inherit her father's vast estate, consume its bounty, and sell it for cash. Nor is Irving ambiguous in his portrayal: Crane is not a native of Sleepy Hollow, but a Yankee intruder from Connecticut, the old Puritan colony founded by Thomas Hooker. What renders him most ridiculous, however, is his regard for the Puritan archvillain, Cotton Mather: Crane "was a perfect master of Cotton Mather's History of New England Witchcraft, in which, by the way, he most firmly and potently believed" (276).

Thankfully, Crane is driven from Sleepy Hollow by the hale and hearty Brom Van Brunt, who successfully exploits Crane's laughable credulity and subsequently marries Katrina Van Tassel. Here, the fate of the Puritan mind is one of stagnation, cowardice, and hypocrisy, and the appropriate place for such a mind is not as a member of the established land-owning community but rather (as Irving, ever the urbane humorist, tells us) in the fields of politics and law, where its qualities can be of good use. At the close of the story, we learn that Crane "had changed his quarters to a distant part of the country; had kept school and studied law at the same time; had been admitted to the bar; turned politician; electioneered; written for the newspapers; and had finally been made a justice of the Ten Pound Court" (296). This classic American tale, which appeared in the sixth installment of *The Sketch Book of Geoffrey Crayon, Gent.* in 1820, followed upon a number of Irving's amiable reflections on English culture and society, all of which were written in England, and all of which made evident the ability and willingness of Americans to refine themselves, renounce their puritanic superstitions, write in proper English, and appreciate the topography, culture, and society of their British counterparts. The exorcism of Ichabod Crane serves as a particularly colorful illustration of the transition that Britons were pleased to see, and Americans were pleased to pride themselves on, in the years following the War of 1812.

Likewise, the tales of Edgar Allan Poe that were published throughout the 1830s and 40s were rife with the European trappings of gothic romance: castellated abbeys, underground catacombs, princes and courtiers, and any number of disaffected patrician narrators. Was Hawthorne trying to undo the progress that Americans had made? By what manner of anachronism could an author so influenced by the British Romantics, the novels of Walter Scott, and the refined American prose of Washington Irving read a new kind of Gothicism, a Dark Romanticism, into the Puritanism of the Massachusetts Bay Colony in the 1600s? One can only imagine what must have been the sense of strangeness to British readers of *The Scarlet Letter* who were unfamiliar with short stories like "Young Goodman Brown" (1835) and "The Minister's Black Veil" (1832) to encounter not an irreverent ghost tale in the manner of Irving, or a "seriotragicomic" tale in the high sumptuous style of Poe, but rather the eerie plainness of New England Puritans gathered outside a prison-door: "A throng of bearded men, in sad-colored garments and gray, steeple-crowned hats, intermixed with women, some wearing hoods, and others bareheaded, was assembled in front of a wooden edifice, the door of which was heavily timbered with oak, and studded with iron spikes" (1: 47).

The unease with which Britons were initially struck by the subject matter of the novel was still evident more than twenty years later in Lady Juliet Pollock's "Imaginative Literature of America" from the August 1873 issue of the *Contemporary Review*. "The plot works itself out among a small group of characters whose relations to each other are the most disagreeable that can well be conceived," she writes, "a disgraced wife—her seducer—her husband—her illegitimate child, all living near together in the same settlement of New England, where puritanic manners, puritanic society, puritanic coldness, cruelty, and hypocrisy combine to bear down upon a woman's fault." Nevertheless, by this time *The Scarlet Letter* is "perhaps the best known of the author's romances," though it is also "the most persistently painful of them all" (359). To explain what Trollope later termed Hawthorne's "weird, mysterious, thrilling charm," Pollock supposed that an obsessive psychological morbidity and fascination with death could explain the uncanny quality of his work: "The physical process of death was at once alluring and appalling to him. He was fastened to it by the horror it inspired; a state of mind which, in a highly-strung nervous system and poetical temperament, it is easy to conceive." In other words, the moral gloom is the result of a mental imbalance, for which Hawthorne sought relief and expression in the world of fiction. "He shielded himself from his gloomy impression by invoking the aid of spiritualism," Pollock concludes, "an environment of mystic supernatural agencies served to cast into shadow that which he saw so keenly and shuddered to see" (363). Here, Hawthorne is portrayed as a damaged genius with the vulnerable and unpredictable sensibility of a Poe, or a *Dejection*-era Coleridge, whose intellect drifts into obsession and eccentricity. Knowing what we now know of Hawthorne's biography—his happy marriage, his cool reserve, his many longtime friendships, his practicality and formality, his healthy enjoyment of food, alcohol, and all the pleasures of the natural world—this conception seems ludicrous, and yet it was undoubtedly preferable to believing that Hawthorne may have truly confounded himself in his creation of Hester Prynne, or that he could believe along with Hester that in her physical circumstances lie the genesis of a new agency, that in accepting her ignominy she had found the creation and acceptance of her very self: "Here had been her sin; here, her sorrow; and here was yet to be her penitence" (1: 263). Is this satire? Tragedy? Even Trollope, who had met Hawthorne, and noted that he had "seen him very happy over canvas-back ducks, and [had] heard him discuss, almost with violence, the superiority of American vegetables," conceived that his strangeness must have emanated from some aberrant, but not Puritan, inner self: "And yet his imagination was such that the creations of his brain could have been other than such as I have described" (207).

That one's identity could be inexorably shaped by moral imperfection, scandal, or indiscretion was by no means new to Romanticism: this had been the theme of Wordsworth's *Tintern Abbey*, Coleridge's *The Rime of the Ancient Mariner*, and Byron's *Manfred*, to name only a few. But never had anyone so explicitly tied this painful process of self-determination to traditional Puritan conceptions of sin, shame, and penance, or had with such a specifically American historical consciousness and sense of moral ambiguity portrayed a protagonist's journey of becoming as one that ends without redemption, escape, or the reconstitution of the self as something greater than it had been before its fracture. Instead, Hester believes in a future prophetess unburdened by the sin that has come to define her: "The angel and apostle of the coming revelation must be a woman, indeed, but lofty, pure, and beautiful; and wise, moreover, not through dusky grief, but the ethereal medium of joy; and showing how sacred love should make us happy, by the truest test of a life successful to such an end!" (1: 263). Such moral asceticism, if read in the spirit of Melville's "Puritanic gloom" rather than in James's "tone of the picture" or Trollope's "weird, mysterious, thrilling charm," also presents the reader with a reimagining of the relationship between British and American identity that runs counter to Irving's narrative, which posits the disavowal of any and all remnants of Puritanism as a key trait of the new American consciousness—out with Edwards, in with Franklin. Instead of this, however, Hawthorne presents us with a heroine who chooses the shame of her American identity over the comfort and freedom from public scorn available to her in England, suggesting a metamorphosis whereby the struggle and confrontation with the Puritan conception of Original Sin actually provides a more realistic and nuanced understanding of human nature and responsibility rather than a perverse obsession with secret sin.

Glossing over the nationalist implications of the disagreement between Melville and the Britons in *The Province of Piety*, Michael

J. Colacurcio nevertheless highlights the inevitability of reading Hawthorne on his own terms: "Hawthorne is *significantly* addressed as a moral historian . . . Far from explaining away the burdens of depravity, the Hawthornean histories precisely locate that universal problem in a particular American time and space" (35). Another way of looking at it would be to say that Hawthorne's invocation of Puritan history and moral experience in *The Scarlet Letter* effectively renovates and reintroduces the Puritan consciousness of depravity to its British readers in the nineteenth century, expanding the scope of Romanticism to include a dark American counterpart that may even claim historical primacy. For, unlike Irving, Hawthorne invites us, even compels us, to read the history of New England as a gothic text, intimating that the elements of Dark Romanticism featured in his fiction are derived, in large part, from the concerns of the New England mind as it developed from the arrival of the Puritans in the 1620s to the years leading up to the American Revolutionary War. In contrast, then, to the gothic mode of texts like Keats's *Isabella* and *Lamia*, Coleridge's *The Rime of the Ancient Mariner*, Byron's *The Giaour*, or even Poe's "The Cask of Amontillado," which all employ exotic locations and time periods to evoke a sense of artifice, Hawthorne fixes his focus on the very aspect of American history that had been held up for censure and cast aside, making an unexpected link between the authoritarian regime of the Puritans and the evolution of a Romantic consciousness. "The leitmotifs of *The Scarlet Letter* are indeed modern," Colacurcio writes, "or at least Victorian-feminist, as Hawthorne makes good his promise that the moral of 'Mrs. Hutchinson' might easily find nineteenth-century application; but its theme is as Puritan as the antinomian sources it re-enacts and vivifies" (32). More than anything, this explicit historical linkage lends a measure of authenticity to a genre that had hitherto acknowledged its province as one of fantasy and historical abstraction as it also supplants the narrative of Puritan obsolescence and an obliging American regard for British manners and customs with a potent defense of the unique cast of mind that had emerged from the colonial era.

Yet, as Laura Doyle points out, the most obvious cause for the drama that unfolds in *The Scarlet Letter* is Hester Prynne's departure from England to the Massachusetts Bay Colony on her own: "Critics have long noted the offstage locale of Hester's and Dimmesdale's act of passion, but none has noted the novel's elision of the original condition for that passionate act: the transatlantic migration of Hester Prynne *alone*. It is *this* fact that determines Hester's 'fall'" (301). In this way, *The Scarlet Letter* not only replaces the caricature of Puritanism evident in a figure like Ichabod Crane with a more realistic and sympathetic model, it also provides an account of the transition from British to American identity. For Hester, this transition seems to occur all at once as she stands upon the scaffold following her release from prison and recalls her journey from girlhood in England to shame and public censure in New England:

> Standing on that miserable eminence, she saw again her native village, in Old England, and her paternal home; a decayed house of gray stone, with a poverty-stricken aspect, but retaining a half-obliterated shield of arms over the portal, in token of antique gentility . . . Lastly, in lieu of these shifting scenes, came back the rude marketplace of the Puritan settlement, with all the townspeople assembled and levelling their stern regards at Hester Prynne—yes, at herself,—who stood on the scaffold of the pillory, an infant on her arm, and the letter A, in scarlet, fantastically embroidered with gold thread, upon her bosom!
>
> Could it be true? She clutched the child so fiercely to her breast, that it sent forth a cry; she turned her eyes downward at the scarlet letter, and even touched it with her finger, to assure herself that the infant and the shame were real. Yes!—these were her realities,—all else had vanished! (1: 58-59)

Here, Hester moves in her mind from the "antique gentility" of her British origins to the "rude marketplace" of Puritan New England, obliterating her past in a harrowing acknowledgement of her present circumstances. That she chooses to return to her home in the settlement and accept this identity at the close of the novel underscores Hawthorne's emphasis on Romantic individualism as a traumatic process of forced independence, which is no doubt a response to the lofty ideals of transcendentalism as well as to the egotistical excesses of British Romanticism. In Joseph Rezek's view, at a time when "the growth and nationalization of American publishing and the emergence of a truly British publishing industry split between Edinburgh and London began to erase the unevenness that made similarities among writers from Ireland, Scotland, and the United states so apparent" (186), even Hester's needlework is a statement of Hawthorne's aesthetic lineage, which finds a place for itself in the Puritan colonies: "In putting to work for American culture the 'gorgeous,' the 'fantastic,' the 'fairy charm' of an English taste that Hester's needlework embodies, Hawthorne bypasses recent British literary history and claims a direct line of descent from the age of Shakespeare to himself" (196).

Hawthorne had also been developing this notion of a distinctly American identity that had emerged from the wreckage of a social and existential crisis for some time. The early meditative sketch "Mrs. Hutchinson" (1830) had reflected upon the trial and fateful expulsion of Anne Hutchinson from the Massachusetts Bay Colony, and the publication in 1838 of "Endicott and the Red Cross" had presented readers with their first glimpse of Hester Prynne as one among a group of sinners sentenced to various punishments by the Puritan authorities:

> There was likewise a young woman, with no mean share of beauty, whose doom it was to wear the letter A on the breast of her gown, in the eyes of all the world and her own children. And even her own children knew what that initial signified. Sporting with her infamy, the lost and desperate creature had embroidered the fatal token in scarlet cloth, with golden thread, and the nicest art of needle-work; so that the capital A might have been to mean Admirable, or any thing rather than Adulteress. (9: 435)

Anticipating the moral admonishment with which he concludes *The Scarlet Letter* ("Be true! Be true! Be true!"), Hawthorne's developing fascination with this character at this time also included an explicit defense of Puritan scrutiny and public censure as a more transparent method of relating to one another. "Let not the reader argue, from any of these evidences of iniquity, that the times of the Puritans were more vicious than our own, when, as we pass along the very street of this sketch, we discern no badge of infamy on man or woman," he writes, "It was the policy of our ancestors to search out even the most secret sins, and expose them to shame, without fear or favor, in the broadest light of the noonday sun. Were such the custom now, perchance we might find material for a no less piquant sketch than the above" (9: 435-36).

Prior to Hester Prynne, however, perhaps the most striking example of the way in which the formation of the American mind could be figured not as a proud declaration of one's independence, but as an experience of personal rupture is "My Kinsman, Major Molineux," which appeared in *The Token and Atlantic Souvenir* in 1832, but remained uncollected until its publication in *The Snow-Image and Other Twice-Told Tales* in 1851. In this tale, which the narrator tells us takes place in a settlement of the Province of Massachusetts Bay sometime in the 1730s, a young man named Robin travels from the country to call upon the favor of his father's cousin, Major Molineux. Unbeknownst to Robin, however, the townspeople have rejected British authority and are planning to tar and feather Molineux and drive him from town. Like Hester upon the scaffold, he also has a vision of his former home as he watches his family "go in at the door; and when Robin would have entered also, the latch tinkled into its place, and he was excluded from his home." But as Robin comes to understand that the entire town has been waiting to see his reaction to his kinsman's humiliation, and that they are now laughing at him, he suddenly erupts in laughter himself: "The contagion was spreading among the multitude, when all at once, it seized upon Robin, and he sent forth a shout of laughter that echoed through the street; every man shook his sides, every man emptied his lungs, but Robin's shout was the loudest there" (11: 230). According to historian Alan Taylor, "nothing done since by historian or novelist conveys the internal essence of the revolution. Hawthorne recognized that the struggle was our first civil war, rife with divisions, violence, and destruction . . . Robin's laugh represents the decision made by thousands when they helped disgrace Loyalists as enemies to American liberty" (2-3). But what if Robin's "decision" is largely compelled—a result not of any conscious choice, but of acquiescence in the face of horror and estrangement from one's former self?

Though Hester eventually chooses to suffer her fate willingly, Robin is prevented from attempting to recover his former identity—at least for the present. When he asks for directions to the ferry his request is denied, and he is given the following counsel: "'Some few days hence, if you continue to wish it, I will speed you on your journey. Or, if you prefer to remain with us, perhaps, as you are a shrewd youth, you may rise in the world, without the help of your kinsman, Major Molineux'" (11: 231). Here, the way in which one becomes American is by a forceful severing of family ties and a complicity in the excesses of mob justice, which stresses both the personal anguish of accepting one's place in a new social order as well as the overlap between Puritan authoritarianism and the ideals and attitudes that led to war and national independence. Read in this context, *The Scarlet Letter* is most accurately viewed not strictly as a work that appealed to British and American audiences alike due to the mysterious charm of Hawthorne's somber tone, but rather as a novel that is both firmly entrenched in the transatlantic world of the Massachusetts Bay Colony in the 1600s as well as the competing ideological currents of a nascent transcendentalism and a vestigial Puritanism in New England in the middle of the nineteenth century. Focused as it finally is on who Hester becomes, or what she chooses to accept as she crosses and recrosses the Atlantic, *The Scarlet Letter* rests somewhere in the space between Puritanism and Romanticism, the ineluctable and the ideal.

Works Cited

Colacurcio, Michael J. *The Province of Piety: Moral History in Hawthorne's Earlier Tales*. Harvard UP, 1984.

Doyle, Laura. *Freedom's Empire: Race and the Rise of the Novel in Atlantic Modernity, 1640-1940*. Duke UP, 2008.

Hawthorne, Julian. *Hawthorne and His Circle*. 1903. Archon, 1968.

_____. *Nathaniel Hawthorne and His Wife*. 1884. 2 vols. Archon, 1968.

Hawthorne, Nathaniel. *The Centenary Edition of the Works of Nathaniel Hawthorne*. Edited by William Charvat et al. Ohio State UP, 1962-1997. 23 vols.

Irving, Washington. *The Sketch Book of Geoffrey Crayon, Gent*. Edited by Haskell Springer.Twayne, 1978.

James, Henry. *Hawthorne*. Macmillan, 1902.

Longfellow, Henry Wadsworth. *The Letters of Henry Wadsworth Longfellow*. Edited by Andrew Hilen. 6 vols. Belknap P of Harvard UP, 1966-82.

Melville, Herman. *Piazza Tales and Other Prose Pieces, 1839-1860*. Edited by G. Thomas Tanselle et al. Northwestern UP, 1987.

Pollock, Lady Juliet. "The Imaginative Literature of America." *Contemporary Review*, vol. 22, 1873, pp. 347-71.

Rezek, Joseph. *London and the Making of Provincial Literature, 1800-1850*. U of Pennsylvania P, 2015.

Scharnhorst, Gary. *Julian Hawthorne: The Life of a Prodigal Son*. U of Illinois P, 2014.

Taylor, Alan. *American Revolutions: A Continental History, 1750-1804*. Norton, 2016.

Trollope, Anthony. "The Genius of Nathaniel Hawthorne." *The North American Review*, vol. 129, no. 274, 1879, pp. 203-22.

Nathaniel Hawthorne's *The Scarlet Letter* and the Form of American Romance_____

Casey R. Pratt

> During the period I have alluded to there was a comfortable, good-
> humoured feeling abroad that a novel is a novel, as a pudding is a
> pudding, and that this was the end of it.
>
> —Henry James, *The Art of Fiction*

The aphoristic moral appearing near the conclusion of Nathaniel Hawthorne's tale of Hester Prynne—"Be true! Be true! Be true!—has been celebrated for the way it crystallizes major moral concerns of *The Scarlet Letter*. But the second part of the injunction, viewed in relation to some of Hawthorne's own theorizing about his aims and motives, significantly obscures the picture: "...Show freely to the world, if not your worst, yet some trait whereby the worst may be inferred." There is clearly a pessimistic implication here that living "truly" involves keeping "our worst" on public display; but simultaneously, there is the suggestion that such public display may be or seem impossible, presumably either because it is prohibited, or more provocatively, because what is worst may be something inner, something psychological, something with no precise material reality. In such cases, the voice of the moralizing narrator advises readers to show (here, some creativity may be required) some outward characteristic that hints at the worst of the inner, psychological or spiritual, disorder. In short, there is a specific claim here about the nature of reality: what is real, and true, may need to be transfigured by some symbolic process before it can be perceived by others. If that were all, it would be a moderately sophisticated, if eccentric, summation of Hester's story. But in his maturity as a writer, Hawthorne had developed a theory of fiction—even a theory of psychology—that encouraged readers not to settle for mildly profound moral propositions. Instead, Hawthorne hoped that some readers might, as he puts it near the beginning of "The Custom-

---

House," "understand him, better than most of his schoolmates and lifemates" (3). For Hawthorne, explicitly, this proposed relationship with an ideal reader, replete with symbolic signifying and unspoken moral, psychological, even theological insinuations, formed the cornerstone of his highest authorial hopes, and the bedrock of what he believed to be a distinct form of fiction that he insisted on calling a romance.

Not all studies of the romance genre have focused on the reader-writer relationship. More often, whether in criticizing the genre, as Henry James did, or defending it, as critic Richard Volney Chase did in the 1950s, critics have tended to define the romance thematically (emphasizing epistemological uncertainty and metaphysical instability) or in terms of its style of symbolic and "mythopoetic" representation. James's well-known description of the romance qualified it as, at best, an "amusing" genre:

> The art of the romancer is, "for the fun of it," insidiously to cut the cable [from "the balloon of experience"], to cut it without our detecting him… the experience here represented is the disconnected and uncontrolled experience—uncontrolled by our general sense of "the way things happen"—which romance alone more or less successfully palms off on us. (*Art of the Novel*, 34)

Chase would have accepted the terms, but differed in his evaluation of what such a genre allows the author to accomplish. "The romance," wrote Chase in 1957, "following distantly the medieval example, feels free to render reality in less volume and detail. It tends to prefer action to character" (13). He continued,

> In American romances it will not matter much what class people come from, and where the novelist would arouse our interest in a character by exploring his origin, the romancer will probably do so by enveloping it in mystery… the romance will more freely veer toward mythic, allegorical, and symbolistic forms. (13)

A well-known cadre of mid-twentieth-century critics, including F.O. Matthiessen, Charles Feidelson, Jr., Leslie Fiedler, and Joel

Porte, refined these definitions and provided a framework for analyzing the romances of Hawthorne, Melville, and others who wrote in the same mode. By the 1980s, the definition of romance, and the central status of romance, would be challenged by a subsequent group of critics for whom the question of genre was secondary to the political work these so-called romances were (or weren't) doing.

Roused by the proposed distinction between a novel and a romance, the critics have had their say ever since. But before wading into downstream waters, we will let the author speak a bit further for himself. Two years after the publication of *The Scarlet Letter*, in his Preface to *The House of the Seven Gables*, Hawthorne condensed the thinking he presented in "The Custom-House." After distinguishing between the romance and the novel in the opening sentence, Hawthorne elaborated:

> Many writers lay very great stress upon some definite moral purpose, at which they profess to aim their works. Not to be deficient in this particular, the author has provided himself with a moral;—the truth, namely, that the wrong-doing of one generation lives into the successive ones.... In good faith, however, he is not sufficiently imaginative to flatter himself with the slightest hope of this kind. When romances do really teach anything, or produce any effective operation, it is usually through a far more subtile process than the ostensible one. (xiv)

This is a rather loud and direct note of caution to would-be hasty readers of Hawthorne's fictions: the "ostensible" moral presented in these romances is downplayed, even effaced. The reader of romances should focus not on any Aesopian moral that may be summarized in a word or two; rather, the ideal romance reader will be attuned to some less definite "operation" or "process" that may allow an elusive communion between author and reader to emerge from "below" the words themselves, and the "native reserve" of the author may be overcome "without violating either the reader's rights or [the author's]." If such claims strike us as mystical, pretentious, or even paranoid we are not alone—has such delicacy ever been required as we open any other sort of book? It is worth noting here the apparent elitist, antidemocratic nature of the romance form. Indeed, "The Custom-House" has been widely despised by casual readers, as Hawthorne's preface to the second edition makes clear. But rather than accept "the public disapprobation," Hawthorne stubbornly refuses to change a single word (5). The essay stands as a rather significant barrier to entry for many readers, and Hawthorne seems to be quite aware of its difficulty and function. Clark Davis argues that "the ethical basis of Hawthorne's work... rests upon an acknowledgement of otherness, an insistence upon separation as a precondition for any sort of meaningful connection" (54). For Davis, Hawthorne's "shyness" may be "not merely a flaw," but "a philosophy, for instance, a way of seeing the self and its approach to the world" (30). If Hawthorne is going to indulge his autobiographical impulse, he will do so only among readers who have, so to speak, "earned" it—and he will do so only indirectly, only symbolically. In his "Custom-House" introduction, Hawthorne speaks of his own efforts at effective reading in relation to the dusty old box containing the scarlet letter and related documents. He says,

> [I should have tried] ...to spiritualize the burden that began to weigh so heavily; to seek, resolutely, the true and indestructible value that lay hidden in the petty and wearisome incidents, and ordinary characters, with which I was now conversant. The fault was mine. The page of life that was spread out before me seemed dull and commonplace, only because I had not fathomed its deeper import. (37)

The apparent elitism of the romance mode is offset by the fact that the door stands open to all classes of readers, to any who would make the effort to meet the challenge posed here by Hawthorne, to any who would read the romance *properly*. This passage acts as a preemptive defense against superficial criticism, and stands as a warning to any incautious skimmer who might shrug and claim not to see what all the fuss is about: the fault in that case, Hawthorne anticipates, is the reader's.

Given this complex and demanding dynamic between reader and writer, it is not surprising to find that separation is thematically pervasive in *The Scarlet Letter*: in Hester's separation from

Chillingworth, in her separation from her village, from Dimmesdale, from the meeting-house, and also in the reader's separation from the scene of her sin, and from a straightforward relation of the facts. The "hypothetical narration" appearing near the beginning of the romance, in the first paragraph of Chapter 2, forces readers to sustain an "unknowing" even as they are led from one scene to the next. Hawthorne writes,

> the grim rigidity that petrified the bearded physiognomies of these good people would have augured some awful business at hand. It could have betokened nothing short of the anticipated execution of some noted culprit... It might be that a sluggish bond-servant, or an undutiful child... was to be corrected at the whipping-post. It might be, that an Antinomian, a Quaker, or other heterodox religionist, was to be scourged out of the town, or an idle and vagrant Indian... was to be driven with stripes into the shadow of the forest. It might be, too, that a witch... was to die upon the gallows. (49)

As we read, of course, each scene comes into focus, but never without some lingering question as to what has transpired morally, or symbolically, psychologically, or "inwardly." According to Richard Chase, whose 1957 book, *The American Novel and its Tradition*, remains perhaps the definitive modern defense of the romance, it is, at least in part, "the perception and acceptance not of unities but of radical disunities" that sets the romance apart (6-7). Time and again in *The Scarlet Letter* we are asked what the letter means and how we can know what it means, and each time we are separated from a conclusive answer. These are the "ultimate concerns" of romance—the theoretical interest in metaphysics and epistemology that do not necessarily occupy a central position in novels. When we are given any definitive view of the central mysteries of the narrative, we are shown only subjective perceptions, as when, after some years, we are told that "many people refused to interpret the scarlet A by its original signification. They said that it meant Able; so strong was Hester Prynne, with a woman's strength" (161). In this manner, Hawthorne's narrative style "teaches" readers—though only through a "subtile process"—to sustain and endure a kind of epistemological uncertainty that may be understood as a prerequisite to the ethical relationship Clark Davis suggests that Hawthorne tried to manifest between himself and his readers. The theme of epistemological uncertainty, of separation from knowledge, is present simultaneously in Hester's story, and through the story as an aesthetic product. If Hester is estranged from Dimmesdale, the reader is similarly estranged from the narrator.

This theme of separation and estrangement, manifesting as a sustained interest in interpretive ambiguity, is present in much of Hawthorne's body of work, from the 1836 parable, "The Minister's Black Veil," through to his last completed novel, *The Marble Faun*. In the former, Hawthorne describes the scene that follows the first sermon delivered by the eccentric minister on the day that he first appeared in public wearing the ambiguous symbol:

> At the close of the services, the people hurried out with indecorous confusion, eager to communicate their pent-up amazement, and conscious of lighter spirits the moment they lost sight of the black veil. Some gathered in little circles, huddled closely together, with their mouths all whispering in the centre; some went homeward alone, wrapt in silent meditation; some talked loudly, and profaned the Sabbath day with ostentatious laughter. A few shook their sagacious heads, intimating that they could penetrate the mystery; while one or two affirmed that there was no mystery at all, but only that Mr. Hooper's eyes were so weakened by the midnight lamp, as to require a shade. (*Tales* 374)

The congregation hears a single sermon, but interprets it variously and contradictorily. Moreover, the narrator of the story refuses to settle, for readers, the question of the meaning of the veil, and the motive of the minister is never fully disclosed. The metafictional element here, where the reader relates to the story precisely as the congregation relates to the sermon, reveals that even early in his career, Hawthorne was acutely aware of constructing a unique relationship with his readers, a theoretical relationship that proved to be as much an ideal as a practice. In many respects, Hawthorne never altered this aim, and only refined his efforts. As the epigraph to a chapter in his book, *The Half-Vanishing Structure: Hawthorne's Allegorical Dialectics* Magnus Ullén cites the following excerpt from a letter Hawthorne wrote to Francis Bennoch on January 27, 1860: "I somewhat doubt whether your dull English public will quite appreciate its excellencies. It depends upon the view a reader happens to take of it, whether it shall appear very clever or very absurd" (qtd. in Ullén 265).

Within this context, it is no surprise to read of Hester's "spiritualized" hearing at the scene of Dimmesdale's Election Day sermon. The narrator reports that Hester "listened with such intentness, and sympathized so intimately, that the sermon had throughout a meaning for her, entirely apart from its indistinguishable words... she caught the low undertone" (243). All metafictional indicators here indicate that Hester has, presumably through her sin and suffering, attained the ability to listen to (or "read") rightly; she hears what others cannot hear. Hawthorne demands the same of his readers. This apparently "elitist" element of the American romance has been something of an embarrassment to literary critics, and has often gone awkwardly ignored. But the antecedents are consistent and plentiful, both in the texts themselves and in the prefaces and letters that frame the romances. Hawthorne's infamous and condescending comment about his literary competition—that "damned mob of scribbling women"—is perhaps only slightly more often cited as an example here than Melville's increasingly tense, defiant, and aloof relationship with his own readers after the publication of *Moby-Dick.* While Melville's sources tended to be, as Arthur Versluis has shown, esoteric and even Gnostic, Hawthorne's own elitist themes present themselves almost as parables, as, in fact, "The Minister's Black Veil" explicitly does in its subtitle. Edgar Allan Poe's comment on the story in his review of "Twice-Told Tales" hits on the theme of literary elitism: "...to the rabble its exquisite skill will be caviare. The obvious meaning of this article will be found to smother its insinuated one" (574).

This apparently *politically embarrassing* insistence on an elitism within the American romance has been used by some critics to argue for diminishing the genre's status in American literary history.

But the elitism of American romance is a particularly American sort of elitism—not an aristocratic elitism, but, to speak romantically, a democratic elitism. Ralph Waldo Emerson spoke in similar terms in his 1838 essay, "Self-Reliance":

> Expect me not to show cause why I seek or why I exclude company. Then, again, do not tell me, as a good man did to-day, of my obligation to put all poor men in good situations. Are they my poor? I tell thee, thou foolish philanthropist, that I grudge the dollar, the dime, the cent, I give to such men as do not belong to me and to whom I do not belong. There is a class of persons to whom by all spiritual affinity I am bought and sold; for them I will go to prison, if need be. (135-36)

This "spiritual affinity" seems to be the desired foundation for reader-writer understanding in the American romance mode, and if it does not apologize for itself, it is because there seems to be no correlation between spiritual affinity and economic or social class. Theoretically, at least, the romance seems to cut across, and aspire to undermine, conventional social hierarchies and class stratifications. The "rabble" referred to by Poe in his review of "The Minister's Black Veil" is not a simple reference to "the poor." Hester was not able to hear "the low undertone" of Dimmesdale's sermon because of her high social status. And Pip, for comparison, in *Moby-Dick*, did not find welcome in Captain Ahab's cabin because of his aristocratic birth. Instead, perhaps, like Jesus' parables, these narratives seem to have been intentionally constructed to reach a specific, rather than a universal, reading audience. Jesus cites Isaiah 6:9-10 as his warrant for speaking in parables: "You will be ever hearing but never understanding; you will be ever seeing but never perceiving. For this people's heart has become calloused" (Mt 13:14-15). Jonathan A. Cook has demonstrated very effectively that the comparison to Jesus is not cultish critical hyperbole but is very important for understanding how these writers conceived of their literary project. Cook wrote,

> … in his review [of Hawthorne's *Mosses*] Melville assumes the role of a critical St. Paul to proclaim Hawthorne as America's long-awaited

literary messiah. Moreover, Melville's pseudonymous "Virginian" frames the essay as a kind of literary conversion experience, comparable to the well-known conversion of Saul to Paul on the road to Damascus. (63)

As Christian soteriology is most commonly understood, all were welcome to recognize Jesus' divinity, but neither social class nor theological training served as any advantage in the process of recognition and conversion. The ideal disciple, like the ideal reader, could come from any social strata. Cook goes on to point out that Melville then criticizes his fellow Americans in the same way that Jesus criticized those Jewish contemporaries who failed to recognize him as the divine being: "Nathaniel Hawthorne is a man, as yet, almost utterly mistaken among men" (qtd. in Cook, 65). Hawthorne himself put the point only slightly differently in *The Marble Faun*, where his narrator remarks, of the paintings in the great Italian galleries: "Let the canvas glow as it may, you must look with the eye of faith, or its highest excellence escapes you" (242). If the reader achieves the capacity to read—to borrow Poe's terminology—both at the level of "insinuation" and simultaneously at the level of the "obvious," then the author may responsibly undertake and indulge the autobiographical impulse by way of the romance genre. In such light, Hester's story comes into focus as Hawthorne's own story, in some sense. Further, because the reader has connected these dots, she may come to understand Hester's story as her own at the "inner" level, psychologically and symbolically. When all these cylinders are firing together, the alchemy of the romance produces its proper fruit.

Other writers of the period, less often considered in relation to the romance genre, but bona fide American romantics, offered similar equations. Emily Dickinson's injunction to tell the truth "slant" seems to mirror Hawthorne's theory of romance almost exactly: tell the truth, but, because such telling is sometimes forbidden, or because such telling requires equally refined hearing (or for other plausible reasons), speak circuitously in order to achieve the desired effect. In his well-known study, *American Romanticism and the Marketplace*,

Michael T. Gilmore emphasized the tension produced in a capitalist society when an author is torn between his artistic impulses and his need to generate sales. "Symbolism," writes Gilmore, "is the effort of the literary imagination to impose significance upon the world of things from which capitalist production has banished the human element" (16). In Gilmore's view, Dickinson's "telling it slant," and especially the "artisanal versions of author-audience relations [of Hawthorne and Melville] were fated to be disappointed" (17). Gilmore sees profound pressures arising from both American capitalism and democracy, pressures that shape the way authors manage their highest themes. Whether the blame falls on capitalism, or a fallen human nature, or some combination of both, it is clear that many of America's best-known writers of the mid-nineteenth century felt a need to communicate at two "levels." Captain Ahab's wild Quarter-Deck speech in Chapter 36 of Herman Melville's *Moby-Dick* succeeded immediately in persuading his crew, but every careful reader recalls that convincing Starbuck would require "a little lower layer" (139). It may be that, like Starbuck, readers of the American romance postured themselves in a resistant attitude; to overcome this resistance, the practitioners of the romance form strove to develop and refine particular habits of narrating and reporting that would overcome their audience's reluctance.

The fact that this "elitist" dynamic, where sacred recognition between reader and author only occasionally creates a complete circuit, manifests not only in letters *about* the great American romances, but also thematically, in the stories themselves, suggests that the writers of romance were highly self-conscious of the dynamic. Indeed, it is possible to deduce from the pervading presence of the themes of separation, hiddenness, and recognition, a hope that a carefully crafted romance may (like a religious parable?) subconsciously catalyze the sort of "literary conversion" noted above by Cook, perhaps by incentivizing the reader to *believe* ("look with the eye of faith") that very close reading will be rewarded by a moment, or some moments, of heightened recognition. A supremely clear and still underappreciated instance of this converted seeing appears at the very end of *The Scarlet Letter*. Douglas Greenwood proficiently summarizes the complicated and "elitist" dynamic at work on the final page of the book; he writes,

> ...the concluding sentence is to be read in heraldic terms, with "field" the heraldic term for "shield," "sable" the graphic representation for black, and "gules" the term for red. The colors, of course, do not appear on the tombstone, but the manner of the engraved lines represents these colors so that one versed in heraldic terminology could easily determine the colors of the device... To the uninitiated, it simply looks like a shield with an A on it, but to a herald it has dimensions of color as well. (208)

The difference in perception between a person who knows how to read heraldry and the person who does not know how to read heraldry could hardly be more significant. The "uninitiated" sees only a tombstone-colored letter *A* with vertical lines etched into it upon a shield etched with perpendicular lines. The image appears drab and prisonlike. But for the initiated ideal reader, for the one who has not been turned away by the superficial difficulties of the text, the image appears wholly different: a blazing red *A* on a black shield. It is an astonishingly clever device that not only embeds thematic questions of elitism (what is more elite and aristocratic than the special knowledge of reading heraldry?), but that simultaneously rewards those careful readers who take the time to understand. Greenwood ends his short article by noting that "[Hawthorne] leaves us with the 'simple slab of slate,' knowing that the curious investigator will linger before it, ponder its meaning, and 'perplex himself with the purport'" (210). While the hasty and incautious skimmer of the romance may miss these deeper levels of meaning altogether, the romance writers themselves hold out hope that one reader here and there may "quite appreciate its excellencies."

Not all readers, or scholars, have been persuaded that such excellencies inhere in the romance form. Some very accomplished critics, led by Nina Baym and Jane Tompkins, have gone so far as to deny, seemingly, that the romance genre properly exists as distinct from the novel. In her preface to the 2003 Penguin edition of *The Scarlet Letter*, Baym summarized decades of her thinking about

Hawthorne's place in the canon of American Literature. Having quoted Hawthorne's preface to *The House of the Seven Gables*, Baym wrote,

> Hawthorne's careful distinction between his type of fiction, the romance, and another type, called the novel, is one that we no longer observe today, when any long fiction is called a novel. But Hawthorne's words guide us to the perception that he was writing about what goes on inside people, "the truth of the human heart," rather than what goes on outside and around them. Today we would label such writing "psychological...." (Baym xv)

Perhaps the "we" Baym refers to in her first sentence is less monolithic and cohesive than she wanted to believe, but in any case, this critical intervention seems more a matter of nomenclature than a careful examination of literary genre. Perhaps describing Hawthorne's books as "psychological" is more appropriate terminology in our era, but the distinction remains.

If we avoid the term *romance* as a way of distinguishing this genre from the novel, then we will speak instead of Hawthorne's books as "more psychological" than the more popular and typical novels of his day. But Jane Tompkins argued convincingly in *Sensational Designs*, that Hawthorne's stories were, "to Hawthorne's contemporaries... indistinguishable from the surrounding mass of magazine fiction" (6). Tompkins asked a reasonably difficult question in support of her essential thesis that literary reputation was as much political as it was an indicator of greatness; she wrote,

> This indifference to what we now regard as Hawthorne's finest tales requires an explanation. If an author's reputation really does depend upon the power of his art to draw attention to itself regardless of circumstances, then why did Hawthorne's first readers fail utterly to recognize his genius as we understand it, or would later understand it? (6)

To try to answer Tompkins's question, we might think along with Hawthorne's ostracized Mistress Hibbins, whose own darkness,

---

fallenness, seems to allow her to see what the rest of the Puritans, so ensconced in propriety, have missed at every turn: "Dost thou think I have been to the forest so many times, and have yet no skill to judge who else has been there" (*Tales* 210) Hibbins, herself marginalized, an outcast, is perhaps Hawthorne's first ideal reader, and she comes not from the luminary class that Tompkins demonstrated to have helped bolster Hawthorne's reputation. The flash of recognition in "the weird old gentlewoman" seems to be what allows her to understand "the low undertone" of the entire situation. But a single answer is not particularly required. The critical dispute that Baym and Tompkins initiated led to a profound and fruitful rethinking of the American literary canon. Texts assumed to be "masterpieces" in an earlier era were now printed in anthologies alongside the better-selling, though long-forgotten, novels and stories of Hawthorne's contemporaries. Not everyone, in either camp, was convinced that anything had been settled. For a definitive study of the American romance controversy from a perspective that tries to preserve the novel-romance distinction, see G. Richard Thompson and Eric Carl Link's book, *Neutral Ground: New Traditionalism and the American Romance Controversy,* which provides a substantial foundation for retaining Hawthorne's original distinction without necessarily privileging one form over the other. Thompson and Link arrived at a compromise that seems to have sufficed for nearly two decades: the comparison should continue. They asked,

> Does not setting Rowson, Tenney, Rush, Sedgwick, Child, Fern, Wilson, Jacobs, Stowe, Warner, Fuller, Douglass, and others alongside Brown, Cooper, Irving, Poe, Hawthorne, or Melville produce a grouping of texts that gives a changed tone and approach to the idea of American romance? (176)

Thompson and Link perceive that the former set seems better defined in terms associated with the novel, and suspect that the latter group may require terminology from romance criticism. But Baym, Tompkins, and many others, have won enough of a victory that it seems now hopeless, and unnecessary, to aim to award one genre more prestige than the other.

Nevertheless, understanding the American romance as incorporating an "interest in mythopoesis, along with an almost obsessive concern for experimental form, linguistic play, indeterminism, and self-reflexivity" (20), and further understanding it as arriving at a particular form of democratic literary elitism arising from its murky settings, thin characterizations, and difficult language and syntax—this comprehending of the aims of the genre as sufficient to constitute a genre—all of this produces the impression that the romance has indeed survived through American history. The work of Hawthorne and Melville, and perhaps some of the earlier work of Charles Brockden Brown, James Fenimore Cooper, Washington Irving, and—and later productions by the likes of Harold Frederic, William Faulkner, Flannery O'Connor, E.L. Doctorow, Toni Morrison, and Cormac McCarthy all share certain unmistakable themes and styles, and all seem to invite any reader to attempt clearing the high bar set by the symbolic and lyrical language commonly deployed by these writers. In thinking of the romance as challenging the reader, it seems likely that some preparation may allow readers to "look with the eye of faith," so that they may see, or hear, with Mistress Hibbins and like-minded critics, the "low undertone" that many readers have failed to appreciate.

Works Cited

Atkinson, Brooks, editor. *The Essential Writings of Ralph Waldo Emerson.* Modern Library, 2000.

Baym, Nina. Preface. *The Scarlet Letter: A Romance.* Penguin, 2003.

Chase, Richard Volney. *The American Novel and Its Tradition.* Doubleday, 1957.

Cook, Jonathan A. "Melville's *Mosses* Review and the Proclamation of Hawthorne as America's Literary Messiah." *Leviathan,* vol. 10, no. 3, 2008, pp. 62–70. doi:10.1111/j.1750-1849.2008.01312.x.

Davis, Clark. *Hawthorne's Shyness: Ethics, Politics, and the Question of Engagement.* Johns Hopkins UP, 2005.

Emerson, Ralph Waldo. *Emerson's Prose and Poetry.* Norton Critical Edition. Edited by Joel Porte and Saundra Morris. W. W. Norton, 2001.

Gilmore, Michael T. *American Romanticism and the Marketplace*. U of Chicago P, 1988.

Greenwood, Douglas. "The Heraldic Device in The Scarlet Letter: Hawthorne's Symbolical Use of the Past." *American Literature*, vol. 46, no. 2, 1974, p. 207. doi:10.2307/2924694.

Hawthorne, Nathaniel. *The Centenary Edition of the Works of Nathaniel Hawthorne*. Edited by William Charvat et al. Ohio State UP, 1962-1997. 23 vols.

_____. *The House of the Seven Gables*. Barnes & Noble, 2000.

_____. *Tales and Sketches*. Literary Classics of the United States, 1982.

James, Henry. *The Art of Fiction: and Other Essays*. Edited by Morris Roberts. Oxford UP, 1948.

_____. *The Art of the Novel: Critical Prefaces*. Scribner's, 1973.

Melville, Herman. *The Piazza Tales and Other Prose Pieces, 1839–1860*. Edited by Harrison Hayford, Alma A. MacDougall, and G. Thomas Tanselle. Northwestern UP and The Newberry Library, 1987.

Poe, Edgar Allan. "Review of Twice-Told Tales." In *Poe: Essays and Reviews*. Edited by G. R. Thompson. Library of America, 1984.

Thompson, Gary Richard, and Eric Carl. *Neutral Ground: New Traditionalism and the American Romance Controversy*. Louisiana State UP, 1999.

Tompkins, Jane P. *Sensational Designs: The Cultural Work of American Fiction: 1790-1860*. Oxford UP, 2013.

Ullén, Magnus. *The Half-Vanished Structure: Hawthorne's Allegorical Dialectics*. Lang, 2004.

Versluis, Arthur. *The Esoteric Origins of the American Renaissance*. Oxford UP, 2001.

Whitman, Walt. *Poetry and Prose*. Library of America, 2010.

Discovering Hester Prynne: *The Scarlet Letter* and the American Renaissance_____

Christopher N. Phillips

In "The Custom-House," Nathaniel Hawthorne seems thoroughly disenchanted with his current world. A literary man who gives in to political patronage for money, he finds his job as customs inspector tedious, his employees and neighbors even more so. The city of Salem is mildly depressed and more than mildly oppressive, and his creative abilities are atrophying like unused muscle. Only two things can rescue him from this misery. The first is crass, mundane, and not entirely unexpected: a new election brings about a mass firing of previous political appointees, Hawthorne included. The second lifeline is much more accidental and surprising: the discovery of a mysterious, embroidered letter *A* in the custom house attic, along with an old manuscript giving an account of the letter's history, involving a colonial woman named Hester Prynne. Hawthorne immediately feels a powerful connection to the letter, even before he knows the story of it; when he absentmindedly puts the letter on his own chest, "It seemed to me…that I experienced a sensation not altogether physical, yet almost so, as of burning heat; and as if the letter were not of red cloth, but red-hot iron (32)." His creative powers reawaken with this discovery, and his unemployment affords him the time to use them in "expanding" the manuscript into what he calls a *romance*.

Of course, the discovery itself is part of the romance. While Hawthorne presents the first-person narrator of "The Custom-House" as himself and fills the story with details of real-life Salem, Massachusetts, there was no historical Hester Prynne, no scarlet letter hidden in an attic for him to find. Yet the fantasy of finding "a most curious relic" (33) of the early colonial days stranded in the humdrum routine of modern life was an attractive one in the nineteenth century. Massachusetts was the first state to organize a historical society to gather and study antiquities from its quickly fading past. As a result, new scholarship as well as reprints of early accounts was plentiful on the topic of New England's Puritan history, and Hawthorne read widely in that material.

Even Hawthorne's narrator persona had antiquarian roots. A generation earlier, Washington Irving launched a new era of American literature precisely by looking into the past with an imaginative lens. His breakthrough work was a satirical *History of New York*, narrated by the cantankerous historian Dietrich Knickerbocker who sifted his state's colonial past under both Dutch and English rule for humorous anecdotes and political intrigues. The two stories that brought Irving his greatest fame, "Rip Van Winkle" and "The Legend of Sleepy Hollow," both turned to the colonial past as well. And in fact, the eponymous narrator presented these stories in *The Sketch Book of Geoffrey Crayon* as Knickerbocker manuscripts that Crayon had found. Hawthorne's invented manuscript wasn't nearly as humorous as those Irving "discovered," but American readers enjoyed a good trip down memory lane, whether the memory was accurate or not.

Indeed, a later excitement over discovering seventeenth-century treasures in nineteenth-century America helped make *The Scarlet Letter* central to the canon of American literature. In 1941, F. O. Matthiessen published a book titled *American Renaissance* that would establish a canon of American literary origins; it still has profound influence over the teaching and study of American literature. Trained originally as a scholar of English Renaissance drama, Matthiessen made a compelling case for the inclusion of American literature in the college curriculum, an idea that still faced much resistance just before World War II. He argued that elements of the style, symbolism, and tragic form that made English authors such as William Shakespeare, Edmund Spenser, and John Milton so masterful were also at work in the writings of Herman Melville, Henry David Thoreau, Ralph Waldo Emerson, Walt Whitman, and Hawthorne. Focusing on the years 1850 (the year of *The Scarlet Letter*'s publication) to 1855, Matthiessen described a moment of highly original literary creation that nonetheless took its inspiration from the great literature of the late sixteenth and early seventeenth centuries. By 1940, American Puritanism was quickly becoming an important topic in American history and literary study thanks to Matthiessen's Harvard colleague Perry Miller, but *American Renaissance* found the transatlantic sources of American art even more important than the colonial experience. Rather than discovering an embroidered letter in a Harvard attic, Matthiessen perceived Spenserian emblems in the character of Pearl, Miltonic tragedy in Hester's struggle with sin, and the theatrical space of the scaffold as the quintessential setting for Hawthorne's moral drama. *The Scarlet Letter*'s deep seventeenth-century roots, thus reimagined, helped to reframe Hawthorne as a major thinker engaged in the great themes and tropes of Western thought, not simply a New England romancer with an antiquarian streak.

Even Hawthorne's preference for *romance* as his word for the kind of fiction he wrote aligned him with authors of poetical romance like Spenser over more modern authors of the much later term *novel*. The romance had less directly to do with love (as in our current phrase *romance novel*) than with adventure, dramatic events, and even the supernatural. As a narrative form, it traced its origins as far back as Homer's *Odyssey*, a genre that shared something of the epic's power while allowing for freer structure and less idealized heroes than the epic required. The old stories of King Arthur and other brave knights were generally romances, as were the popular historical novels of Sir Walter Scott and his American counterpart, James Fenimore Cooper. Against the strict realism of the novel as practiced by writers like Jane Austen, Charles Dickens, and Henry Fielding, the romance celebrated the imagination's ability to embellish real life. Hawthorne would go on to explain some of what he meant by *romance* in prefaces to his next novels, *The House of the Seven Gables* and *The Blithedale Romance*, but he began to develop his idea of the genre in "The Custom-House":

> Moonlight, in a familiar room, falling so white upon the carpet, and showing all its figures so distinctly,—making every object so minutely visible, yet so unlike a morning or noontide visibility,—is a medium the most suitable for a romance-writer to get acquainted with his illusive guests.... [familiar] details, so completely seen, are so spiritualized by the unusual light, that they seem to lose their actual

substance, and become things of intellect. Nothing is too small or too trifling to undergo this change, and acquire dignity thereby. (35)

In this passage, Hawthorne emphasizes the power of moonlight to make real things visible while also "spiritualizing" them, making them mean something beyond their literal existence—in other words, to turn them into symbols.

This symbolizing power is not reserved solely for great, lofty, or striking images, but can also act on the "small" and "trifling"; even something as small as an embroidered letter, measuring "precisely three inches and a quarter in length," could become "the groundwork of a tale" (31, 33). As Hawthorne tries to account for the placement of the scarlet letter and its manuscript in the attic, he points out that they were "not official, but of a private nature," and that when colonial authorities fled Massachusetts during the American Revolution, "this package, proving to be of no public concern, was left behind, and had remained ever since unopened" (30). It is the story of a woman, of moral and family drama, one seemingly disconnected from policy, finance, and other matters of "public concern," and thus both ignored by history and susceptible to the spiritualizing that Hawthorne aims to do in his story. The moonlight of romance becomes a way of getting at truth that those interested in the public, masculine history of nations are ill-equipped to see or tell.

Hester, the American Heroine

As a woman Hester Prynne necessarily inhabits the private, the domestic, the details in her Puritan culture, making her a fitting subject for a Hawthorne romance. She is introduced to the reader as a figure suffering her forced removal from the private to the public in her exposure on the scaffold. The jail, where she had recently given birth to her daughter, is a poor sort of domestic space, but it at least kept her concealed, under official surveillance yet free to care for her baby without the prying eyes of the town. On the scaffold, however, she must now construct a persona, choosing a face to put forward to her leering neighbors. This first step of public self-making is also her first into the pantheon of great American characters, those who define themselves by their resistance to injustice and inauthenticity to create a new possible world for themselves, whether they can hold it together or not. As with male characters like Cooper's Natty Bumppo or Twain's Huck Finn, she finds herself more at home in wilderness spaces like the forest and the seashore than in human society. She identifies with the Indian, the outcast, the infirm, the suffering. Marked by the state for her exposed sin, she seems to offer redemption for others, particularly young women, with moral struggles. Faced with attack from all sides, and attached to a daughter whose uncontrollability is a daily reminder of her own sin, Prynne becomes a patient saint, but also a prophetess of new womanly power in the New World.

To find a strong female character in a canonical novel—in the 1940s, that almost necessarily meant one written by a man—was something of a surprise to a number of the (male) scholars of the American Renaissance, and the political possibilities of a strong heroine in a male-dominated age weren't lost on them. Isn't *The Scarlet Letter*, asked one scholar, "a feminist tract" (Chase 73)? That scholar, Richard Chase, was careful to temper his answer by asserting that "no coherent politics is to be derived from Hawthorne" (74), but Hester Prynne's independence of thought, her living by her own labor, and her refusal to let the town's condemnation of her be the last word in her social standing have long made her a feminist heroine. Her stigmatization becomes the source of her freedom, even her American individualism:

> Standing alone in the world...she cast away the fragments of a broken chain. The world's law was no law for her mind. It was an age in which the human intellect, newly emancipated, had taken a more active and a wider range than for many centuries before. Men of the sword had overthrown nobles and kings. Men bolder than these had overthrown and rearranged—not actually, but within the sphere of theory, which was their most real abode—the whole system of ancient prejudice, wherewith was linked much of ancient principle. Hester Prynne imbibed this spirit. She assumed a freedom of speculation, then common enough on the other side of the Atlantic, but which our

forefathers, had they known of it, would have held to be a deadlier crime than that stigmatized by the scarlet letter. (164)

Hester Prynne becomes an intellectual rebel, a theorist rather than a revolutionary, but in this rebellion she becomes more modern than her surroundings. She does not agitate for social change, but instead imagines it, performing the political work that Hawthorne seems to desire for the romance: a new way of seeing the world, one potentially even leading to a new ethic, but one in which "thought suffices...without investing itself in the flesh and blood of action." The importance of her retaining custody of Pearl is clearly a motive for Prynne's keeping her radicalism quiet, but it also seems somehow to manifest itself in the child's refusal to recognize social norms. Pearl in this way is a manifestation both of her mother's passion and of her thought.

Wild spaces provide the scene for such freedom. The forest especially provides private, wild space for the Prynnes, as well as an alternative space for Hester Prynne and Dimmesdale not only to admit but to enjoy their connection to each other. Dimmesdale speaks freely to her only here, even resting his head on her chest in his exhaustion. Mistress Hibbins, self-identified as the leading witch of the area, repeatedly teases Hester Prynne by saying she can tell she has been to the forest and, therefore, with "the Black Man," meaning the Devil. Yet Hibbins never sees Prynne there personally, despite the widow's own admissions of making visits to the Devil to do her witchcraft in the forest. If Prynne draws attention to herself by her trips into the forest, it does not seem to affect her reputation much; the residents of Boston may see her as evil, but few are willing to consider her a witch. She thus possesses a peculiar power: she can freely enter the forest without becoming a witch, as Mistress Hibbins assumes must be the result of such wanderings. Hester Prynne's forest is a secular one, where the only "Black Man" she meets is a robed, off-duty minister and where she can reach for the joy of Eden as easily as others seem to reach for darkness. She renounces Puritan suspicions of the spiritual and physical dangers of the wilderness and finds a life for herself on the frontier of her society, still within the bounds of curse and blessing but not necessarily from human sources. In the wild, her own mind seems to have become her own church, to borrow Thomas Paine's phrase.

One of the odd things about Hester Prynne's Boston, though, is that the town in some ways is less Puritan than she is. While Hawthorne from the opening scene of "The Prison-Door" characterizes these early Bostonians as "bearded men, in sad-colored garments and gray, steeple-crowned hats" (47), those who condemn Hester Prynne as wicked display a decidedly eclectic sense of identity. Their clothing is austere, except for the frilly lace and embroidered accessories that the town elites commission from none other than Prynne, whose extravagant needlework in her scarlet letter becomes a kind of walking advertisement. Similarly, the rejection of formal ceremonies in religious life gives way to the need for English-style pomp on election days and other great occasions of state. Governor Bellingham himself lives in a well-lit house, with walls sparkling with glass-coated stucco and a lush garden that even the great ministers of the town examine with knowing admiration. Chillingworth, for his outward show of piety, seems to have little sympathy for the Puritan "errand in the wilderness," and rather more with the old alchemical practices of European universities. Even the pious Dimmesdale, with his ruthless regimen of self-mortification through fasts, vigils, and even flagellation, seems not so much Puritan as weirdly Anglo-Catholic, and his education at the conservatively Anglican Oxford rather than the more Puritan-friendly Cambridge is a curious detail of his background.

By contrast, Hester Prynne embraces not only liberty of conscience and of thought but also affirmation of sexual love's consecrating power, the importance of inner as well as outer piety, and of respect for the social order that she nonetheless critiques— all classic Puritan qualities. While Hawthorne often refers to her simply as Hester, laying emphasis on her given name, he has chosen a Puritan's Puritan for her namesake. William Prynne was a Puritan lawyer whose extreme Calvinist views and penchant for controversy landed him in frequent legal trouble before the English Civil War. Besides fines and imprisonment, he was condemned to have both his ears cut off and, eventually, to have the letters *S. L.* branded on both his cheeks for "seditious libel." While in prison following his branding, Prynne wrote poems interpreting his letters as *stigmata laudi,* translated either as *marks of praise* or *marks of Laud,* the Archbishop of Canterbury who led many prosecutions against Prynne (see Kirby). Hawthorne would surely have known William Prynne's history, and using such a name for his independent heroine, marked by a frequently reinterpreted letter by the authorities of her day, reconfigures her outsider role as a lonely stance for truth in the face of power.

And yet, perhaps like her Puritan namesake, the question remains for Hester Prynne: why does she stay to take so much punishment? And furthermore, why does she return after her departure for Europe at the end of the book? For all of Hester Prynne's independence of thought and her ability to make a life for herself, even to plan her own escape with Pearl and Dimmesdale on a ship where she has personal contacts, she can't seem to find her way to, as Huck Finn would say, "light out for the territory." Only in the city of Boston does her punishment hold; presumably, she could throw the scarlet letter into the nearest body of water on her way out of town. As Hawthorne's narrator points out, it "may seem marvellous" that she should not leave and "hide her character and identity under a new exterior, as completely as if emerging into another state of being" (79), and yet she stays.

The first possible explanation exemplifies Hawthorne's penchant for using confusing behavior to illustrate moral truths: "[T]here is a fatality, a feeling so irresistible and inevitable that it has the force of doom, which almost compels human beings to linger around and haunt, ghost-like, the spot where some great and marked event has given the color to their lifetime; and still the more irresistibly, the darker the tinge that saddens it" (79-80). This sounds like a second explanation of the mystery that Hawthorne sought to address in "The Custom-House": why did he return to Salem? "This old town of Salem," he says, "possesses, or did possess, a hold on my affections, the force of which I have never realized during my seasons of actual residence here. Indeed, so far as its physical aspect is concerned...

it would be quite as reasonable to form a sentimental attachment to a disarranged checkerboard. And yet, though invariably happiest elsewhere, there is within me a feeling for old Salem, which, in lack of a better phrase, I must be content to call affection" (8). Fatality may be that better phrase, but easier to attach to Hester Prynne's experience than to Hawthorne's; he uses indirection and deflection throughout "The Custom-House" to keep the reader from penetrating too deeply into his secrets. As he says, "It is scarcely decorous...to speak all, even where we speak impersonally...[A]n author, methinks, may be autobiographical, without violating either the reader's rights or his own" (4).This issue of rights, particularly the right to be left alone, does not seem to apply to Prynne, as the narrator specifies that it is "[h]er sin, her ignominy," which are "the roots which she had struck into the soil" (80). Yet reading back into "The Custom-House," this language connects directly with Hawthorne's "affection," which he says is "probably assignable to the deep and aged roots which my family has struck into the soil" (8). His following account of family history initially implies that those roots were those of settlement as new immigrants, but his description of his "first ancestor" as a "steeple-crowned" Puritan who proved to be a "bitter prosecutor" who ordered the deaths of Quakers, and whose son oversaw "the martyrdom of the witches" in the infamous Salem Witch Trials change the tenor of the root-soil metaphor to something much closer to the admission of family sin along the lines of Hester Prynne's personal sin. She thus becomes a stand-in for the author who finds himself unwillingly bound to a place he would rather not remember, much less inhabit.

Another possibility presents itself, however. In characteristic qualifications and questionings, the narrator suggests: "It might be, too,—doubtless it was so, although she hid the secret from herself... that another feeling kept her within the scene...There dwelt, there trode the feet of one with whom she deemed herself connected in a union that, unrecognized on earth, would bring them together before the bar of final judgment"—in other words, she stays for Dimmesdale (80). Hester Prynne, refusing to believe this reason directly, evolves it into "half a truth, half a self-delusion," that she must work out her penance (a very Catholic, and hence un-Puritan notion) in the place of her sin (80). The tie to Dimmesdale does seem more believable than other explanations as the narrative unfolds: when Prynne finally makes plans to leave, it is in the company of Dimmesdale, and she cancels her plans in the wake of his death, leaving only after receiving an inheritance from Chillingworth following his death some months after.

Then, in the space of a page, "the wearer of the scarlet letter disappeared, and Pearl along with her," enough time passes that the "story of the scarlet letter grew into a legend," and then "Hester Prynne had returned, and taken up her long-forsaken shame" (261-62). This return has long frustrated critics, as has the argument Matthiessen and other influential readers of Hawthorne have made that Hester Prynne's great moral accomplishment is to convert her passion into patience. The narrator offers an explanation, stripped of the earlier qualifications for her remaining: "[T]here was a more real life for Hester Prynne here, in New England, than in that unknown region where Pearl had found a home. Here had been her sin; here, her sorrow; and here was yet to be her penitence" (262-63). This much barer reason is precisely what the narrator had earlier attributed to Hester as "half truth and half self-delusion," but that does not seem to matter now. Instead, the narrator focuses on the new, saintly aura around the scarlet letter, which "ceased to be a stigma," and on Prynne's new role as a source of "counsel" and of a prophecy that, "in Heaven's own time, a new truth would be revealed, in order to establish the whole relation between men and women on a surer ground of mutual happiness" (263). She has also come back to die, as it turns out, and the ambiguity of her burial gives one last twist to the symbol of the scarlet letter: though buried near Dimmesdale, Prynne's grave is clearly separate, and yet the two share a headstone with the scarlet letter used for an armorial crest in imitation of those of Boston's first families, which becomes a "motto and brief description" of the entire story. The letter glows "gloomier than the shadow" against a black background, ending with a tone of sorrow, but also of the uncanny, as if the letter had a luminous power of its own, just as people had whispered the original letter had as Hester

Prynne first stepped out of the prison with it years before (264). Hester Prynne's return only deepens the mystery of the scarlet letter that has come to define, and redefine, her.

Another View of the Renaissance

As much as readers and critics (many of them male) have delighted in the depths of symbolic ambiguity that give Hester Prynne and her eponymous feature so much meaning, decades of feminist interpretations (most of them by women) have pointed out the ways that Hawthorne writes his heroine so as to silence and discount women, particularly the "damned mob of scribbling women" he infamously referred to in a letter to his publisher. The fact was that, though Hawthorne built such a strong reputation for himself that he has never been out of the canon of American literature since 1850, a number of female authors of his time outsold him by orders of magnitude. Susan Warner's coming-of-age story *The Wide, Wide World* was the hit of the year *The Scarlet Letter* was published, and two years later Harriet Beecher Stowe's *Uncle Tom's Cabin* would change everyone's definition of a bestseller. And Warner and Stowe were merely two of the best known of the writers of sentimental fiction, largely female and religious, who did more than any other group of authors—certainly more than the male authors Matthiessen used to define the American Renaissance—to make individual novels a mass reading experience for hundreds of thousands simultaneously. The whole country did not read *The Scarlet Letter* in the 1850s, which was in fact banned for inappropriate content (i.e., adultery) in some places. Jane Tompkins makes a compelling argument in *Sensational Designs* that Hawthorne was as indebted to the female language of sentiment for the success of his novel as he was to the circle of male publishers and critics who bolstered his reputation. This section offers insights from scholarship since Tompkins that has cast Hester Prynne, Pearl, and Hawthorne into new light as the American Renaissance as a democratic movement has recently been redefined in light of the achievements of women and minority writers overlooked in earlier studies.

Wendy Martin has argued that, like Eve in *Paradise Lost*, "heroines of American fiction are fallen women" (qtd. in Barlowe 14). Tellingly, this is much more the case with male authors of the American Renaissance than with female authors. Ellen Montgomery carefully preserves her virtue and her self-respect as she navigates the perils of growing up in *The Wide, Wide World*; even the figure of Cassy in *Uncle Tom's Cabin*, who has been forced into a life of sin by her lustful owner, Simon Legree, stands not as a moral warning but a sign of how deeply depraved the system of slavery was—and she is the exception in a novel in which virtuous white women act to protect virtuous black women, some of whom have run away or hidden themselves to avoid sexual violation. Martin's critique holds, rather, for women such as the incestuous Isabel Banford in Herman Melville's *Pierre* or the mysterious Alice Pyncheon in Hawthorne's *House of the Seven Gables*. Plenty of male characters also define themselves by their transgressions, from Rip Van Winkle to Huck Finn, but they are not marked as "fallen" by their actions, but rather as interesting or sympathetic.

Hawthorne seems determined to move Hester Prynne beyond "fallen woman" status by continually revising the meaning of her badge of shame, the scarlet letter. Her thought life, her struggles with her daughter and with the men in her world, certainly help make her interesting. But she is only interesting to readers (including Hawthorne) to begin with because of her sin, and one of the ways it becomes impossible for her to overcome that fact is simply because the complex symbolism of the scarlet letter, as well as the plot it drives, is predicated on everyone staring at Hester Prynne's chest. From the first scene on the theatrical platform of the scaffold, Prynne's bosom is put on public display. She initially tries to defend herself from the unwanted gaze of the crowd by a move not to hide her face but to hide the letter on her bodice by covering it with Pearl, who is continually made to double the letter throughout the novel, both by Prynne and by Hawthorne. The punishment of the letter is the devising of the ruling, male authorities, and the women of Boston protest that the punishment does not harm her body sufficiently—branding, beating, and even execution are suggested in the crowd as they await "Madame Hester" to "show [her] scarlet letter in the market-place" (54). When she appears, the initial reaction is admiration for her needlework, quickly followed by indignation at her extravagant display as a "brazen hussy" (54). The shaming starts with the women, but continues everywhere; Chillingworth, whose arranged marriage to young Hester may border on what we now call statutory rape, reaches out twice to touch the letter on her chest, despite his refusal to publicly acknowledge their marriage (see Haviland).

Another kind of unwanted attention occurs at Governor Bellingham's house, where Pearl's gaze into the "polished mirror" of the governor's breastplate attracts her mother's attention: "Hester looked...and she saw that, owing to the peculiar effect of this convex mirror, the scarlet letter was represented in exaggerated and gigantic proportions, so as to be greatly the most prominent feature of her appearance. In truth, she seemed absolutely hidden behind it" (106). This optical illusion, comically exaggerating the letter and thus Prynne's bosom, makes the rest of her disappear; the distorting mirror thus captures what the governor and indeed the rest of the town see when they look at Hester: a pair of breasts with a mark of sexual shame upon them. Her aim in seeking the governor is to persuade the government not to take away custody of Pearl, which has been rumored as planned by those fearing a fallen woman could not properly raise a Christian child. It falls to Dimmesdale, at Prynne's urging, to convince the authorities that Pearl would be best kept with her mother; Prynne has no standing to make such an explanation herself, as her letter on her sexualized body renders her silent before the law.

Jamie Barlowe has argued that a key part of the legacy of *The Scarlet Letter* has been a cultural practice of what she calls "Hester-Prynne-ism," using the fallen woman as a moral cautionary tale and thereby ignoring and denigrating the truth of her own moral experience. Again, the combining of alphabetic message and sexualized body gives this practice power in Hawthorne's book. When Hester enters a church service, "trusting to share the Sabbath smile of the Universal Father, it was often her mishap to find herself the text of the discourse" (85). She is merely something for the leaders to interpret, to imbue with the meaning they wish her to have. Both Chillingworth and Dimmesdale accuse Hester Prynne of sinning against them, and thus driving them to their admittedly greater sins of revenge and hypocrisy, and she refuses to contest their condemnation of her. And yet, given the opportunity, she recasts the meaning of her sexual sin: "What we did had a consecration of its own. We felt it so! We said so to each other" (195). Dimmesdale agrees, but only in private. Just as he repeatedly refuses to confess his shared guilt publicly, he also refuses to admit the sacred bond he shares with his lover.

Pearl understands this refusal, and refuses Dimmesdale as a result, running away from him and washing off the unwelcome kiss he plants on her forehead. She serves here not only as a living version of the scarlet letter but also as something like Hester Prynne's "anger translator," giving voice to the emotions that form part of her mother's bond with her father but that Prynne herself finds impossible to express. Pearl seldom exhibits any social filters, any superego: rather, she shows the powerful emotions of her home life, reflecting herself as well as her mother, so forcefully that Dimmesdale recoils from one of her outbursts, shouting petulantly to Prynne: "Pacify her, if thou lovest me!" (210). Pearl is indeed quite difficult for adults to stand, but particularly for men; she mystifies governors and terrifies her father, entertaining rough sailors who nevertheless perceive that she is well beyond their control or comprehension, while a visiting Indian meeting her on the streets of Boston "grew conscious of a nature wilder than his own" (244).

Male critics have had even more trouble with Pearl over the years. Even as Matthiessen ultimately argues that Pearl is "based on exact psychological notation" (279), he begins his discussion of Pearl by offering two possibilities of understanding her, both shocking: "She is worth dissecting as the purest type of Spenserian characterization, which starts with abstract qualities and hunts for their proper embodiment; worth murdering, most modern readers of fiction would hold, since the tedious reiteration of what she stands for betrays Hawthorne at his most barren" (278). If Pearl is not to be simply flattened into an allegorical figure, Matthiessen says, she should be removed as a character—the violence of the verb "murder" indicates more than aesthetic uselessness, however. There is often a visceral reaction against Pearl in male critics' accounts of *The Scarlet Letter*, and wrapped up in this is not only something of a wider fear of (uncontrolled) children but also a repugnance toward the feminine; not long after Matthiessen attacks Pearl and then defends her as a shrewd psychological portrait, he makes a broader comment on Hawthorne's approach to morality: "His usual firm moral perception is vitiated very rarely by such overtones of the era of *Godey's Lady's Book* and the genteel female" (280). Matthiessen praises Hawthorne for not giving in to the female-style moralizing epitomized by the periodical and novel writers that Hawthorne famously condemned. Just before *American Renaissance* was published, another early champion of American literary studies, Fred Lewis Pattee, published *The Feminine Fifties*, in which he argued that 1850s American literature was plagued by sentimentalism and overwhelmed by pandering to female middle class sensibilities; according to Pattee, Melville was both artistically great and economically defeated by rejecting femininity altogether, while Hawthorne tainted himself with female sentimentalism. If male critics tend to see Hester Prynne as "morally deficient," their responses to Pearl reveal even deeper rejections of female presence in American literature.

Decades of scholarship, largely written by women, has pushed against this Hester-Prynne-ism, but as Barlowe argues, one of the greatest examples of Hester-Prynne-ism is the fact that male critics of *The Scarlet Letter* have nearly always ignored female scholarship on the novel. As Barlowe says, each mainstream interpretation "becomes another attempt to control Hester Prynne" (48). Thus one of the most important meanings of *The Scarlet Letter* as a canonical text of the American Renaissance today is the ways in which it speaks to the experiences of women and their struggle against the masculine gaze of society. Among women scholars the meaning of Hester Prynne herself has varied widely: some condemn her internalization of Boston's view of her as a fallen woman, others celebrate her liberation from sexual and familial limits. She is, after all, the strongest and most sympathetic single mother in all of American literature. And Pearl might be seen as more liberated still. The citizens of Boston feel an urgent need to find a father for Pearl, most explicitly in the first scaffold scene and in the custody battle. It is worth noting, however, that Pearl herself does not feel the need for a father. She blithely repeats Mistress Hibbins's declaration that she is the daughter of "the Prince of the Air" (245) as a way of threatening those that would harass her; she even denies God's fathering of her, as she "announce[s]" during Reverend Wilson's examination of her catechesis "that she had not been made at all, but had been plucked by her mother off the bush of wild roses, that grew by the prison-door" (112).

If previous generations have had difficulty in tolerating the weird power of Pearl, a new generation of readers may be ready to reconsider the psychological accuracy Matthiessen perceived in Hawthorne's characterization. And Hester Prynne herself, who begins the story as a young woman, suffering not only under public condemnation but also under the pain of a loveless, arranged marriage at a young age, has new things to tell us in a time when gender norms and the experiences of women have become much more open questions than they were in either 1850 or 1940. *The Scarlet Letter* continues to make its power felt among readers, but what that power amounts to is for each rising generation to determine for itself.

Works Cited

Barlowe, Jamie. *The Scarlet Mob of Scribblers: Rereading Hester Prynne.* Southern Illinois UP, 2000.

Chase, Richard. *The American Novel and Its Tradition.* Doubleday Anchor, 1957.

Haviland, Beverly. "What It Betokened: Waiting for Hester in *The Scarlet Letter.*" *Common Knowledge*, vol. 21, no.3, Sept. 2015, pp. 420-36.

Hawthorne, Nathaniel. *The Scarlet Letter.* Edited by William Charvat et al. Centenary Edition, Vol. 1. Ohio State UP, 1962.

Kirby, Ethyn Williams. *William Prynne: A Study in Puritanism.* Harvard UP, 1931.

Matthiessen, F. O. *American Renaissance: Art and Expression in the Age of Emerson and Whitman*. Oxford UP, 1941.

Pattee, Fred Lewis. *The Feminine Fifties*. Appleton, 1940.

Tompkins, Jane. *Sensational Designs: The Cultural Work of American Fiction 1790-1860*. Oxford UP, 1985.

Popular Fiction and *The Scarlet Letter*

Nancy F. Sweet

According to his son, Julian, Nathaniel Hawthorne first developed a taste for narrative by listening to the adventure tales of his own father, a sea captain who died when Nathaniel was just four years old:

> When his tall, grave father came home, he would take little Nathaniel between his knees, and tell him tales of the sea and of foreign countries; how, once, he helped an English merchant captain fight off a French sloop of war in the south Atlantic; how palms and orange trees and mahogany grew in the West Indies like elm and spruce in New England; how, in the remoter Indies, were strange temples and dark-skinned, turbaned myriads of people speaking outlandish tongues. (16)

With their faraway settings, wartime exploits, and exotic characters, the chronicles of Captain Hathorne (who spelled his name without the *w* that Nathaniel would later add) whetted his child's appetite for the popular romance fiction that he would eagerly devour as a young man. Although Julian Hawthorne didn't credit his grandfather with much storytelling skill—he was too cold and puritanical to be an effective narrator, according to his grandson—nevertheless it was the romance mode of exotic adventure and faraway fantasy that was the first literary influence of the author of *The Scarlet Letter*.

As David S. Reynolds argues in *Beneath the American Renaissance*, the highly literary works of nearly all the authors we today think of as the major figures of nineteenth-century American literature—Hawthorne, Poe, Dickinson, Melville, Thoreau, Whitman, and Emerson—incorporated and reworked elements of popular fiction in their novels and poetry. A prolific reader from an early age, Hawthorne wrote fiction reflective of diverse literary sources. The influence on his writings of English classics such as Edmund Spenser's *The Faerie Queen*, (1590), John Milton's

Paradise Lost (1667), and John Bunyan's *Pilgrim's Progress* (1678), has been well documented by literary scholars. But Hawthorne's reading frequently ranged beyond the canon of great English works to what he called "good-for-nothing books" (Julian Hawthorne 64), the mass-marketed tales of pirates, cannibalism, Indian captivity, monastic prisons, high crime, and thrilling adventure that likely reminded him of his father's fireside stories. Gothic works in English, French, and even a little German rounded out Hawthorne's reading, along with annals of New England Puritan history, many of which also read like gothic fantasies, with their lurid tales of murder, Indian warfare, and witchcraft. If *The Scarlet Letter* has antecedents in the great Christian allegories of sin and redemption written by Bunyan, Spenser, and Milton, so too does it emerge from Hawthorne's knowledge of a variety of forms of popular antebellum literature, particularly the seduction novel, the Indian captivity narrative, and convent escape fiction. Indeed, *The Scarlet Letter* embeds these popular fiction types at its very foundations, but all toward the surprising end of inverting their structure and logic.

Consider the opening scenes of *The Scarlet Letter*, for instance, which take up where the plots of seduction stories and Indian captivity narratives typically leave off. An unwed mother with a three-month-old baby in her arms, Hester Prynne first appears in Hawthorne's novel as a version of the disgraced, "fallen woman" who inhabited such American best sellers as Susanna Rowson's *Charlotte Temple: A Tale of Truth* (1791) or Hannah Foster's *The Coquette; or the History of Eliza Wharton* (1797). Among the very first novels published in America, these two works pioneered a new genre form, the American seduction narrative, and together they would assert their influence over fiction writers for decades to come. They share a common plot, whereby an unsophisticated and emotionally needy young woman succumbs to the sexual machinations of an older, predatory male. She soon becomes pregnant and dies in childbirth, a plotline adapted from English seduction novels such as Samuel Richardson's *Clarissa* (1748) and *Pamela: Or Virtue Rewarded* (1740), which records show Hawthorne checked out multiple times from the Salem Athenaeum in the 1820s and 30s. The novels of

Rowson and Foster build gradually to the climactic consummation of the illicit sexual relationship, and then close quickly, their fallen heroines erased from their final pages as their stories culminate in shame and death. In an era when a woman's sexual chastity was perceived as mystically connected to her moral worth as a human being, such novels served as cautionary tales for young women who, in the parlance of the day, could be "ruined"—morally, spiritually, and physically—by the sexual pressures of devious males who promise attention, love, and security to impressionable young women.

American novels published in the wake of these eighteenth-century prototypes often embed seduction narratives within their larger plotlines. In Charles Brockden Brown's *Ormond; Or the Secret Witness*, and Catharine Maria Sedgwick's *Hope Leslie*, for instance, secondary female characters live out the prototypical seduction story, but their stories serve to contrast with those of the novels' heroine-protagonists, whose quick wit and bold independence enable them to prevail over the seducer-males whose predations lead to the deaths of less self-possessed women. Set shortly after the founding of Puritan Boston, Sedgwick's novel features the eponymous Hope Leslie. A young, dark-haired woman with strength of mind and a defiant streak displeasing to the colony's Puritan leaders, she is also a forerunner of Hester Prynne. Hope Leslie befriends but also pities a gullible and pliant young woman named Rosa, who is ensnared in an illicit sexual relationship with the novel's villain and who ultimately commits suicide in her hopeless shame. In drawing such a contrast between Hope and Rosa, Sedgwick establishes Hope's keen intelligence and feisty independence as rightful features of American femininity, against the passive, quiet submissiveness expected of women in a Calvinist culture. Similarly, Constantia Dudley, the heroine of Charles Brockden Brown's *Ormond*, is a model of American virtues: industrious, resourceful, and smart, she also contrasts with a weak-minded counterpart, Helena Cleves, who becomes easy prey for the novel's villainous seducer, Ormond. For both authors, dependency is envisioned as inimical to feminine virtue and well-being. The seduction stories that Brown and Sedgwick embed in their plots thus enable them to advance a new vision of American femininity, built upon autonomy and self-reliance.

When Nathaniel Hawthorne commences *The Scarlet Letter* with Hester's exposure as a fallen woman, he thus silently invokes a plotline that nineteenth-century readers knew well: that of the ingénue beguiled by a conniving male who has lured her into an unwise sexual relationship that should be her final downfall. But Hawthorne's novel inverts the seduction-novel formula in both its form and its underlying gender presumptions. In a contrast to seduction-novel plots, which dwell on the lengthy process of seduction, the exact events that lead up to Hester's sexual congress with Arthur Dimmesdale precede the action of the novel and are never clearly delineated. Did the minister pursue Hester doggedly, over the course of months, as Major Sanford does Eliza Wharton in *The Coquette*, exploiting her self-doubts and offering an emotional support she finds nowhere else? Did he deceive her with false promises of security o rtake advantage of her financial vulnerability with assurances to be her provider, as does Ormond with Helena Cleves in Charles Brockden Brown's novel? Since *The Scarlet Letter* never shows us how the relationship came to pass, the various explanatory plotlines of seduction narratives are all subtly in play; nineteenth-century readers knew how the story goes and that it inevitably signals the moral, emotional, and intellectual weakness of the seduced victim. But ultimately, Hawthorne upends these presumptions as Hester emerges as a character of strength, integrity, and intelligence, whose worth is not contained by her sexual history.

Whereas seduction novels linger over the process of the fallen woman's succumbing to temptation, Hawthorne's novel is entirely engaged with the aftermath of the illicit sexual relationship, which, for Hester, is not exile and death as it is for seduction-novel heroines, but independence and new life. When the ordeal of her public exposure on the town scaffold is finished, Hester turns quietly to work; her skillful needlecraft soon becomes, however ironically, "the fashion" (1: 82) and earns her not only a subsistence for herself and her thriving daughter, but enough disposable income to dispense as charity in her community. Hester's financial independence corresponds with her growing autonomy of thought: "she assumed a freedom of speculation," Hawthorne writes, as she measures the "whole system of ancient prejudice"—patriarchy, classism—that determines not only her own suffering but that of women more generally (1: 164). Far from being morally ruined, a "dishonest woman," as unchaste women were termed in popular fiction, Hester in her post-seduction life manifests a "genuine regard for virtue" (1: 160). She also gains a powerful capacity for empathy; her nature "showed itself warm and rich; a well-spring of human tenderness, unfailing to every real demand, and inexhaustible by the largest" (1: 161). Far from losing all goodness or integrity, Hester in her supposed fallenness is the sole character in the novel who appears to take seriously the call to charity, fellowship, and selflessness issued to the Massachusetts Bay Colony by John Winthrop in his famous founding sermon, "A Model of Christian Charity."

Although Hester in her sexual unchastity shares a sisterhood with the seduced victims of *Charlotte Temple* or *The Coquette*, in character she has far more in common with the strong-minded personalities of Constantia and Hope Leslie, the resourceful, self-confident heroines who easily see through the machinations of predatory males. A woman of endurance and patience, Hester does not fade away to an obscure death, but rather establishes her financial security, provides for her child, and, of course, defies the patriarchal Puritan authorities who would impose on her a sense of moral worthlessness in the wake of her sexual ruination. As Nina Baym has argued, *The Scarlet Letter* is truly "an anti-seduction novel," (121) one that imagines an intelligent, independent woman not as immune to sexual exploitation but that also refuses to consign its "fallen" protagonist to obscurity, worthlessness, and death. Hawthorne has thus subverted not only the structure of the seduction narrative in *The Scarlet Letter* but also transfigured its underlying gender ideologies by dismantling the twin assumptions that only weak, naïve women are vulnerable to sexual exploitation, and that a woman's worth can be measured by her chastity.

If the prototypical seduction narrative sits at the headwaters of *The Scarlet Letter* only to be inverted as the novel unfolds, so does another American sensation genre: the Indian captivity narrative. When Roger Chillingworth makes his first appearance in Chapter 3 of the novel, he is newly delivered to the English settlement by Indian captors who now seek a ransom for his return. Having sent his wife, Hester, across the Atlantic before him, Roger has followed after her in the intervening two years, only somehow to fall into the hands of Native Americans. Just as the seduction events have happened offstage, so do Roger's capture and sojourn in the wilderness, but Hawthorne counts on his readers' knowledge of the popular genre in order to fill in the missing story. *The Scarlet Letter* commences at the culminating point of the traditional Indian captivity narratives: at the moment of the captive's restoration to civilization. But in establishing the intertexual link between *The Scarlet Letter* and the Indian captivity genre, Hawthorne also undermines the colonialist ideologies at the heart of the genre.

As tales of contact between unlike cultures, captivity narratives often served, as Gordon M. Sayre explains, to "rally 'us' around the figure of the innocent captive held in bondage by 'them,' . . . [the] mysterious villains in our midst" (1). Literary scholars often credit the Indian captivity narrative with being the first truly American genre to emerge in the new world (Kolodny 6), born of white anxieties over coexistence with indigenous people so apparently unlike themselves. Mary Rowlandson, whom Sayre credits with the creation of the genre (9), published the most famous of these narratives in 1682, under the title *A True History of the Captivity and Restoration of Mrs. Mary Rowlandson, A Minister's Wife in New England.* Her narrative opens with what she depicts as the unmotivated, random destruction of her frontier Puritan village by Wampanoag Indians, and then recounts her subsequent eleven-week captivity with the Indians, or, as she calls them, "murderous wretches" (137), "hellhounds" (139), and "black creatures in the night" (140). Forcibly marched 150 miles through the winter wilderness, Rowlandson concludes her story with her return to Boston, where she is redeemed for twenty pounds and restored to "the benevolence of Christian friends" (175). Rowlandson's narrative and those that follow its model emphasize Calvinist values of endurance and faith in time of trial; as her editor (likely the Puritan minister Increase Mather) put it, Rowlandson's story "is a narrative of the wonderfully awful, wise, holy, powerful and gracious providence of God" (134). But it is also a story that represents Indians as subhuman, even demonic, and that served the larger purpose of justifying English appropriation of native lands, and the extermination of a people and culture it cast as thoroughly violent and debased. In fact, the conflict called King Philip's War, which gave rise to the attack on Rowlandson's village, would ultimately leave several New England tribes, including the Wampanoag and Narragansett, utterly decimated.

Hawthorne was particularly intrigued by another captivity narrative, that of Hannah Dustan, taken hostage by Abenaki Indians in 1697. As told by Increase Mather's son, Cotton, whose histories of New England life Hawthorne studied in depth, Dustan was captured during a raid on her village, together with a nurse and ten other white settlers, some of whom were subsequently murdered. As Cotton Mather relates the story, Dustan heroically seized an opportunity to kill her captors in their sleep, slicing their scalps from their heads, before returning to an English settlement, where the General Assembly rewarded her with fifty pounds for the set of scalps. Hawthorne doesn't share in Mather's celebration of the Puritan woman's retaliatory violence against her captors, however. Indeed, in a sketch he published in the *American Magazine of Useful and Entertaining Knowledge* in 1836, he lambastes Dustan as an "awful woman" and a "bloody old hag" (397), and he extends admiration and sympathy for the Indians whom she killed:

> These Indians, like most with whom the French had held intercourse, were Catholics; and Cotton Mather affirms, on Mrs. Duston's authority, that they prayed at morning, noon, and night, nor ever partook of food without a prayer; nor suffered their children to sleep, till they had prayed to the Christian's God. Mather, like an old hard-hearted, pedantic bigot, as he was, seems trebly to exalt in the destruction of these poor wretches, on account of their Popish superstitions. Yet what can be more touching than to think of these wild Indians, in their loneliness and their wanderings, wherever they went among the dark, mysterious Woods, still keeping up domestic

worship, with all the regularity of a household at its peaceful fireside. (396)

In his esteem for the Indians' Christian devotion and their domestic closeness with nature, Hawthorne rejects the premise at the heart of Mather's version of the tale, that the Indian "Idolaters" deserve the vengeance that a godly Dustan wreaks (184). Indian captivity narratives such as Dustan's and Rowlandson's are typically driven by a colonialist belief in the innate superiority of white Protestants over the supposedly uncivilized, dark-skinned inhabitants of "the dark, mysterious Woods." Their dehumanizing representations of merciless and violent Indians perpetuate a colonialist ideology that enabled white Protestants to view as natural and right their takeover of North American lands and their elimination of native tribes. Just as Hawthorne rejects these notions in his correction to Cotton Mather's lionizing of the vengeful Hannah Dustan, so does he reject the racial and cultural prejudices stoked by the captivity narrative genre even as he weaves its generic form into the plot of *The Scarlet Letter*.

Although both men and women were taken captive by Indians in colonial America, the captivity genre disproportionately foregrounded women's experience, thereby magnifying the contrast between vulnerable, white captives, and brutal Indian captors. But Hawthorne's novel features a male captive, who, in his sojourn with the native peoples, appears not to have suffered, but to have benefited from his cross-cultural interactions. Indeed, when we first see Roger Chillingworth emerging out of the woods with his supposed captor, he sports a "heterogeneous garb," "a strange disarray of civilized and savage costume" (1: 60), dress indicative of his adoption of Native American customs. He stands "by the Indian's side, and evidently sustaining a companionship with him" (1: 60), a description that sounds less like the coercible relationship of captor and captive than of compatriots.

That Roger's "captivity" has been experienced as a relationship of contact and exchange is also signaled by the enrichment of his medical skills through the adoption of Indian practice. When he concocts a calming draught for baby Pearl, for instance, he tells Hester, "I have learned many new secrets in the wilderness, and here is one of them,—a recipe that an Indian taught me, in requital of some lessons of my own, that were as old as Paracelsus" (1: 72). Roger's reference to Paracelsus hints that his own European medicine might owe something to alchemy and black magic, which whites often associated with Native American healing techniques. Roger now applies a more earthly knowledge of "the properties of native herbs and roots" in ministering to his fellow English settlers, and it is to the blending of these European and Indian modes of healing that he attributes the honing of his skills. Roger tells Hester, "My old studies in alchemy. . . and my sojourn, for above a year past, among a people well versed in the kindly properties of simples, have made a better physician of me than many that claim the medical degree" (1: 71). His life with the Indians has thus provided Roger with practical and useful expertise from which the entire community now benefits.

With its many references to the satanic "Black Man" who haunts the wilderness tempting wayward white Christians to sin, *The Scarlet Letter* might appear to subtly indict the New England Indians as the "hell-hounds" that Rowlandson imagined them to be. As Mary Beth Norton remarks,

> The association among Indians, black men, and the devil would have been unremarkable to anyone in the Salem Village meetinghouse. English settlers everywhere on the continent had long regarded North America's indigenous residents as devil worshippers and had viewed their shamans as witches. Puritan New Englanders, believing themselves a people chosen by God to bring his word to a previously heathen land, were particularly inclined to see themselves as antagonists of the "devilish" Indians. (59)

But while Hawthorne's Puritan characters might associate Indians with Satan, the novel never bears out their prejudice, and indeed suggests that the "Black Man" tempting the various characters is none other than the hypocrisy the Puritans find within themselves. As a people "well versed in the kindly properties of simples," the

Indians, as Hawthorne represents them, are a rational, resourceful people, skilled in the very human art of healing, and who contrast with the Puritans, whose cemetery and prison-building speak to their deficiencies in these same arts.

The Native Americans of *The Scarlet Letter* are never identified by tribal affiliation, nor individuated, and they lurk entirely on the margins of the novel's action. One attends Roger Chillingworth in observing Hester's exposure on the scaffold at the beginning at the novel. Again at the novel's conclusion, "a party of Indians" is on hand (1: 232), standing apart from the crowd, to witness Arthur Dimmesdale's procession into church and his quasi-revelation of his relationship to Hester and Pearl on the scaffold. Oblique references to Indian presence are sprinkled throughout the text. Although the Indian characters are thus never fully developed, nevertheless, as spectators who reside at the edges of the Puritan world, the Native Americans are situated much like Hawthorne's narrator, or even Hawthorne himself—a rational, detached observer who does not share in Puritan values or beliefs, but who is caught up in the Puritan story. The novel thus evokes a narrative form that by its very nature casts Indians as depraved and barbarous, standing in the way of God's work, and deserving of white vengeance, but ultimately, the novel bears out none of the racial or cultural prejudices woven into the generic form.

Hawthorne builds *The Scarlet Letter* upon elements of yet another type of popular "good-for-nothing book," the convent escape narrative. Published tales of runaway nuns fleeing the spiritual seduction that Roman Catholicism often represented in nineteenth-century Protestant discourse became a literary craze in the antebellum years. With titles such as *The Rescued Nun; Or, a Convent and its Wrongs, Danger in the Dark: A Tale of Intrigue and Priestcraft,* and *The Veil Lifted; or The Romance and Reality of Convent Life,* convent escape narratives sold into the hundreds of thousands of copies between 1833 and 1860, and functioned as a mass marketing of anti-Catholic sentiment in an era of sweeping socioreligious change. The popularity of these narratives grew in tandem with escalating Protestant fears over the dramatic midcentury growth of the Roman

Catholic Church in the United States. With rising immigration from predominantly Catholic countries, the Roman Catholic Church was fast becoming a dominant force in US society while its churches, schools, and convents became an increasingly visible presence in cities from Boston to Cincinnati. Convent escape narratives seek to reveal the supposedly sinister inner workings of Catholicism for unsuspecting and vulnerable Protestants. Isaac Kelso, the author of *Danger in the Dark*, writes, for instance, that his goal is to

> unvail [sic] the dark designs, insidious movements, and hidden policy, of the Papal Hierarchy, and at the same time bring to light the duplicity, craft, and trickery practiced in our midst by the order of Jesuits—a brotherhood of pious assassins, the vilest and most despicable of our race; who in every land, as well as our own, are the sworn enemies of civil and religious liberty. (v)

As David S. Reynolds explains, "The story of early anti-Catholic fiction is one of increasing xenophobic outrage on part of nativists who felt that the growth of Roman Catholicism in America must be stopped at any cost" (*Faith in Fiction* 180). With their prodigious sales, the narratives served as Protestant propaganda, and also became a tidy source of profit for authors and publishers alike.

The best known convent escape narrative, *The Awful Disclosures of the Hotel Dieu Nunnery*, is also the most lurid. A book-length tale ghostwritten by male Protestants in 1836 for Maria Monk, a woman who claimed to have fled a Canadian house of horrors fronting as a Catholic convent, the work was marketed as a factual exposé of the purported evils of monasticism—no less than infanticide, rape, and murder. The Monk text, by some estimates, outsold all other works in the antebellum United States but *Uncle Tom's Cabin* and the Bible, and its popularity attests to readers' fascination with the hidden interiors of the Church's seemingly medieval institutions and power structures. Although immediately debunked, the claims of the Monk text contributed to a growing anti-Catholic bigotry in the United States that would climax with the coming to power of the Know-Nothing party, which gained control of several state

---

legislatures and won seventy-five seats in the US Congress in 1854, largely on a platform of anti-Catholic intolerance (Massa 28).

The Scarlet Letter is set in seventeenth-century New England, where there was virtually no Roman Catholic presence, but the novel abounds with references to Roman Catholicism and is informed by convent escape tropes. When Hester stands atop the scaffold at the outset of the novel, for instance, Hawthorne imagines an observer, a hypothetical "Papist among the crowd" (1: 56), who would see in the display of mother and child a likeness to the Madonna, "but only by contrast, of that sacred image of sinless motherhood" (1:56). Arthur Dimmesdale, wracked with guilt over his sexual improprieties, makes recourse to bloody self-scourging, a practice commonly featured in convent escape narratives, and which Hawthorne describes as "more in accordance with the old, corrupted faith of Rome, than with the better light of the church in which he had been born and bred" (1: 144). Mr. Wilson asks the brightly bedecked Pearl if she might be "one of those naughty elfs or fairies, whom we thought to have left behind us, with other relics of Papistry, in merry old England" (1: 110). Although, at first glance, these references appear consistent with the denigration of Catholicism that is innate to the convent escape genre, the novel again refuses to bear out the prejudices the underlying genre invokes. That Dimmesdale adopts the violent practice of self-flagellation, for instance, suggests that, despite his ostensible Calvinism, it is to the old rituals of Roman Catholicism that he turns for actual solace in his sins. His self-scourging is a tragic gesture that speaks as much to the inadequacy of his Protestantism as it does to Hawthorne's anti-Catholicism. Moreover, the imagined "Papist among the crowd" is another version of the Indians who lurk in the margins of the story, observing its action without participating in Puritan belief, much like the detached Hawthornian narrator himself.

While convent escape narratives typically feature women who renounce their vows after discovering Catholicism to be a corrupted faith, Hester undergoes a transformation that inverts that formula. The scarlet letter imposed on Hester by the Protestant leaders of her community comes to set Hester apart, nunlike, with "the effect of the cross on a nun's bosom. It imparted to the wearer a kind of sacredness, which enabled her to walk securely amid all the peril" (1: 163). After years of ministering to the needy and sick in the village, Hester seems a self-ordained "Sister of Mercy; or, we may rather say, the world's heavy hand had so ordained her . . . The letter was the symbol of her calling" (1: 161). Of course, the only calling ordinarily available to Protestant women was the vocation of wifedom and motherhood. That Hester has a calling beyond the confines of domesticity is indicative of the autonomy and agency she gains in her sisterlike role.

In most convent narratives, Catholic sisters are portrayed as captive in their cloisters and wasting their lives in meaningless hours of rote prayer and social isolation. As purported escaped novice Josephine Bunkley explains, the convent teaches that

> to be truly "*religious*," signifies . . . not to illustrate the principles of the Gospel in all those humble but sanctified employments that belong to the lot where God has placed us, but to fly from the scene of trial, and to abandon the relations of our providential position, and to waste, in a condition of passivity and mental vacuity, the precious moments of probation. (33-34)

So unhealthy is the sisters' "unremitting observance of the oppressive routine of useless forms" in Bunkley's convent that many succumb to sickness and early death (102). In his portrayal of Hester's living out a calling tending to the needs of the poor and the downtrodden, Hawthorne hits much closer to the reality of Catholic religious' lives in the antebellum United States, where the sisterhood most often entailed active work within communities, especially in teaching, nursing, and caregiving, rather than in the cloistered, contemplative life common to monasticism in medieval Europe. While convent narrative nuns languish in monastic prisons, Hester, as Sister of Mercy, acquires so much vitality that by the climactic forest scene, Arthur Dimmesdale cries out to her, "Think for me, Hester! Thou art strong. Resolve for me!" (1: 196), a plea that utterly transposes the usual gender roles both of convent escape narratives and of seduction novels.

The celibacy of avowed sisters is typically cast as unnatural and cruel in convent narratives. As one disappointed lover puts it in *Danger in the Dark* after his beloved enters a convent,

> She is lost! Alas! My fair one is lost!—lost to her friends, to society, and to herself; lost to the world and to me; lost to happiness, to usefulness; lost to a life of active benevolence, for which her generous heart and noble nature so eminently fitted her! Influenced by an intriguing Jesuit, she has forgotten the pledges of her love, and been led, blindfold, into the mazes of an absurd, stupefying and soul-withering theology! (58)

Lost to wifedom, the convent narrative nun is imagined as a cipher whose life no longer serves any purpose. But while Hawthorne suggests that the repression of Hester's sexuality has indeed come at an emotional cost, her life as a single woman confers on her a freedom generally unavailable to women of her community. Again, her experience mirrors that of actual nineteenth-century US sisters, who often found their vows empowering. As Carol K. Coburn and Martha Smith explain,

> The vow of chastity prohibited sexual thoughts or behavior, but it also provided a buffer against male sexual advances as well as heterosexual marriage, and allowed sisters access to isolated settings on the frontier and other male-dominated milieus with less fear of scandal or unwanted sexual attention. They used this vow . . . to gain moral superiority, public space, and agency over their bodies and activities. (83-84)

Similarly, Hester can come and go with impunity at any time of the day or night, as when she crosses the town marketplace after her midnight ministering to the dying John Winthrop and comes across Arthur Dimmesdale, performing an ineffectual penance alone on the scaffold. When Hawthorne attests that the scarlet letter had "the effect of a cross on nun's bosom," shielding Hester from "peril," the implication is that she, like Catholic nuns, enjoys the rare ability to exist in the world free of sexual harassment or fear of violation, one of the most powerful enforcers of patriarchal power. Whereas the convent escape genre reinforces Protestant stereotypes of nuns as living vacuous lives, devoted to meaningless superstitions and blind obedience to corrupt superiors, Hawthorne's self-ordained Sister of Mercy lives out Gospel values of charity and love, enjoys a unique autonomy and freedom, and is guided, seemingly uniquely in the novel, by her "genuine regard for virtue."

In each of these cases of Hawthorne's adoption of popular genre forms, he inverts the plot structure and the underlying social prejudices of the genre and, in so doing, calls out the false ideologies on which the genre is premised. The seduction narrative, for instance, reinforces a belief in the all-important nature of a woman's chastity, which, if lost even in coercive sexual contact, signals the concomitant loss of her virtue and worth. The Indian captivity narrative reifies belief in white racial superiority and seeks to justify the vanquishing and even the eradication of native peoples. The convent escape narrative represents Catholicism as an un-Christian mockery of true religion, its sisters living wasted, meaningless lives. *The Scarlet Letter* turns these social beliefs inside out, insisting on the dignity of the "fallen" Hester, no matter her sexual history, exploring cultural contact between Native Americans and the English as an enriching source of knowledge and possibility, and envisioning the Catholic sister's life as ennobling, vital to the well-being of her community, and perfectly consonant with Christian values. Hawthorne's novel thus shows the falsehoods woven into the very conventions of these popular narrative forms so well known to his readers.

If Hawthorne rejects the underlying social premises of these popular forms of fiction, then why embed them in his own novel? Why, indeed, build these popular generic forms, with their inbuilt social prejudices, into the very foundations of his own work? David S. Reynolds suggests that Hawthorne felt pressure to compete in the popular literary market-place (*American Renaissance* 249), but perhaps he also grappled with the problem of writing in ways that anticipate the ideas of Roland Barthes, who claims that the idea of "an author" is a delusion, since every text is, after all, a copying and borrowing of texts that have come before it. "The text is a tissue of

---

quotations," Barthes writes, "drawn from the innumerable centres of culture," and the author's "only power is to mix writings, to counter the ones with the others, in such a way as never to rest on any one of them" (86). That is, according to Barthes, individual authors are not the real creators of texts; they instead build texts out of the mixing and matching of preexisting narrative forms, conventions, vocabularies, and values. Hawthorne's conceiving of the writer's activity as more a matter of borrowing than authoring is suggested in his description of "finding" the story of Hester Prynne among the attic papers of the long deceased Surveyor Pue in "The Custom-House." In fact, Hawthorne fashions himself in his preface to *The Scarlet Letter* as little more than the editor of the story that he has purportedly found, although he admits to having "dress[ed] up the tale," and allowed himself "as much license as if the facts had been entirely of my own invention" (1: 33). What he has "found," are as much the various narrative forms he adopts as any actual story of an extraordinary woman who had "flourished" during the days of the Puritans (1: 32). Hawthorne's genius was more than just the capacity to rework and dress up formulaic genres interwoven with oppressive cultural beliefs; it was to radically transform the building blocks out of which the American novel was constructed in order to reveal a "new truth" and a "surer ground" of human happiness (1: 263) in the racial and cultural tolerance and gender equity that the novel envisions.

Works Cited

Barthes, Roland. "The Death of the Author." *Critical Theory: A Reader for Literary and Cultural Studies*. Edited by Robert Dale Parker. Oxford UP, 2012.

Baym, Nina. "Revisiting Hawthorne's Feminism." *Hawthorne and the Real: Bicentennial Essays*. Edited by Millicent Bell. Ohio State UP, pp. 107-24.

Brown, Charles Brockden. *Ormond; Or the Secret Witness*. 1799. Broadview, 1999.

Coburn, Carol K., and Martha Smith. *Spirited Lives: How Nuns Shaped Catholic Culture and American Life, 1836-1920.* U of North Carolina P, 1999.

Foster, Hannah. *The Coquette; or the History of Eliza Wharton.* Oxford UP, 1987.

Hawthorne, Julian. *Hawthorne Reading.* The Rowfant Club, 1902.

Hawthorne, Nathaniel. *The Centenary Edition of the Works of Nathaniel Hawthorne.* Edited by William Charvat et al. Ohio State UP, 1962-1997. 23 vols.

_____. "The Duston Family." *American Magazine of Useful and Entertaining Knowledge,* vol. 3, 1836, pp. 395-97.

Kelso, Isaac. *Danger in the Dark: A Tale of Intrigue and Priestcraft.* Rulison, 1857.

Kolodny, Annette. *The Land Before Her: Fantasy and Experience of the American Frontiers, 1630-1860.* U of North Carolina P, 1984.

Massa, Mark, S.J. *Anti-Catholicism in America: The Last Acceptable Prejudice.* Crossroad, 2003.

Mather, Cotton. "A Notable Exploit; Wherein Dux Faemini Facti." Sayre, pp. 183-85.

Norton, Mary Beth. *In the Devil's Snare: The Salem Witchcraft Crisis of 1692.* Vintage, 2002.

Reynolds, David S. *Beneath the American Renaissance: The Subversive Imagination in the Age of Emerson and Melville.* Oxford UP, 1998.

_____. *Faith in Fiction: The Emergence of Religious Literature in America.* Harvard, 1981.

Rowlandson, Mary. *A Narrative of the Captivity and Restoration of Mrs. Mary Rowlandson.* Sayre, pp. 137-82.

Rowson, Susanna. *Charlotte Temple: A Tale of Truth.* Oxford UP, 1987.

Sayre, Gordon, editor. *American Captivity Narratives.* Houghton Mifflin, 2000.

Sedgwick, Catharine Maria. *Hope Leslie; or Early Times in the Massachusetts.* Penguin, 1998.

The Scarlet Letter as Utopian/Dystopian Fiction_____

Steven Petersheim

"The founders of a new colony, whatever Utopia of human virtue and happiness they might originally project, have invariably recognized it among their earliest practical necessities to allot a portion of the virgin soil as a cemetery, and another portion as the site of a prison" (1: 47). With these words, the first chapter of *The Scarlet Letter* is injected simultaneously with the expansive seeds of hope and with the unfortunate reality of human frailty. The brooding shade of skepticism that colors the second part of Hawthorne's statement is a characteristic of Hawthorne's writing that has led readers like Lauren Berlant to interpret Hawthorne's romances as endeavors "to prove the failure of utopian theory" (59). The displacement of utopia with dystopia in Hawthorne's work, however, is rarely complete or final. And certainly dystopia does not entirely erase the attempts at utopia that his works recall—those prospects of a "Utopia of human virtue and happiness." In *The Scarlet Letter,* neither dystopia nor utopia gets the final word. Instead, we are left with a kind of balancing act that retains the seeds of utopian hope even while dealing with the stultifying aftereffects of the dystopian reminders of death and crime.

Utopia is not new to literature, and neither is dystopia. Beginning with the publication of Thomas More's *Utopia* in 1516, the "discovery" of lands without European civilization have frequently been imagined as an opportunity to start over again—a chance to create the perfect society. Etymologically, utopia can be defined as uo- (no) or as eu- (good) +topia (place) (OED, *utopia, eutopia*). A perfect society may in fact be equivalent to no place, and thus utopian literature from its inception already bears within it the seeds of *dsytopia*—bad or broken place (OED, *dystopia*). A perfect society may be an ideal one that exists only as a fiction. And yet even a fiction like More's imaginary island of Utopia may inspire the pursuit of social goods that have not been achieved in one's present sociopolitical environment. Utopian writers after More included other features Hawthorne seems to have incorporated into *The Scarlet Letter.* Margaret Cavendish's 1666 novel *The Blazing World* also gives us a "new world" utopia that evokes the newly colonized land of America, and the blazing stars from which this world gets its name portend great things, much as the meteor in Hawthorne's *Scarlet Letter* is taken by its observers as a portent bearing various divergent messages. Like Hawthorne's text, Cavendish's text features a remarkable woman as the central figure whose story opens and closes the text. In the eighteenth century, Jonathan Swift's *Gulliver's Travels* employed utopian and dystopian tropes to investigate imagined good societies and bad societies in order to satirize his contemporary situation. Hawthorne's scathing satire of the Puritans is obvious, and his reading of Jonathan Swift and the "new worlds" discovered by Gulliver gave him a pattern of critiquing his own society by traveling elsewhere. For Swift, as for More and Cavendish before him, it is an imagined journey into other contemporary worlds, but for Hawthorne it is an imagined journey into the past. Perhaps traces of utopia can be found there where the dream of utopia was reborn in an actual place also thought of as a "new world" for the Puritans and other European settlers.

The Scarlet Letter reminds us that the Puritan colonization of the New World was conceived in hope by founders such as the past governor John Winthrop, who dies along with his utopian vision in Hawthorne's romance. The New World was not a paradise, as he had imagined in his famous 1630 sermon "A Model of Christian Charity." Stern discipline had become the rule of the new world Puritans, Hawthorne points out in the "Custom-House" introduction, calling one of his own Puritan ancestors "a bitter persecutor" and describing them as a group as "stern and black-browed... shadows of my forefathers" (1: 9-10). It was not Puritans like Winthrop, Hawthorne suggests, but the second generation of American Puritans who became so dark as to stamp out utopian dreams, for many years at least: "Their immediate posterity, the generation next to the earliest emigrants, wore the blackest shade of Puritanism, and so darkened the national visage with it, that all the subsequent years have not sufficed to clear it up. We have yet," the narrator continues, "to learn again the forgotten art of gayety" (1: 232).

Hawthorne finds something more admirable in the Puritans whose utopian dreams are dashed by the hard realities of crime and death than in those dark brooding Puritans who become "persecutors" of others and stern "black-browed" individuals. And he suggests that it is to our benefit to recover some of that utopian vision—at least "the forgotten art of gayety." E. Shaskan Bumas connects this statement convincingly to Hawthorne's earlier short story "The May-Pole of Merry Mount," in which "Jollity and gloom were contending for empire" (9: 54). In this story, Bumas characterizes the standoff between the Massachusetts Bay Puritans and Thomas Morton's carnivalesque New World as Hawthorne's way of "giv[ing] credence to the possibility, now extinct, that Merry Mount *might have* determined the character of Americans, as they would later call themselves" (2-3). Given this earlier depiction of the struggle between the New World utopia and the Puritan iron fist, we ought to give greater consideration to the lighter more hopeful hints in this work too that is often characterized only in terms of its dark symbolism.

Lauren Berlant's study of utopia as a construction of nationhood that Hawthorne depicts and critiques has set the stage for considerations of *The Scarlet Letter* and utopia. Berlant clearly links Hawthorne's literary work to the "national fantasy" of the so-called new world as a potential utopia. While Berlant convincingly shows that the dream of an American utopia typically took form as an intense, predominately male "national fantasy," it is worth noting the more laudatory elements of utopian literature as the aspirations of individuals or groups pursuing the good of the community in an extraordinary environment. The gloss of nationalist patriarchal egomania reveals where utopian ideals went wrong in American history, as Berlant argues, but it does not follow that utopia is identical to egomania.[1] Indeed, in *The Scarlet Letter,* some of the Puritan leaders as well as some of the most disenfranchised individuals aspire toward the good of the community. This common cause is hinted at in Hawthorne's references to the dying ex-governor John Winthrop alongside his treatment of Hester Prynne's most admirable qualities. These two characters allow for an alternate, more optimistic understanding of utopia in Hawthorne's romance.

In recent years, Frederic Jameson has similarly drawn attention to the slighting of utopia in favor of dystopia but sees in this trend a misunderstanding of utopia: "it is a mistake to approach Utopias with positive expectations, as though they offered visions of happy worlds, spaces of fulfillment and cooperation." Instead, Jameson argues, we ought to recognize "the diagnostic interventions of the Utopians" (12). Rather than representing naïvety or a guise for the will to power, then, the utopian urge is sometimes best understood as an attempt to intervene in a world where not all is well. Examined in that light, it is easy to see how Winthrop's attempt to intervene in his world—to keep the new world settlers from making the same mistakes that he saw being made in Europe—may have given rise to his utopian ideals. And whether or not Hester saw herself intervening in the Puritan world, it is clear that she did intervene as a "Sister of Charity," leaving an impact on individual lives even if the community as a group was suspicious of her intervention.

Following Hester Prynne from the prison-door where she first appears, we find the backstory of her life a picture of the new world as a utopia where she has a tryst in the woods with a young lover. But since Hester is married to another man, the hinted memory of utopia in Hawthorne's text has already crumbled into the crime of adultery. Hawthorne's romance opens with the scene of Hester experiencing the new world as a dystopia from behind prison bars. The brunt of the punishment imposed by the community—being imprisoned and standing in infamy on the scaffold—was soon past, but Hester's ongoing infamy as a "spoiled" woman was marked by the scarlet letter she had to wear as well as by the child she had to raise. As Margaret Brantley puts it, Hester stands uneasily in the community as a "sinner living as part of the moral utopia" (350). Her imperfections are evident to those who have no visible mistakes or sins. This is no utopia. But even here are signs of a world that could have been utopia—the "wild rose-bush... with its delicate gems," emanating its "fragrance and fragile beauty" (1:48). The child Pearl is described as "a lovely child... worthy to have been brought forth in Eden." She exhibits both "a native grace" in her actions and "faultless beauty" in her bodily form (1: 89-90). Fittingly, Pearl is drawn to the rose bushes in Governor Bellingham's garden and even begins "to cry for a red rose" before being interrupted by the arrival of the governor and his train passing "adown the vista of the garden-avenue" (1: 107).

But Hester does not see the new world as utopia anymore. The shadows seem to chase her and the sun blazes only on the red letter on her bosom even when she is out in the woods with Pearl. But for a moment, it all disappears again when she happens upon Dimmesdale, Pearl's father, and they decide to run off together. Flinging the scarlet letter away, she seems to bring back the utopian dreams of "what men call the irrevocable past" as "happiness" replaces the "gloom" that had followed her and the natural world seems in tune with utopia as well: "All at once, as with a sudden smile of heaven, forth burst the sunshine, pouring a very flood into the obscure forest, gladdening each green leaf, transmuting the yellow fallen ones to gold, and gleaming adown the gray trunks of the solemn trees... Such was the sympathy of Nature—that wild, heathen Nature of the forest, never subjugated by human law, nor illumined by higher truth—with the bliss of these two spirits!" (1: 202-203). Rather than reflecting the Puritan fears associated with the forest as the place of the devil—made famous by Hawthorne's story "Young Goodman Brown"—the natural world has returned to the old myths of Arcadia, a place of natural happiness without the fear of transgression against gods or humans. Thus, Hawthorne resituates the pastoral tradition of a utopian past on the North American continent—even for two Puritans like Hester and Dimmesdale.

And while their dreams of a life away from the Puritan community are dashed by Dimmesdale's death, Hester has learned to hope again. She returns to Europe for a time and procures a good life for Pearl there before returning to New England to end her days in her cottage, serving as a counselor for Puritan women seeking sympathy. And she is convinced that "in Heaven's own time, a new truth would be revealed, in order to establish the whole relation between man and woman on a surer ground of mutual happiness" (1: 263). And here it is that Hester's utopian hope moves from the past to the future: "The angel and apostle of the coming revelation must be a woman indeed, but lofty, pure, and beautiful; and wise, moreover, not through dusky grief, but the ethereal medium of joy; and showing how sacred love should make us happy, by the truest test of a life successful to such an end" (1: 263). The utopia of the past, if it ever existed, was now part of "the irrevocable past." The utopia of the future, however, is something still to be anticipated. On this note, Hawthorne ends his text. Old utopian dreams have become a memory, but new utopian dreams will take us on to the next phase of humanity.

Joseph Alkana argues that "Hawthorne's gesture toward the future at the conclusion of *The Scarlet Letter* conforms to an American rhetoric of progress... based on a historical outlook that criticized the Puritans while it simultaneously preserved the Puritan ideal of America's special mission" (82). While it is clear that Hawthorne gestures toward some notion of progress, a kind of utopian hope, this notion of progress is clearly chastened by the experience of Hester in his fiction as well as in the experience of Hawthorne reflected in his harsh critique of his Puritan ancestors' outlook in the introduction. What he seems to admire is the utopian hopes of the first generation, those like John Winthrop who promote policies and practices based upon charity rather than rigid legalism.

Winthrop never actually appears in Hawthorne's text, but Hester and Pearl and some of their severest detractors gather respectfully together around his "death-chamber," his "death-bed" (1: 150, 152). What is it about this leader that draws people together like this? As Matthew Holland points out, the narrator of *The Scarlet Letter* never accuses Winthrop as he does the other Puritan leaders; instead, his "striking absence" during these scenes may be one of the reasons Hester was motivated to linger at his bedside when he was dying (6). In his probing historical study of Winthrop, as relates to Hawthorne's characterization of him, Holland finds that Hawthorne's other fictional depictions of Winthrop also suggest "that Hawthorne considered Winthrop a political ruler with admirable and redeeming qualities," not the least of which was his leniency with repentant lawbreakers and his generosity to the poor (7). Although Holland is focused primarily on the political philosophy espoused and practiced by Winthrop, he does recognize the impact of "charity" on Hawthorne's depiction, noting that "it does appear that Winthrop's personal application of principles of Christian love may help to redeem him to some degree in the eyes of Hawthorne..." (12). What is clear is that Hawthorne is acquainted enough with the historical Winthrop and his emphasis on "charity" and goodwill to recognize him as the rare exception to Puritan hard-heartedness. When he dies, one Puritan claims that Winthrop "was made an angel this past night" (1: 158). Hawthorne represents Winthrop in death as in life a noble exception to the menacing intransigence of other Puritan leaders.

Michael J. Colacurcio also notes that the nineteenth-century narrator of *The Scarlet Letter* is apparently well-versed in "the Puritan world of the 1630s and 1640s" and that his story represents a "rewriting" of the kind of "Utopia" for which Winthrop's sermon "served as moral groundplan and exemplar" (103-04). Although Winthrop's words about the Puritan settlement as "a city upon a hill" are often quoted as an example of American exceptionalism, his words within the context of the whole sermon serve as a caution against "deal[ing] falsely" rather than as a promotion of Puritan pride. His sermon actually revolves around what he calls "the two rules whereby we are to walk one towards another: Justice and Mercy." Interestingly, "Justice" is only explicitly mentioned four more times in his sermon while "Mercy" appears in thirteen other instances. And "love" (or "loue") is referenced more than seventy times, suggesting that establishing a community that operates out of "charity" or love" really is the focus for Winthrop. *The Scarlet Letter* tests Winthrop's thesis on charity against the life of a Puritan like Hester Prynne, and she comes out redeemed in the end even though the next generation of Puritans abandons Winthrop's utopian virtue of charity.

Like the historical Winthrop presented by Holland and recent biographers of Winthrop, Hester Prynne also serves others until she dies, practicing the kind of charity Winthrop advocates even if he falls short. Hawthorne makes the connection between Winthrop's call for charity and Hester more explicit by calling her a "self-ordained... Sister of Mercy" (1: 161) and "a self-enlisted Sister of Charity" (1: 215). When she returns from her trip abroad, she again takes up a life of service for the community by serving as a counselor and comforter to those who were troubled: "Women, more especially,—in the continually recurring trials of wounded, wasted, wronged, misplaced, or erring and sinful passion... came to Hester's cottage, demanding why they were so wretched, and what the remedy! Hester comforted and counseled them, as best she might" (1: 263). While Hester's status in the community is at the opposite end of the spectrum from Winthrop's, she exemplifies the virtues of Mercy and Charity championed by Winthrop. And she does so without embracing "all the Puritanic traits, both good and evil" that Hawthorne ascribes to his own ancestors (1: 9).

Given the typical view of Hawthorne as a dark brooding writer, it may seem odd to draw attention to Hawthorne's representation of the mixed qualities of Puritans. Hawthorne was not always seen as a dark brooding writer, however, and his contemporary Herman Melville first drew attention to a "mystical blackness" in Hawthorne in order to challenge then-prevalent notions of Hawthorne as a writer who "witche[s] by his sunlight" (108). Instead of seeing simply "the Indian-summer sunlight on the hither side of Hawthorne's soul," Melville insists that we also notice "the other side... shrouded in blackness" (107). Today the situation is much the reverse. We have become so versed in Hawthorne's dark imagination that we miss the sunlight of his imagination. In terms of utopia, we have become so fixated on dystopian effects that we assign to the desire for utopia little more than the certainty of a dystopian ending. In her study of Hawthorne's most direct investigation of utopian aspirations, *The Blithedale Romance,* Judith Shklar emphasizes that Hawthorne's critique of utopians' shortcomings does not equate his dismissal of their aspirations for the good life: "He had no traditional or radical scheme of his own, and did not, therefore, blame the Blithedalers for following another path. He took no pleasure in their failures, even though he understood it with a chilling clarity" (217-18). Similarly in *The Scarlet Letter*, the narrator does not celebrate the death of Winthrop and his utopian dream but instead imagines a hopeful space for Hester Prynne to exist and even to flourish in a limited fashion despite the demise of utopian aspirations.

The celebratory relish of life often attendant upon utopia is also found in other characters as well, but mostly as a memory of the old country. The governor and the old clergyman John Wilson both recall it when they see Pearl prancing about in her colorful red outfit. "The old clergyman, nurtured at the rich bosom of the English Church, had a long established and legitimate taste for all good and comfortable things; and... the genial benevolence of his private life had won him warmer affection than was accorded to any of his professional contemporaries" (1: 109). While the Reverend Wilson is reminded of the bright colors of birds in stained glass windows back in England, so Governor Bellingham relates Pearl's outfit to old England: "I profess, I have never seen the like, since my days of vanity, in old King James's time, when I was wont to esteem it a high favor to be admitted to a court mask! There used to be a swarm of such apparitions, in holiday-time; and we called them children of the Lord of Misrule" (1:109). Court masques and quasi-pagan celebrations might be smiled upon by Anglican priests—but not by Puritan pastors—and Pearl's colorful spirited presence reminded them of these almost forgotten days.[2] Dreams of the happy life, like dreams of utopia, had once inspired at least some of these Puritans who retained England in their memories.

But in these early years, some festivities remained even in the Puritan colonies of New England. The parade of Election Day was a celebratory affair that was awaited with merriments that recalled bits and pieces of old world festivities, including wrestling competitions and the like. These early Puritans, the narrator reminds us, "had not been born to an inheritance of Puritanic gloom. They were native Englishmen, whose fathers had lived in the sunny richness of the Elizabethan epoch; a time when the life of England, viewed as one great mass, would appear to have been as stately, magnificent, and joyous, as the world has ever witnessed" (1: 230). On this day, the Puritans were joined in the open "market-place" by adventurous frontiersmen as well as by "Indians—in their savage finery of curiously embroidered deer-skin robes, wampum-belts, red and yellow ochre, and feathers, and armed with the bow and arrow and stone-headed spear" (1: 232). But they were joined also by sailors described almost as pirates—"mariners... from the Spanish Main,— who had come ashore to see the humors of Election Day," the one day when even "the Puritan elders, in their black cloaks, starched bands, and steeple-crowned hats, smiled not unbenignantly at the clamor and rude deportment of these jolly seafaring men" (1: 232-33). This reprieve allowed for hints of utopia—a time of relative freedom and frolicking—for one day each year in the early days of the Puritan colony.

In the end, however, the narrator calls the second generation of Puritans "the most intolerant brood that ever existed" (1: 94), "the blackest shade of Puritanism" (1: 232). John Winthrop dies. So do the other old folks. Dissidents like Hester Prynne die out and their descendants flee to other places, as little Pearl goes off to Europe. As the death of John Winthrop indicates that a bid for utopia has been lost, so the erasure of a tale like Hester's shows that a darker Puritanism has blotted out any lighter views that existed. And it is this loss of possible utopia as much as the emergence of the sternest of Puritan visions that Hawthorne mourns. His ancestors have strong qualities that allow them to endure and persevere through the hardships of the new world, but they also have "the persecuting spirit" of his witch trial judge ancestors (1: 9). Utopia was firmly pushed aside by such second-generation Puritans.

Like the nineteenth-century Custom House that serves as a site of narrative meaning making in Hawthorne's introduction, so the seventeenth-century Puritan community serves as a site of meaning making for the United States. And Hawthorne ominously tells us that "[n]either the front nor the back entrance... opens on the road to Paradise" (1: 13). The front entrance led to the seafront, where Hawthorne's ancestors had arrived years earlier, where

Hawthorne's father had taken ships on voyages around the world when Hawthorne was very young, where Hester had arrived and departed and returned in Hawthorne's story, the gateway to England and other places abroad. Paradise was not to be found there. And the back door of the Custom House led into the town of Salem or perhaps beyond into the woods where Hester and Dimmesdale found a kind of sanctuary away from the Puritans or perhaps even beyond to westward expansion of the nation. These places did not provide the paradise they promised either, being wrought with wrongdoing and fear and guilt. The utopia seemingly promised by the new world scene was thus but a dream—a happy dream at first perhaps but chastened by the cold, hard realities of a world that could be bent but not completely shaped to one's will. Thus, utopia is seen as already turned to dystopia at the outset of *The Scarlet Letter.* But that does not mean utopia is without any redeeming qualities; it has allowed the space for at least some people to hope and act out of a desire for the common good even if we inevitably fall short in our strivings for utopia.

Notes

1. Berlant characterizes this "national fantasy" in Hawthorne's writing as "the promise of millennial and secular collective perfectibility to create a sphere of projected political experience and knowledge that competed with and even sublated the pressure of material political realities" (7). Berlant does, however, argue that Hawthorne's work represents "an attempt to break the frame of national hegemony itself" (9). While she makes this argument by attacking utopia, I make a similar argument by seeing utopia as a potential good for the many (rather than the few) and instead of simply representing an egocentric fantasy of patriarchal nationhood.

2. Such a scene plays out in the early New England landscape of "The May-Pole of Merry Mount" before the stern Puritan imprint establishes itself in the new world.

Works Cited

Alkana, Joseph. *The Social Self: Hawthorne, Howells, William James, and Nineteenth-Century Psychology.* UP of Kentucky, 1997.

Berlant, Lauren. *The Anatomy of National Fantasy: Hawthorne, Utopia, and Everyday Life,* U of Chicago P, 1991.

Brantley, Margaret. "Interpretive Notes." *The Scarlet Letter,* Pocket, 2004.

Bumas, E. Shaskan. "'The Forgotten Art of Gayety': Masquerade, Utopia, and the Complexion of Empire." *Arizona Quarterly,* vol. 59, no. 4, 2003, pp. 1-30.

Colacurcio, Michael J. "'The Woman's Own Choice': Sex, Metaphor, and the Puritan 'Sources' of *The Scarlet Letter. New Essays on The Scarlet Letter*. Edited by Michael J. Colacurcio. Cambridge UP, 1985, pp. 101-36.

"dystopia, n." *OED Online*. Oxford UP, June 2017. Accessed 8 August 2017.

"eutopia, n." *OED Online*. Oxford UP, June 2017. Accessed 8 August 2017.

Hawthorne, Nathaniel. *The Centenary Edition of the Works of Nathaniel Hawthorne*. Edited by William Charvat et al. Ohio State UP, 1962-1997. 23 vols.

Holland, Matthew. "Remembering John Winthrop—Hawthorne's Suggestion." *Perspectives on Political Science,* vol. 35, no. 1, 2007, pp. 4-14.

Jameson, Frederic. *Archaeologies of the Future: The Desire Called Utopia and Other Science Fictions.* Verso, 2005.

Melville, Herman. "Hawthorne and His *Mosses.*" 1850. *Nathaniel Hawthorne: The Contemporary Reviews*. Edited by John L. Idol Jr. and Buford Jones. Cambridge UP, 1994, pp. 104-15.

Shklar, Judith. "Hawthorne in Utopia." *In the Presence of the Past: Essays in Honor of Frank Manuel*. Edited by Richard T. Bienvenu and Mordechai Feingold. Kluwer, 1991, pp. 215-32.

"utopia, n." *OED Online*. Oxford UP, June 2017. Accessed 8 August 2017.

Winthrop, John. "A Model of Christian Charity." 1630. *Collections of the Massachusetts Historical Society,* 1838. Scanned 1996. https://history.hanover.edu/texts/winthmod.html.

The Scarlet Letter and Film Adaptation: Feminism and Fidelity_____

David Greven

Nathaniel Hawthorne's most famous and widely read novel, an American classic routinely taught in high school and a narrative familiar enough to be referenced in popular culture without ever even having been read, *The Scarlet Letter* has not very often been adapted for film since its first film version in 1908. Several silent shorts exist, but the most famous silent era version is the 1926 one starring Lillian Gish, famous for her roles in D. W. Griffith movies, and directed by the Swedish émigré Victor Sjöström. Hollywood made a sound version in 1934 starring Colleen Moore as Hester Prynne. But this was a low-budget production in a decade of plush literary adaptations of nineteenth-century classics such as *Little Women, David Copperfield, A Tale of Two Cities*, and *Pride and Prejudice*. It would not be until the 1970s that the novel received renewed filmic attention. In 1973, the great German director Wim Wenders made a German-language movie version, *Der scharlachrote Buchstabe*, and a four-part PBS miniseries produced by WGBH Boston aired in 1979. Finally, in 1995, the Roland Joffé-directed version starring Demi Moore as Hester, Gary Oldman as Arthur Dimmesdale, and Robert Duvall as Roger Chillingworth. This effort is widely, and rightly, seen as a disaster. My essay will focus on the Gish/Sjöström, Wenders, and Joffé versions, the latter being fascinating in the ways it fails.

At the outset, let me establish that I share Robin Wood's view, expressed with characteristic eloquence in his study of a film adaptation of Henry James's novel *The Wings of the Dove*, that

> literature is literature, film is film. It's really as simple as that. There is no such thing as a faithful adaptation. When people talk about faithful adaptations they usually seem to mean that the film follows the plot of the novel. This represents a profound (if doubtless well-

intentioned) insult to great literature, the greatness of which resides in the writer's grasp of the potentialities of language... To reduce a great novel to its plot is merely to reveal a total incapacity to reading it. But the notion of the faithful adaptation is equally insulting to film. It implies that film is the inferior art, and should be content (or even proud) to reproduce precisely what it can never hope to reproduce: the movement of the author's words on paper. (7-8)

While I am a partisan of Wood's view on both counts, I also believe that it is important to consider where and why, how and for what purpose, a film adaptation interprets its source text. For in the choices of an adaptation lie its political appraisal and measure of engagement with its source material. Specifically, my concern throughout this chapter is with film's engagement with Hawthorne's depiction of his heroine's desire for a man she wants but cannot possess.

Filming Female Desire

Lillian Gish was one of the major Hollywood stars of the silent era. She is best known for her work with the legendary director D. W. Griffith, appearing in his most notable films: *The Birth of a Nation* (1915), *Intolerance* (2016), *Hearts of the World* (1918), *Broken Blossoms* (1919), *True Heart Susie* (1919), *Way Down East* (1920), and *Orphans of the Storm* (1921). By the mid-1920s, Gish had transitioned from Griffith's productions at American Mutoscope and Biograph Company to MGM. There, she had the ability to choose star vehicles; she actively pursued *The Scarlet Letter* as a film project. But first, Gish had to fight for the right to have the film made at all. Religious groups frowned on Hawthorne's source material as too sexually provocative; she personally had to reassure these groups that the film would be morally upstanding and also that she would take full responsibility for the finished product. It was her decision to employ Sjöström because she believed that the Swedes had a clearer understanding than contemporary Americans of Puritan New England.

As Anke Brouwers has shown, this version of the *The Scarlet Letter*, made during the Jazz Age, and its depiction of femininity intersected with a new model of female sexual liberation in the United States at this time embodied in the image of the flapper, immortalized by F. Scott Fitzgerald in his fiction. An icon of the Roaring Twenties and the Jazz Age, the flapper was a newly liberated postwar woman, representing "female youthfulness and the future. She was associated with short hair, short skirts, dropped waistlines, a flat chest, in fact a look that was decidedly androgynous." The flapper also represented "immorality, generational challenge, and the erosion of stability, particularly in relation to gender relations and the family" (Bland 3-4).

Frances Marion, one of the most famous female screenwriters of early Hollywood, who would go on to win two Academy Awards for screenwriting (the first won by a woman), wrote the screenplay adaptation of Hawthorne's novel. Marion successfully retooled the source text for Jazz Age audiences, creating a modern heroine who fought for sexual liberation, the inherently cautionary nature of Hawthorne's work providing the necessary moralistic ending to assuage religious watch guards. This was a pre-Code film, not bound to the Production Code, which regulated film content from 1930 to the 1960s. Nevertheless, clearly, the studios were eager to appease those who monitored film for moral transgressions. (The Motion Picture Production Code was applied by the Hays Office, which, overseen by Joseph Breen, began to monitor content in earnest beginning in 1934. The strict regulations of content did not loosen until the 1960s, with films such as the expletive-filled *Who's Afraid of Virginia Woolf?* released in 1966 by Warner Brothers, challenging the strictures.)

Anke Brouwers makes a persuasive and illuminating case for Marion's success in updating the novel for modernity. One limitation of Brouwers's valuable analysis is that she tends to cast Hawthorne as a repressive force from which Marion, and to a certain extent Gish and Sjöström, liberate the ardent heroine. Hawthorne's own work, which indubitably has conservative elements, is committed as well to a model of female sexual liberation. That the film pursues, in a manner distinct to it, a similar model does not invalidate the source material's perspectives on female sexuality and critique of the constraints placed on its expression. Indeed, in some respects Hawthorne's work remains the more transgressive vision, as I will show.

Marion's strategy is to emphasize the romance between Hester and Arthur Dimmesdale, the tremulous minister with whom she shares an illicit, adulterous sexual relationship, and to do this she devises a considerable backstory for the lovers' relationship. Hester is depicted as a social rebel long before her and Dimmesdale's illegitimate daughter, Pearl, is born. At the very least, she is perceived as such by her fellow New England Puritans. Strangely, Marion casts Mistress Hibbins not as a witch, her role in the novel, but instead as a pious busybody, constantly policing Hester's behavior, essentially the reverse of Hawthorne's depiction of the real-life Ann Hibbins, hanged for witchcraft in Boston, Massachusetts, on June 19, 1656, an event presaging the Salem witch trials of 1692. Hibbins was the sister-in-law to Massachusetts governor Richard Bellingham, and Governor John Endicott, Hawthorne's model for Puritan severity, handed down her sentence. In *The Scarlet Letter*, Mistress Hibbins is a lively, cackling witch who, seizing on Hester's newfound infamy and especially the social vulnerability that comes with it, attempts to enlist the scorned young woman and later Pearl too in her satanic arts.

In the movie, Mistress Hibbins leads a group of sin monitors at the start of the narrative to the transgressive Hester's door. Her crime? Her caged canary is singing on the Sabbath day. When Hester runs out of her house to find the bird after it flies away, her transgressions multiply, and she is placed in the stocks for revelry on the Sabbath, her act of running after her bird seen as undue physicality. Seeing her in the stocks, the compassionate Dimmesdale tends to her, freeing her from the device and public humiliation. In a strange depiction of Puritan sexual morality, the women of the town wash their undergarments in a stream. Dimmesdale inadvertently spies on Hester in the act, like an innocent Actaeon happening upon the goddess Diana in her nudity. Hester tries to hide her undergarments, holding them behind her back, but Dimmesdale ardently insists on seeing them. And so their passion kindles.

Very important to the film, Hester's marital status is unknown to the town or to Arthur. This makes Roger Prynne's appearance after Hester's public shaming on the scaffold, where she is exhibited holding her newborn infant before the town after having been jailed for being pregnant out of wedlock, all the more shocking. Chillingworth, as Prynne calls himself to keep his identity hidden as he routs out the identity of Pearl's father, is played by Henry B. Walthall, and made to look like an ersatz aged John the Baptist who has long given up gospelizing. With his long, scraggly, mountain man beard and fierce looks, this Chillingworth is clearly the villain of the piece, a stark contrast to the smooth, bland features of the Swedish actor Lars Hanson, who plays Dimmesdale.

The film removes the entire subplot of Chillingworth inviting the troubled Dimmesdale to move in with him, so that, unbeknownst to the young minister, he can spy on him and confirm his suspicions that Dimmesdale is Pearl's father. By removing this crucial aspect of the novel, the film jettisons Hawthorne's signature theme of fraught male-male relations, and the sinister tones of a predatory homoerotic fascination with the beautiful young man, further heterosexualizing the plot. Indeed, by adding the scenes of Hester and Dimmesdale's romantic and sexual passion before Pearl's birth, the film removes much of the novel's enigmatic, haunted quality of an unrecapturable and unrepresentable passion between the thwarted lovers.

The most bizarre decision on the film's part remains the transformation of Mistress Hibbins into her opposite, a pillar of Puritan rectitude. Later in the film, she is framed for witchcraft, but clearly not guilty of it. What ensues is the oddest moment in this cinematic rendering of Hawthorne's novel: Mistress Hibbins, on trial for being a witch, is repeatedly dunked into the water to see if she will float, thereby confirming her satanic powers. While this was an actual method used to determine whether someone was a witch, the film plays this entire sequence for laughs, as the outraged, falsely accused, matronly older woman is repeatedly dunked into a pond.

Another important dimension of Hawthorne's novel that the film largely jettisons is Hester's complicated, agonized relationship to her daughter, her Pearl of great price. Indeed, one would not have any inkling of the beguilingly weird, vexatious nature of Hawthorne's Pearl, drawn from the author's close observations of his daughter Una, from the film. If the movie admirably puts forth a positive image of adult female sexuality, it does so at the cost of eradicating Hawthorne's depiction of nonnormative childhood energies and a difficult, challenging mother-daughter relationship. As Maureen Turim writes, "Pearl is above all a vehicle for Hawthorne's irony, as he juxtaposes her wild innocence to the guilt that surrounds her, including her mother's fear that her child will be corrupted, indeed damned, by her heritage. The film adopts an attitude more consonant with later American Protestantism," especially in scenes such as the baptism of Pearl by Dimmesdale invented for the film, anointing Dimmesdale, Hester, and Pearl "with a born-again goodness of spirit quite outside of Hawthorne's attitude toward his characters" (175). As Turim observes, the novel is rarely understood as a nineteenth-century work looking back at Puritan culture, "nor do most readers follow the complications of voice in Hawthorne's writing, turning instead to the memorable scenes of punishment and confrontation. Yet the film largely changes even the key scene of Hester's public humiliation" by delaying a full eight minutes into the film the depiction of Hester's shaming, in Chapter 2, on the scaffold after she is led from the jail while holding Pearl, the invented scene of Hester in the stocks being punished for "running and playing on the Sabbath" occurring first (171-72, 174).

Much of the film's lasting power comes from two sources: Gish's luminous portrayal, especially her ability convey the heroine's archetypal suffering, and Sjöström's uncannily poetic direction, which evokes the Puritan past even as Marion's screenplay renders it a cartoon. In the scene in which Hester, infant Pearl in her arms, walks to the scaffold for the first time, Sjöström "edits the scene focusing on shots of characters looking silently at each other, deliberately exposing tensions and anguish through an impassive immobility that resonates with the viewer" (Turim 174). Surely the shot of Gish's Hester, holding her child and standing on the scaffold, looking both defiantly and plangently out at the pitiless crowd but crucially looking upward, as if in divine appeal, is one of the indelible shots of the cinema.

The film deserves its acclaim for its evocation of Puritan New England and for Gish's performance, but despite remarkable moments it stands as a diminution and distortion of Hawthorne's compelling portrait of a desiring woman who faces opprobrium for her desires. As I argue in *Gender Protest*, Hawthorne depicts Hester as a woman willing to defy her society to find both romantic and sexual fulfilment with Arthur, the first letter of his name one of the many possibilities for what the *A* signifies. Much of the novel's power derives from Hawthorne's steady, unflinching analysis of Hester's deterioration within the unyielding atmosphere of her community and especially as a result of Dimmesdale's neglect of her, stemming from his pusillanimous inability to stand alongside her and Pearl before the community as Pearl's father. The film, rendering the Puritans buffoonish, as will the 1934 sound version, and emphasizing the spritelike, flapperlike qualities of Hester as rebel, eschews a great deal of the somberness and loneliness that makes Hawthorne's work endure. While Sjöström conveys these qualities through his expressionistic cinema, the screenplay opts for a more facile and ultimately blander treatment of the costs of female sexual autonomy. Again, this is not to insist on the fidelity model of screen adaptation. There is an affecting moment at the climax when Arthur, standing on the scaffold to deliver his Election Day sermon, bares his chest for all to see and confessing his sins and his paternity of Pearl. A giant *A* visibly marks the flesh of his chest. As he lies dying in Hester's arms, her woven scarlet letter—which she tried to take off in the forest scene where she and Arthur make their plans for escape, before Pearl retrieves the discarded symbol from a brook and puts it back on her mother's breast—falls from her bosom onto his fleshly majuscule. Her material emblem of sin and his corporeal one momentarily merge, a poignant image of connection and disconnection at once. Hawthorne leaves it entirely ambiguous whether or not Dimmesdale has an *A* on his chest or if his would-be confession is heard as such by his congregation. The film invents the effect of the two *A*s momentarily meeting one another, but creates a poetic effect. In such moments, the film sings, even if out of tune with Hawthorne.

A Woman Escapes

Wim Wenders's version of Hawthorne's novel, the 1973 international production *Der scharlachrote Buchstabe*, filmed in Spain, uses the Galician coast, rocky and sandy, to substitute for Hawthorne's New England coastline. This is only one of several and significant alterations to Hawthorne's text. Wenders's film is a second-wave-feminist era updating of Hawthorne's novel that reframes Hester Prynne as a sexual revolutionary. That is not entirely out of keeping with elements of Hawthorne's characterization of his heroine—her intransigence and daring. But Wenders's film goes much further than Hawthorne ever would have in imagining a defiant Hester who not only challenges but actively escapes her repressive Puritan community. Not for Wenders's Hester a self-sacrificing, penitent return to her Puritan community; this Hester (Senta Berger) sets out, with her daughter, Pearl (Yella Rottländer), at film's end for the freedoms of Providence, Rhode Island. Hester follows Anne Hutchinson's example, which she extols midway through the film in a conversation with her daughter.

Wenders was disappointed that his producers' budget stipulations forced him to film in Spain rather than in New England. Galicia's craggy coastline, however, adds a gritty natural world ambience to the film that fits in nicely with its sense of Hawthorne's narrative as an elemental, timeless drama about fierce individualism's battle against authoritarian, repressive control. The forbidding Puritan elders here are less specific to colonial America than they are archetypes of this controlling menace. That having been said, Wenders treats the characters with much more realism than other adaptations do. Chillingworth (Hans Christian Blech), in contrast to the shaggy-haired medieval wild man of the 1926 version and the gone-native madman of the 1995 version, is neither craven nor misshapen but instead an aging blond man of science with a certain amount of virility and heft, a wanderer with physical stamina. Wenders also depicts an element of the novel left out of other film adaptations, the crucial male-male dynamic of Chillingworth and Dimmesdale's living arrangements. Determined to learn the incontestable truth that Dimmesdale is Pearl's father, Chillingworth moves in with the young, agonized minister, treating him as a seeming friend whose wracked state the older physician attempts to ameliorate, a diabolical yet intimate relationship that I have described as Hawthorne's parody of same-sex intimacy and a bad marriage (*Men* 126). Hawthorne shares with Melville a fascination with the predatory older male's manipulation and mistreatment of a vulnerable younger man. At one point in Wenders's film, Arthur Dimmesdale (Lou Castel), a gentle, pale young man with cold, haunted eyes, accuses Chillingworth of having emotionally violated him. This accusation is uttered in the house they uncomfortably share, not in the third scaffold scene as it does in the novel.

Wenders makes very good use of Castel, whose mildness masks a steady intensity. (Born in Bogotá, Colombia, Castel is best known for his roles in *Fists in the Pocket* [1965], *Beware of a Holy Whore* [1971], and Wenders's adaptation of Patricia Highsmith's *Ripley's Game*, *The American Friend* [1977].) He also makes good use of Blech, "an unusual but effective Chillingworth. He is neither satanic nor overtly sadistic, as in the Hawthorne novel. ... In the film... he carries the appearance of a knowledgeable man of the world, whose weathered countenance seems to symbolize his experience and wisdom." His zealous attempt to discover the mystery of Pearl's parentage stems from his scientific curiosity (Keenan and Welsh 176-78). As most adaptations do, this film literalizes what Hawthorne leaves a suggestion: Chillingworth eventually beholds the A carved on the young minister's exposed chest.

Originally, the director intended to cast the Russian-born Yelena Samarina as Hester. The producers once again intervened, opting for the better-known Senta Berger in the lead role. The Austrian star Berger gives an adequate performance, but her high-fashion-model looks seem somewhat out of place here. (While Hawthorne describes Hester's beauty at length, it is the beauty of the Madonna of Renaissance painting, not of the runway. The "passionless quality of the acting" of which Bromley complains, in his critique of the film as too literal minded, "decontextualizing and monological," applies most directly to Berger in the lead [Bromley 15-16]). It is pity that Wenders could not cast the intense and less conventional Samarina as Hester, who instead plays Mistress Hibbins, here the daughter of Governor Bellingham. Wenders's version of Hibbins is strikingly distinct from that in other adaptations. Younger than usual, and endowed with a feral sensuality by the red-haired Samarina, Hibbins evokes a fiery feminist activist at a women's liberation meeting rather than the cackling older woman of Hawthorne's novel. When Hester is brought out, babe in hand, to endure public scorn and the pinning of the *A* to her bosom (the first scaffold scene in the novel; there are no scaffold scenes matching Hawthorne's in Wenders's film), Samarina's Hibbins boldly hails Hester, telling her to come down off of the scaffold and join her in the forest, where they can live independently, free of authoritarian opprobrium. Later, Hibbins engages in a startling piece of performance art, donning the governor's robe and wig, and, in this gender-bending garb, ceremonially walking, long phallic torch in hand, to the scaffold, where she then attempts to set fire to herself in protest, though prevented from doing so. And when Dimmesdale exposes his guilt to the crowd during his Election Day sermon, she moans in ecstasy. Richard C. Keenan and James M. Welsh argue that Hibbins here functions as Hester's "eerie *doppelgänger*" while also serving "a choric function... She appears to be a free spirit, almost demented in her assertion of natural impulses. She has the irrational qualities of a witch... Wenders makes her younger and more comely" than she is in Hawthorne's characterization (Keenan and Welsh 176). Later, Hibbins, her black servant, Sarah (Laura Currie), by her side, once again coaxes Hester and Pearl to make their escape with her into the forest. But Hester and Pearl make their escape alone, boarding a ship bound for Providence "in a newly written denouement. That she achieves this has been cited as evidence of Wenders's 'genuine respect for women'" (Raw 85).

Laurence Raw observes that both Hester and Hibbins evince the "values of the counterculture," which Wenders also "expresses in formal terms, as he deliberately rejects the conventions of classical narrative cinema—specifically its insistence that the plot should be logically structured to ensure maximum comprehensibility for the audience" (86). Perhaps the starkest deviation from the novel is the movie's depiction of Dimmesdale's fate; he is strangled to death by a black-gloved Puritan official after the minister scandalously exposes his complicity in Hester's guilt at the climax.

> After Dimmesdale has revealed his sign of human vulnerability to the Community, the new Governor cannot permit him to rise as a man who has accepted his vulnerability and reconciled his failure. The black-gloved hand that stifles him at the end of the film is the Black Hand of the Theocratic Order.... Hawthorne has Dimmesdale killed by the pressures of society. Wenders makes the Theocratic State more sinister than even Hawthorne presents it—utterly unforgiving, spiritually repressive, inhumanely corrupt. (Keenan and Welsh, 178)

In this regard, it is especially striking that Hester and Pearl can make their way out of Salem and that they do so, pointedly, without Dimmesdale. "In the novel, Chillingworth remains but dies within a year of Dimmesdale; in the film, he watches Hester and Pearl leave the shore, turns away, sheds his puritan coat, and departs with his Native American companion" (Bromley 16). Laurence Raw describes Wenders's preoccupation with an individualism that is gendered as male as a carryover from the classical Hollywood directors Wenders admired, such as John Ford and Nicholas Ray; his depiction of the solitary and rough-hewn wanderer Chillingworth evinces this influence (88). Yet Wenders concludes his version of *The Scarlet Letter* with an image that transfers this fierce male individualism to women and girls, the intransigent intergenerational pairing of Hester and Prynne voyaging out on the sea unaccompanied and unfettered by the men in their lives, seeking out a new community and land.

Apocalypse Now
Having stated at the outset that the fidelity model of film adaptation has little to no traction despite its being the standard response of the literate moviegoer, I am now in the uncomfortable position of

having to impugn a film for a lack of fidelity to its source material. But a consideration of the 1995 Roland Joffé-directed version of *The Scarlet Letter* starring Demi Moore as Hester, Gary Oldman as Arthur Dimmesdale, and Robert Duvall as Roger Chillingworth allows us to expand our discussion of fidelity and its limitations productively. If a movie makes its own case for why fidelity is of little consequence to the pursuit of its own ends, its own vision of the material, then the adaptation must be judged on its own terms and not held to the fidelity standard. Such a work would have to be bold, exciting, and simply interesting enough on its own terms to allow us to dispense with fidelity concerns even if quite serious ones. An example of such an adaptation is Michael Mann's 1992 film *The Last of the Mohicans*, based on James Fenimore Cooper's famous 1926 novel, the third of his five Leatherstocking Saga books featuring his indelible white-man-living-among-the Indians hero, Natty Bumppo. Mann and his screenwriter jettison much that makes Cooper's novel a politically progressive, even resistant text. The mixed racial identity of Cora Munro and the theme of interracial sexual desire that attends her relationships with the good Indian, the Mohican Uncas, son of Chingachgook, and the villain, the Huron Magua, are missing from the film. Moreover, Mann heterosexualizes the notably unmarried, sexually inviolate Natty Bumppo, giving him and Cora, who dies tragically in the novel, a full-blown romance. There are other important changes made in the film. But Mann and his team justify their alterations to the source material by creating a movie that is cinematically dazzling and often daring. A contribution that they do make to interpretations of Cooper's material is the depiction of large-scale violence involving the French and British, the colonists, and the various competing Indian tribes warring against them or on their behalf. Few films more dynamically convey the urgency and unpredictability of war, and no other film one can recall conveys the particular incoherent force of the Seven Years of War with such power. While one indubitably misses, and faults the film for blunting, Cooper's complex racial themes, one can also admire Mann's film on its own successful terms.

Not so Joffé's, which is "freely adapted" from Hawthorne's novel by the screenwriter Douglas Day Stewart. The film fails the fidelity test on two levels, first by being a bad film, second by making adaptive choices that are inscrutable and much less effective than the action Hawthorne envisioned. Specifically, the film blunts the issue of feminism important to the novel by substituting an array of 1990s-specific fantasies of historical female empowerment for Hawthorne's tougher, less sentimental, though always empathetic design. This is to say that the 1995 version self-servingly envisions a feminist utopia specific to its contemporary moment rather than sensitive to the complexities of Hawthorne's vision. That the film does this so flagrantly and consistently is an issue precisely because the film doesn't work, its choices unsound aesthetically, narratively, sociologically, and historically. Indeed, the film so thoroughly rewrites not just Hawthorne but American history as to seem a kind of perverse parody of both rather than an updated adaptation.

Instead of being a solitary heroine as well as an artist who expresses herself through her needlework, Demi Moore's Hester is more like a savvy businesswoman, running a small farm, aided by her black slave girl Mituba (Lisa Andoh). Moreover, Hester enjoys an empowering community of progressive female friendships. The Mistress Hibbins of this film is back to being the older woman of Hawthorne's text, played by the great English actress Joan Plowright. But this Hibbins is a womanist freethinker swathed in plush Elizabethan gowns, a commonsensical earth mother leading group discussions among other progressive Salem women.

The costumes in this film demand a discrete analysis. (They were designed by the notable Gabriella Pescucci, who made the costumes for Martin Scorsese's great film adaptation of *The Age of Innocence* among many other films.) The film jettisons the idea of Hester as artist, but her sumptuous baroque gown in the first scaffold scene conveys something of her aesthetic sensibility. Then again, the film crucially omits the key detail that Hester has magnificently designed the *A* herself, appropriating her own symbol of oppression as artistic statement. Dimmesdale's hipster-Puritan ensemble, wildly anachronistic, suggests him as a transatlantic rock star, his garb evocative of something that the singer Bono might have worn in his U2 heyday. Hence the political significance of the costumes here. Rather than drab and forbidding, the clothing worn by the film's heroic personae defy the plain and stolid sartorial schemes of the Puritans traditionally understood. Indeed, the "praying Indians" aligned with the Puritan freethinkers like Oldman's Dimmesdale look like they have stepped out of the pages of chic bourgeois emporiums' catalogs.

Perhaps the most radical change the 1995 film makes to Hawthorne's text is its heroification of Arthur Dimmesdale. Long seen as weak-willed, tremulous (in a bad way), hypocritical, even misogynistic, and certainly a deadbeat dad, Dimmesdale comes into his own in the movie, a recognizably '90s crunchy, politically correct, otherness-embracing youngish white man who, to use more contemporary parlance, is suitably "woke." This Dimmesdale maintains relationships with the Native American community and heroically translates the Bible into Algonquin, a detail not in Hawthorne's novel to say the least (and Hawthorne certainly knew of the person who did so, mentioning it more than once in his body of works). As Elizabeth Abele details,

> Though Nathaniel Hawthorne refers to the wilderness and Indians in the background of *The Scarlet Letter*, the novel does not have a single Indian character. ... Dimmesdale is one of two white men attending the funeral rites for the former chief Massasoit, though the only one who speaks in Algonquin. ... The new chief Metacomet remarks, "You are the only one who comes to us with an open heart. But your people have murdered my father with their lies." Similarly, the praying Indian John Running Moose introduces Dimmesdale as "my best friend in the colony." ... The screenplay conflates Dimmesdale with the historical figure of Apostle Eliot... Dimmesdale is translating the Bible into Algonquin. (171)

The Puritan missionary and Englishman John Eliot translated the Geneva Bible into Algonquin, and The Eliot Indian Bible, also known as the Algonquian Bible, was first published in 1663, making it the first published Bible in British North America. Making Dimmesdale into Eliot radically transforms Hawthorne's depiction of the minister, especially when we consider that Hawthorne was well aware of Eliot's history, devoting a chapter to it in *Grandfather's Chair* (1840) and mentioning it significantly in *The Blithedale Romance* (1852). (Elizabeth Abele affirms Lucy Maddox's reading of Hawthorne's view of the Algonquian translation as "useless," but that is not at all the attitude that Hawthorne conveys in *Grandfather's Chair.*) Ironically, Eliot also testified against Anne Hutchinson at her trial—given the Hutchinson-ization of cinematic Hesters as defiant free spirits.

Sacvan Bercovitch outlines the politics of historical revision in the film (1991):

> The bad guys are the usual suspects: witch-hunters, moralists, and land-grabbers. The good guys are mainly the marginal and the unrepresented minorities. [The time is purportedly the 1670s,] but the movie actually compresses the three most familiar episodes of seventeenth-century New England: the Anne Hutchinson trial (1630s), Metacomet's War (1670s), and the witchcraft hysteria (1690s). Thus the plot relates intolerance, male chauvinism, colonialism, and, climactically, the racism that explodes in the inter-tribal attack. Hawthorne's novel is set in 1642-1649, in order to emphasize the newness of the venture, and the nature of its errand...a certain social order designed to redirect the radical energies of its adherents. The movie Puritans are an incipiently progressive community under an oppressive regime, a society at odds with its own liberal possibilities. (3)

These liberal possibilities are embodied by the movie's progressive warriors Hester, Hibbins, and especially Dimmesdale, who seeks to forge an alliance with the Native Americans in his midst. While I am not in agreement with many of Bercovitch's readings of Hawthorne as the most eloquent of American proponents of social conformity ("Masculinist Theory" 2008), I believe that he is certainly right in his view of the 1995 film as a kind of temporal vortex with a utopianizing agenda. (If earlier generations of critics worried that Hawthorne may have been right to call himself in his fiction too much of an inveterate allegorist, or that his work was too insubstantial, too evanescent, critics since the late 1980s in particular have worried less about the purported aesthetic defects of Hawthorne's writing and more about the ideological lapses his style foregrounds by hiding. I refer of course to the work pioneered by Jonathan Arac and by Bercovitch in *The Office of The Scarlet Letter*, that reads Hawthorne's ambiguity as a covert aesthetic strategy for political accommodation and conformity, for, on the one hand, expressing by camouflaging ambivalence over the slavery question, or, on the other, complicity with one's own socialization, the great example of this being Hester Prynne, through a seemingly open-ended ambiguous style in which infinite points of view work to "deprive us of choice" [*The Office* 20].)

If the reimagining of Dimmesdale gives one considerable pause, blunting Hawthorne's critique of American masculinity and its failings and limitations, the reimagining of Chillingworth here induces astonishment. The film seems to be paying homage to Duvall's involvement in Francis Ford Coppola's *Apocalypse Now* (1979), his feverish Vietnam War-rendering of Conrad's *Heart of Darkness*. Chillingworth's descent into madness mimics that of Colonel Kurz (Marlon Brando) and Captain Willard (Martin Sheen) in Coppola's film, specifically their act of "going native," as Sylvia Shin Huey Chong discusses in *The Oriental Obscene* (154-55).

While Chillingworth has lived for a time among Indians in Hawthorne's novel, the film treats the cuckolded physician's exposure to Native American culture as an experience that produces bouts of madness, a peculiar form of PTSD that involves masquerade, identity shifts, and murderous violence. Giving vent to his insatiable lust for vengeance, Chillingworth periodically doffs his Puritan wig and reverts to an aboriginal state, wearing feathers in his hair and skimpy "Indian" clothing. (Duvall suggests a denizen of Tompkins Square Park in the New York City of the 1980s; he looks rather punk.) And in this adopted garb Duvall kills with bloodlust. Strangely, the Puritan wig that Chillingworth wears at other times feminizes him, recalling the effect of the minister's black veil in one of Hawthorne's greatest short stories. Overall, Duvall's Chillingworth, with his collage of strained British accent, mixture of modes of menacing masculinity, and schizophrenic cultural allegiances, comes across as a telling index of the film's own confused attitudes about masculinity, not a contrast to the idealization of Dimmesdale but in keeping with it.

As noted at this essay's outset, my chief concern in thinking about the ways in which the cinema translates Hawthorne has been the issue of female sexuality and desire, one that I believe Bercovitch erroneously deemphasizes in his reading of *The Scarlet Letter* as reactionary (*Gender Protest*). While Hester fights for her freedoms of all kinds in this film, and more than once we hear the question "What is a sin in God's eyes?" the film jettisons Hawthorne's view of Hester as complexly grappling with her situation and her desires in favor of depicting Hester as a free love radical from the start. Hence her ability to wield the female desiring gaze early on when she spies, with avidity, a naked Arthur and his Nautilized body swimming. There is no climactic forest scene in which Hester lets down her sensual raven locks to affirm that her and Arthur's love had "a consecration of its own," because the film does not need this scene of erotic reclamation (1: 195). No reclamation is needed because this Hester and Arthur are always already in touch with their carnal and liberating desires. The only impediments are the much more fustily garbed, forbidding Puritan conservatives. (Certainly, the softcore-porn aesthetic of the notorious sex scene in the film in which Hester and Arthur consummate their desires as Mituba effectively masturbates with lighted candles in a wooden bathtub represents a view of sexual liberation quite distinct from Hawthorne's vision, and very specific to a kind of cinematic fantasy that the 1995 version pursues and affirms.)

I want to take a moment to brood on Hawthorne's peculiar and suggestive account of Hester and the workings of her mind as she listens to Arthur's Election Day sermon. Here is Hawthorne:

By this time the preliminary prayer had been offered in the meeting-house, and the accents of the Reverend Mr. Dimmesdale were heard commencing his discourse. An irresistible feeling kept Hester near the spot. As the sacred edifice was too much thronged to admit another auditor, she took up her position close beside the scaffold of the pillory. It was in sufficient proximity to bring the whole sermon to her ears, in the shape of an indistinct, but varied, murmur and flow of the minister's very peculiar voice.

This vocal organ was in itself a rich endowment; insomuch that a listener, comprehending nothing of the language in which the preacher spoke, might still have been swayed to and fro by the mere tone and cadence. Like all other music, it breathed passion and pathos, and emotions high or tender, in a tongue native to the human heart, wherever educated. Muffled as the sound was by its passage through the church-walls, Hester Prynne listened with such intentness, and sympathized so intimately, that the sermon had throughout a meaning for her, entirely apart from its indistinguishable words. These, perhaps, if more distinctly heard, might have been only a grosser medium, and have clogged the spiritual sense. Now she caught the low undertone, as of the wind sinking down to repose itself; then ascended with it, as it rose through progressive gradations of sweetness and power, until its volume seemed to envelop her with an atmosphere of awe and solemn grandeur. And yet, majestic as the voice sometimes became, there was for ever in it an essential character of plaintiveness. A loud or low expression of anguish,—the whisper, or the shriek, as it might be conceived, of suffering humanity, that touched a sensibility in every bosom! At times this deep strain of pathos was all that could be heard, and scarcely heard, sighing amid a desolate silence. But even when the minister's voice grew high and commanding,—when it gushed irrepressibly upward,—when it assumed its utmost breadth and power, so overfilling the church as to burst its way through the solid walls, and diffuse itself in the open air,—still, if the auditor listened intently, and for the purpose, he could detect the same cry of pain. What was it? The complaint of a human heart, sorrow-laden, perchance guilty, telling its secret, whether of guilt or sorrow, to the great heart of mankind; beseeching its sympathy or forgiveness,— at every moment,—in each accent,—and never in vain! It was this profound and continual undertone that gave the clergyman his most appropriate power. (1: 243-34)

The kind of meditative immersion in Hester's thought-making and, I would argue, in her desire for Arthur that Hawthorne displays here would be very difficult to translate to film. Perhaps the 1926 version comes closest to doing so, thanks to Lillian Gish's emotional intensity. Certainly, the films do not come close to conveying the intricacy not only of Hester's desire for Arthur but also of her sympathy for him. Even in the comparatively humane treatment of the characters that Wenders offers, such an intricacy proves elusive.

In Hawthorne, Arthur's voice, its broken but also endlessly suggestive nature, conveys mysteriously more than just his own predicament but also humanity's. Hester's sympathy for him widens into a larger one for others. Moreover, Hawthorne gives us an immersion in the ways that Hester's mind works. There is an intellectual as well as an emotional responsiveness to Arthur's words and vocal register. Even if his voice takes on distinct qualities, the auditor—Hester, specifically—can "detect the same cry of pain" within it. Hester's imaginative empathy with Arthur allows her to find her own levels of loss and longing within his performance of self.

The predicament of film is that it is very difficult to convey a character's inner life as a novelist does. But film conveys such experiences in its own ways, and amply. The moment in the flawed but affecting 1926 film in which Hester's material A falls on the fleshly one engraved on Arthur's chest conveys, through a visual image invented for the film, connection and disconnection at once. The image eloquently translates the paralytic desire thematized in the novel, the ardent but balked nature of the passion between these lovers. But at times a bravura cinematic image can also distort a crucial aspect of a literary work's intentions. The magnificent shot of Hester and Pearl making their sea-set voyage toward freedom in Wenders's film is a testament to a belief in female empowerment, and on these terms a most welcome gesture. Yet the difficulties that Hawthorne incorporated into Hester's complex negotiations of both her desires and her relationship with her larger community are effectively dropped into the waters, drowned away. Good political intentions clash uncomfortably with intractable textual stances. Overall, the truly complexly alive and richly resonant film adaptation of Hawthorne's work waits to be made, even if there are fleeting moments of exciting clarity in the films made by Sjöström and by Wenders.

Works Cited

Abele, Elizabeth. *Home Front Heroes: The Rise of a New Hollywood Archetype, 1988-1999*. McFarland, XXXX, 2013.

Bercovitch, Sacvan. *"The Scarlet Letter*: A Twice-Told Tale." *Nathaniel Hawthorne Review*, vol. 22, no. 2, 1996, pp. 1-20.

_____. *The Office of the Scarlet Letter*. Johns Hopkins UP, 1991.

Bland, Lucy. *Modern Women on Trial: Sexual Transgression in the Age of the Flapper*. Gender in History. Manchester UP, 2013.

Bromley, Roger. *From Alice to Buena Vista: The Films of Wim Wenders*. Greenwood, 2001.

Brouwers, Anke. "The New Mother: Maternal Instinct as Sexual Liberation in Victor Sjöström's *The Scarlet Letter* (1926)." *Quarterly Review of Film and Video*, xxiv, no. 3, 2007, pp. 249-66.

Chong, Sylvia Shin Huey. *The Oriental Obscene: Violence and Racial Fantasies in the Vietnam Era*. Duke UP, 2012.

Greven, David. "Masculinist Theory and Romantic Authorship, Or Hawthorne, Politics, Desire." *New Literary History*, vol. 39, no. 4, 2008, pp. 971-87.

_____. *Gender Protest and Same-Sex Desire in Antebellum American Literature: Margaret Fuller, Edgar Allan Poe, Nathaniel Hawthorne, and Herman Melville*. Routledge, 2016.

_____. *Men beyond Desire: Manhood, Sex, and Violation in American Literature*. Palgrave Macmillan, 2005.

Hawthorne, Nathaniel. *The Centenary Edition of the Works of Nathaniel Hawthorne*. Edited by William Charvat et al. Ohio State UP, 1962-1997. 23 vols.

Keenan, Richard C., and James M. Welsh. "Wim Wenders and Nathaniel Hawthorne: From *The Scarlet Letter* to *Der Scharlachrote Buchstabe*." *Literature Film Quarterly*, vol. 6, no. 2, Spring 78, pp. 175-79.

Maddox, Lucy. *Removals: Nineteenth-Century American Literature and the Politics of Indian Affairs*. Oxford UP, 1991.

Raw, Laurence. *Adapting Nathaniel Hawthorne to the Screen: Forging New Worlds*. Scarecrow, 2008.

Turim, Maureen. "Movies and Divine Stars: Defining Gender." *American Cinema of the 1920s: Themes and Variations*. Edited by Lucy Fischer. Screen Decades. Rutgers UP, 2009, pp. 165-87.

Wood, Robin. *The Wings of the Dove: Henry James in the 1990s*. BFI Modern Classics. British Film Institute, 1999.

RESOURCES

Chronology

1804	Nathaniel Hathorne (the *w* was added later) was born in Salem, Massachusetts, to Captain Nathaniel Hathorne and Betsy Hathorne (née Manning) on the auspicious date of July 4.
1822	Hathorne, as he was still known, began to attend Bowdoin College, where he became friends with Henry Wadsworth Longfellow, America's most famous poet during his lifetime, and Franklin Pierce, a close lifelong friend and future president of the United States.
1827	Nathaniel Hathorne began to identify himself as Nathaniel Hawthorne, providing the name by which we know him today.
1828	Hawthorne, as he was known by this time, published his first novel, *Fanshawe: A Tale*, anonymously.
1837	Hawthorne published *Twice-Told Tales*, his first short story collection.
1838	Hawthorne became close friends with two talented sisters, Elizabeth Peabody and Sophia Peabody, ultimately forming a romantic attachment with Sophia.
1839	Hawthorne accepted a position as inspector at the Boston Custom House. He also met Margaret Fuller for the first time in Boston.
1840	Hawthorne announced his resignation from the Boston Custom House, to be effective at the start of 1841. He published a book of popular history for children, *Grandfather's Chair*, in December.

1841	Hawthorne joined the Brook Farm utopian community, which was founded by George Ripley and included Margaret Fuller among its members. Ralph Waldo Emerson did not join, but consulted with Ripley on the endeavor, which was also strongly supported by Elizabeth Peabody. Hawthorne admired Fuller, even as he seems to have been intimidated by her intellect and outspokenness.
1842	Hawthorne married Sophia Peabody on July 9. They lived together at the Old Manse in Concord, Massachusetts, which they rented from Ralph Waldo Emerson. Hawthorne also befriended Henry David Thoreau at this time.
1843	Sophia Hawthorne suffered a miscarriage in February, and became pregnant again later in the year. Hawthorne wrote steadily, publishing such stories as "The New Adam and Eve," "The Birth-Mark," and "The Celestial Railroad" in periodicals.
1844	Hawthorne continued to publish in periodicals, notably "Drowne's Wooden Image" and "Earth's Holocaust." His eldest daughter, Una, was born in Concord on March 3.
1846	In March, Hawthorne accepted a position as surveyor at the Salem Custom House that would become important in shaping *The Scarlet Letter.* In June, Hawthorne published his second major collection of short stories, *Mosses from an Old Manse*, which included such stories as "Young Goodman Brown," "The Birth-Mark," and "Rappaccini's Daughter." His son, Julian, was born on June 22.

1849	Hawthorne was fired from his position of surveyor at the Salem Custom House on June 8, as part of a political purge of Democratic appointees.
1850	Hawthorne published his first and most famous novel, *The Scarlet Letter*, on March 16. Hawthorne learned in July that Margaret Fuller had drowned as she was returning to the United States from Italy. On August 5, Hawthorne met Herman Melville, a younger writer who would write one of the most influential reviews of Hawthorne's short fiction in "Hawthorne and His *Mosses*," and who, one year later, would dedicate his great novel, *Moby-Dick*, to Hawthorne "in admiration of his genius."
1851	Hawthorne published his second novel, *The House of the Seven Gables*, in April. Hawthorne's youngest child, Rose, was born in May. Rose would convert to Catholicism in adulthood and is presently a candidate for canonization as a Catholic saint. Hawthorne maintained a lively correspondence with Herman Melville throughout the year. *Moby-Dick*, with its dedication to Hawthorne, was published in England in October and in the United States in November. Hawthorne also published *A Wonder-Book for Girls and Boys* in this year.
1852	Hawthorne published his third novel, *The Blithedale Romance*, and his third collection of short stories, *The Snow-Image, and Other Twice-Told Tales*. *The Blithedale Romance* drew heavily on his experience at Brook Farm. He also published a campaign biographical of successful presidential candidate Franklin Pierce, his longtime friend from Bowdoin.
1853	Hawthorne published *Tanglewood Tales for Boys and Girls*, a sequel to *A Wonder-Book for Girls and Boys*.

In July, Hawthorne sailed to Liverpool, England, to take up a position as the American consul there. In 1856, Hawthorne would meet Herman Melville for a memorable discussion of faith and doubt between two of nineteenth-century America's most important literary figures.

1860	Hawthorne published his fourth novel, and the last to be published in his lifetime, *The Marble Faun.*
1862	Hawthorne published "Chiefly about War Matters, By a Peaceable Man," in *The Atlantic.* Many of his friends were critical of his ambivalence toward the Union war effort.
1864	Nathaniel Hawthorne died in Plymouth, Massachusetts, on May 19, in the company of his old friend and former president of the United States, Franklin Pierce.

Major Works

Fanshawe (1828)

Twice-Told Tales (1837)

Grandfather's Chair (1840)

Mosses from an Old Manse (1846)

The Scarlet Letter (1850)

A Wonder-Book for Girls and Boys (1851)

The House of the Seven Gables (1851)

The Blithedale Romance (1852)

The Snow-Image and Other Twice-Told Tales (1852)

Tanglewood Tales for Boys and Girls (1853)

The Marble Faun; or, The Romance of Monte Beni (1860)

Our Old Home (1863)

Septimius Felton; or, The Elixir of Life (posthumous, 1872)

Both the works above and the extensive array of notebooks, letters, and manuscripts that Hawthorne left behind at his death are included in *The Centenary Edition of the Works of Nathaniel Hawthorne*, vols. 1-23 (Ohio State UP, 1963-).

Bibliography

Abel, Darrel. "Hawthorne's Dimmesdale: Fugitive from Wrath." *Nineteenth-Century Fiction*, 11, Sept. 1956, pp. 81-105.

Adamson, Joseph. "'Guardian of the Inmost Me': Hawthorne and Shame." In *Scenes of Shame: Psychoanalysis, Shame, and Writing*. Edited by Joseph Adamson and Hillary Clark. State U of New York P, 1999.

Baughman, Ernest. "Public Confession and *The Scarlet Letter*." *New England Quarterly*, vol. 40, 1967, pp. 532-50.

Barlowe, Jamie. *The Scarlet Mob of Scribblers: Rereading Hester Prynne*. Southern Illinois UP, 2000.

Baym, Nina. *The Shape of Hawthorne's Career*. Cornell UP, 1976.

_____. *The Scarlet Letter: A Reading*. Hall, 1986.

_____. *The Shape of Hawthorne's Career*. Cornell UP, 1976.

Bell, Michael Davitt. *Hawthorne and the Historical Romance of New England*. Princeton UP, 1971.

Bell, Millicent, editor. *Hawthorne and The Real: Bicentennial Essays*. Ohio State U P, 2005.

Bercovitch, Sacvan. *The Office of the Scarlet Letter*. Johns Hopkins UP, 1991.

Brodhead, Richard. *The School of Hawthorne*. New York UP, 1986.

Brownson, Orestes. Review of *The Scarlet Letter*, Brownson's*Quarterly Review* (1850) in *Hawthorne: The Critical Heritage*. Edited by J. Donald Crowley. Routledge, 1970, pp. 175-79.

Budick, Emily Miller. *Engendering Romance: Women Writers and the HawthorneTradition, 1850-1990*. Yale UP, 1994.

_____. *Nineteenth-Century American Romance: Genre and the Construction of Democratic Culture*. Twayne, 1996.

Chase, Richard. *The American Novel and Its Tradition*. Doubleday Anchor, 1957.

Coale, Samuel. *The Entanglements of Nathaniel Hawthorne*. Camden House P, 2011.

Colacurcio, Michael J. *The Province of Piety: Moral History in Hawthorne's Early Tales*. 1984.

Cook, Jonathan A. "'The Most Satisfactory Villain That Ever Was': Charles W. Upham and *The House of the Seven Gables.*" *New England Quarterly*, 88, June 2015, pp. 252-85.

_____. "Melville's *Mosses* Review and the Proclamation of Hawthorne as America's Literary Messiah." *Leviathan*, vol. 10, no. 3, 2008, pp. 62–70. doi:10.1111/j.1750-1849.2008.01312.x.

Coxe, Arthur Cleveland. "The Writings of Hawthorne," *Church Review*, 1851. Crowley, pp. 179-84.

Crews, Frederick. *The Sins of the Fathers: Hawthorne's Psychological Themes.* Oxford UP, 1966.

Dauber, Kenneth. *Rediscovering Hawthorne.* Princeton UP, 1977.

Davis, Clark. *Hawthorne's Shyness: Ethics, Politics, and the Question of Engagement.* Johns Hopkins UP, 2005.

Dryden, Edgar A. *Nathaniel Hawthorne: The Poetics of Enchantment.* Cornell UP, 1977.

Elbert, Monika. *Encoding the Letter "A": Gender and Authority in Hawthorne's Early Fiction.* Haag & Herchen, 1990.

Estrin, Mark W. "'Triumphant Ignominy': The Scarlet Letter on Screen." *Literature Film Quarterly*, vol. 2, no. 2, Spring74, pp. 110-22.

Felski, Rita. *The Limits of Critique.* U of Chicago P, 2015.

Gilmore, Michael T. *American Romanticism and the Marketplace.* U of Chicago P, 1988.

Greven, David. "Masculinist Theory and Romantic Authorship, Or Hawthorne, Politics, Desire." *New Literary History*, vol. 39, no. 4, 2008, pp. 971–87.

_____. *Gender Protest and Same-Sex Desire in Antebellum American Literature: Margaret Fuller, Edgar Allan Poe, Nathaniel Hawthorne, and Herman Melville.* Routledge, 2016.

_____. *Men beyond Desire: Manhood, Sex, and Violation in American Literature.* 1st ed., Palgrave Macmillan, 2005.

Harris, Kenneth Marc. *Hypocrisy and Self-Deception in Hawthorne's Fiction.* UP of Virginia, 1988.

Hawthorne, Julian. *Hawthorne and His Circle.* Archon, 1968.

_____. *Nathaniel Hawthorne and His Wife.* 2 vols. Archon, 1968.

James, Henry. *Hawthorne.* Macmillan, 1902.

Kazin, Alfred. "Hawthorne: The Artist of New England." *Atlantic Monthly*, 1966.

Lathrop, Rose Hawthorne. *Memories of Hawthorne*. Houghton Mifflin, 1897.

Loring, George Bailey. Review of *The Scarlet Letter*, *Massachusetts Quarterly Review*, 1850. Crowley, pp. 168-75.

Matthiessen, F. O. *American Renaissance: Art and Expression in the Age of Emerson and Whitman*. Oxford UP, 1941.

McFarland, Philip. *Hawthorne in Concord*. Grove, 2005.

Miller, Edwin Haviland. *Salem Is My Dwelling Place: A Life of Nathaniel Hawthorne*. U of Iowa P, 1991.

Millington, Richard. *Practicing Romance: Narrative Form and Cultural Engagement*. Princeton UP, 1992.

Moore, Margaret B. *The Salem World of Nathaniel Hawthorne*. U of Missouri P, 1998.

Morrison, Toni. *Playing in the Dark: Whiteness and the Literary Imagination*. Harvard UP, 1992.

Person, Leland. *The Cambridge Introduction to Nathaniel Hawthorne*. Cambridge UP, 2007.

Railton, Stephen. *Authorship and Audience: Literary Performance in the American Renaissance*. Princeton UP, 1991.

Raw, Laurence. *Adapting Nathaniel Hawthorne to the Screen: Forging New Worlds*. Scarecrow, 2008.

Reynolds, David S. *Beneath the American Renaissance: The Subversive Imagination in the Age of Emerson and Melville*. Oxford UP, 1998.

_____. *Faith in Fiction: The Emergence of Religious Literature in America*. Harvard UP, 1981.

Reynolds, Larry. *Devils and Rebels: The Making of Hawthorne's Damned Politics*. U of Michigan P, 2008.

Riss, Arthur. *Slavery, and Liberalism in Nineteenth Century American Literature*. Cambridge UP, 2006.

Stern, Milton R. *Contexts for Hawthorne:* The Marble Faun *and the Politics of Openness and Closure in American Literature*. U of Illinois P, 1991.

Thompson, Gary Richard, and Eric Carl. *Neutral Ground: New Traditionalism and the American Romance Controversy*. Louisiana State UP, 1999.

Tompkins, Jane. *Sensational Designs: The Cultural Work of American Fiction 1790-1860*. Oxford UP, 1985.

Trilling, Lionel. "Our Hawthorne." *Hawthorne Centenary Essays*. Edited by Roy Harvey Pearce. Ohio State UP, 1964, pp. 429-58.

Ullen, Magnus. *The Half-Vanished Structure: Hawthorne's Allegorical Dialectics*. Uppsala University, 2001.

Waggoner, Hyatt H. *Hawthorne: A Critical Study*. Belknap, 1963.

_____. *The Presence of Hawthorne*. Louisiana State UP, 1979.

Wineapple, Brenda. *Hawthorne: A Life*. Knopf, 2003.

About the Editor

Brian Yothers is the Frances Spatz Leighton Endowed Distinguished Professor of English and the Associate Chair of the Department of English at UTEP. His research specialties are early and nineteenth-century American literature, religion and literature, the literature of travel, poetry, and the literature of slavery and abolition. In 2014, he was a recipient of the University of Texas Regents' Outstanding Teaching Award. He is the author of *The Romance of the Holy Land in American Travel Writing, 1790-1876* (2007), *Melville's Mirrors: Literary Criticism and America's Most Elusive Author* (2011), *Sacred Uncertainty: Religious Difference and the Shape of Melville's Career* (2015), and *Reading Abolition: The Critical Reception of Harriet Beecher Stowe and Frederick Douglass* (2016). He has also edited several volumes: *Visionary of the Word: Melville and Religion* (2017), with Jonathan A. Cook; *Billy Budd, Sailor: Critical Insights* (2017); and *Above the American Renaissance: David S. Reynolds and the Spiritual Imagination in American Literary Studies* (forthcoming, 2018), with Harold K. Bush. He presently serves as associate editor of *Leviathan: A Journal of Melville Studies*, coeditor of the travel section of the *Melville Electronic Library (MEL)*, and associate editor of *Melville's Marginalia Online*. He is the editor of the Camden House Press series Literary Criticism in Perspective and has served as the coeditor of the interdisciplinary journal *Journeys*. He is the author of more than fifty published and forthcoming scholarly articles, editions, and reviews, dealing with such topics as Melville's biblical marginalia, Melville's poetry, Poe's poetry and fiction, literary connections between South Asia and the Americas, and the literary cultures of nineteenth-century American missionaries.

Contributors_____

Anupama Arora is associate professor of English at UMass Dartmouth. She moved to UMD in Fall 2008 after spending a few years at Earlham College in Indiana. Her PhD is from Tufts University (Boston). She is the editor, with Rajender Kaur, of *India in the American Imaginary, 1780s-1880s* (Palgrave 2017). Her work has appeared in *The Journal of Commonwealth Literature, Ariel: A Review of International English Literature,* and *Women's Studies,* among other journals.

Brad Bannon is a lecturer in the department of English at the University of Tennessee, Knoxville. He is the author of *Jonathan Edwards, Samuel Taylor Coleridge, and the Supernatural Will in American Literature,* forthcoming from Routledge, and his essays have appeared in the *James Joyce Quarterly, Journal of the History of Ideas, The Cormac McCarthy Journal,* and the edited collection *Melville and Religion: Visionary of the Word.* He is also the coeditor, with John Vanderheide, of *Cormac McCarthy's Violent Destinies: The Poetics of Determinism and Fatalism,* forthcoming from the University of Tennessee Press.

Samuel Coale teaches American literature and culture at Wheaton College in Massachusetts. His most recent books include *The Entanglements of Nathaniel Hawthorne* (2011) and *Quirks of the Quantum: Postmodernism in Contemporary American Fiction* (2012), and he is the coeditor of *Nathaniel Hawthorne in the College Classroom* (2017). He has lectured most recently in Jordan, Lebanon, Japan, Belarus, Romania, Brazil, India, and Pakistan. He is working on a new book on the sublime.

Jonathan A. Cook is the author of *Satirical Apocalypse: An Anatomy of "The Confidence-Man"* (1996), *Inscrutable Malice: Theodicy, Eschatology, and the Biblical Sources of "Moby-Dick"* (2012), and coeditor, with Brian Yothers, of the essay collection *Visionary of the Word: Melville and Religion* (2017). He has contributed essays to *Critical Insights: Herman Melville* (2013) and *Critical Insights: Moby-Dick* (2014). His article on Melville and London will be appearing in the collection *Herman Melville in Context.* He has published widely on Melville, Hawthorne,

Poe, and other nineteenth-century writers. His interviews on various works of Melville and Hawthorne are available on YouTube through the educational platform Noetics. He is chair of the English Department at Middleburg Academy.

Robert C. Evans is I. B. Young Professor of English at Auburn University at Montgomery. He earned his PhD from Princeton University in 1984. In 1982 he began teaching at AUM, where he has been named Distinguished Research Professor, Distinguished Teaching Professor, and University Alumni Professor. External awards include fellowships from the American Council of Learned Societies, the American Philosophical Society, the National Endowment for the Humanities, the UCLA Center for Medieval and Renaissance Studies, and the Folger, Huntington, and Newberry Libraries. He is the author or editor of more than thirty-five books and of more than four hundred essays, including recent work on various American writers.

David Greven is professor of English at the University of South Carolina. His books include *Intimate Violence: Hitchcock, Sex, and Queer Theory* (Oxford University Press, 2017), *Ghost Faces: Hollywood and Post-Millennial Masculinity* (SUNY Press, 2016), *Gender Protest and Same-Sex Desire in Antebellum American Literature* (Ashgate, 2014), *Psycho-Sexual: Male Desire in Hitchcock, De Palma, Scorsese, and Friedkin* (University of Texas Press, 2013), *The Fragility of Manhood: Hawthorne, Freud, and the Politics of Gender* (Ohio State University Press, 2012), *Representations of Femininity in American Genre Cinema: The Woman's Film, Film Noir, and Modern Horror* (Palgrave Macmillan, 2011), *Manhood in Hollywood from Bush to Bush* (University of Texas Press, 2009), and *Men Beyond Desire: Manhood, Sex, and Violation in American Literature* (Palgrave Macmillan, 2005).

Steven Petersheim teaches American literature and poetry at Indiana University East. He has published articles on Hawthorne in journals such as *College Literature, Nathaniel Hawthorne Review,* and *ANQ.* His coedited book *Writing the Environment in Nineteenth-Century American Literature* was published by Lexington Books in the Ecocritical Theory and Practice series, and he is currently working on a monograph on Hawthorne and the

---

236   Critical Insights

environment. From time to time, he roams the New England landscape where Hawthorne walked or hikes and writes poetry in the beautiful Whitewater Valley area in eastern Indiana.

Christopher N. Phillips is associate professor of English at Lafayette College, where he teaches early American and transatlantic literatures, book history, and writing. He is the author of *Epic in American Culture, Settlement to Reconstruction* (Johns Hopkins, 2012) and *The Hymnal: A Reading History* (Johns Hopkins, 2018), and is the editor of *The Cambridge Companion to the Literature of the American Renaissance* (2018). He is also the primary investigator for the Easton Library Company Database, a public digital humanities project analyzing the loan records for the Easton (Penn.) Library Company, 1811-1862.

Casey R. Pratt is an associate professor of English at Wingate University where he teaches classes in Early American literature, world literature, and college writing. He has recently published work in *African American Review* and *Libertarian Papers*. Other recent scholarship includes a coauthored book chapter on Plato's political thought that will appear in a new series by Bloomsbury titled *Textual Moments in the History of Political Thought*.

Nancy F. Sweet is Professor of English at California State University, Sacramento, and Associate Editor of the *Nathaniel Hawthorne Review*, a scholarly journal featuring articles, book reviews, and an annually updated bibliography related to the life and works of Nathaniel Hawthorne.

John Wenke is professor of English at Salisbury University, where he teaches American literature and literary writing and has twice won the university's Distinguished Faculty Award. He received his BA in English from the University of Notre Dame and his MA and PhD in English from the University of Connecticut. His books include *Melville's Muse: Literary Creation and the Forms of Philosophical Fiction* and *J. D. Salinger: A Study of the Short Fiction*. He has published numerous scholarly essays, short stories, chapters, reviews, and creative nonfiction essays. "The Brides of Christ," a memoir essay, recently appeared in *Communion Journal*. He is currently in the final stages of completing *American Proteus: Providence, Self-Fashioning and the Creation of Charles Brockden Brown.*

Jane Zwart teaches contemporary American and postcolonial literatures at Calvin College in Grand Rapids, Michigan, where she is an associate professor of English as well as the codirector of the Calvin Center for Faith and Writing. As a graduate student at Boston University, she wrote her dissertation on twentieth-century retellings of *The Scarlet Letter*. Subsequently, she published an article on Hawthorne's masterplot itself. In addition to other academic articles, Zwart has published edited versions of onstage interviews with Jonathan Safran Foer, Christian Wiman, and Zadie Smith. She writes poems, too, some of which have appeared in literary reviews.

Index